NOBODY'S PERFECT
THE MAKING OF
SOME LIKE IT HOT

'We were pretty sure it would be a good comedy. What we did not know was that it was going to be a great comedy.'

Billy Wilder

NOBODY'S PERFECT

— THE MAKING OF —

SOME LIKE IT HOT

LUCY JANE SANTOS

WHITE OWL

AN IMPRINT OF PEN & SWORD BOOKS LTD.
YORKSHIRE – PHILADELPHIA

First published in Great Britain in 2026 by
PEN AND SWORD WHITE OWL
An imprint of
Pen & Sword Books Ltd
Yorkshire – Philadelphia

Print ISBN 978 1 03613 880 6
ePUB ISBN 978 1 03613 882 0
ePDF ISBN 978 1 03613 884 4

A CIP catalogue record for this book is available from the British Library.

Typeset in Times New Roman 11/14.5 by
SJmagic DESIGN SERVICES, India.
Printed and bound in the UK by CPI Group (UK) Ltd, Croydon, CR0 4YY.

The Publisher's authorised representative in the EU for product safety is Authorised Rep Compliance Ltd., Ground Floor, 71 Lower Baggot Street,
Dublin D02 P593, Ireland.
www.arccompliance.com

For a complete list of Pen & Sword titles please contact

PEN & SWORD BOOKS LIMITED
George House, Units 12 & 13, Beevor Street, Off Pontefract Road,
Barnsley, South Yorkshire, S71 1HN, England
E-mail: enquiries@pen-and-sword.co.uk
Website: www.pen-and-sword.co.uk

or

PEN AND SWORD BOOKS
1950 Lawrence Rd, Havertown, PA 19083, USA
E-mail: uspen-and-sword@casematepublishers.com
Website: www.penandswordbooks.com

MIX
Paper | Supporting responsible forestry
FSC® C013604
FSC www.fsc.org

Contents

Part Four: Creating A Classic

Acknowledgements

Huge thanks to the team at White Owl including Olivia Camozzi, Melanie Burrows, Laura Hirst, Paul Wilkinson (who designed the amazing cover) and to Laura Macdougall, Olivia Davies and Eleanor Horn at United Agents. I was so appreciative of all the support from the librarians, archivists, curators and volunteers at various collections including Maxwell Zupke at UCLA Library Special Collections; Genevieve Maxwell at the Academy of Motion Picture Arts and Sciences, Mary K. Huelsbeck, Wisconsin Center for Film and Theater Research, the team at Alamy and David Leopold at The Al Hirschfeld Foundation. As well as to Matthew Dessem for his assistance when it wasn't possible to visit the archives in person.

To all my family and friends – Mike, Sarah, Alice, Amber, Krishna, Jane, Penny, Katrina, Andrew, Lily, Freya, Shareen, Mark, Sasha, Liam, Ryan, Vanderlei, Zilda, Catherine, Carol, Kate, Kit, Sarah, Anne, James, Charlie, Emma, Billy, Michelle, Fiona, Natalie, Hillary, Lauren, Emma B, Amy, Sam, Cora, Vik, Nigel from Past Preservers and Corey from the New York Adventure Club.

And the biggest thanks of all, to Andy who has continued his dedication to helping me visit the places I write about – although this time with much less radioactivity.

Prologue

Now, I've never written a book about my favourite film before (my previous two books have been about the cultural and everyday history of radioactivity) but everyone seems to expect me to have a neat little anecdote about the first time I saw *Some Like It Hot* which tidily explains why I've written so extensively about it. But whilst the truth is much less obliging it is – in its own way – more instructive.

Because I don't remember it at all.

There is evidence, I think, of the time I may have first encountered the film. A photograph of my teenage bedroom, dated 1993, shows a small newspaper clipping pinned to the wall – Jack Lemmon and Tony Curtis in full Daphne and Josephine mode. So the movie must have meant something to me, or I wouldn't have bothered to cut it out, but, on the other hand, it's just one among hundreds of pinned images in a chaotic mix of my obsessions, so it didn't necessarily mean everything to me at the time – though I do still have it.

And yet, when I later told friends from my early twenties that I was writing this book, their reaction was unequivocal. Of course I was writing about *Some Like It Hot*. Hadn't it always been my favourite film? Hadn't I talked about it constantly? So somewhere between that pinboard and those friendships, something had shifted and the film had become *my* film.

And that uncertainty, as it turns out, illustrates perfectly exactly where my problems began.

Because memory – our own as much as anyone else's – can be a treacherous foundation on which to build history. It is patchy, selective and – perhaps most importantly – largely shaped by what comes after.

And as it turns out when you're writing about something as iconic as *Some Like It Hot* there are no shortage of memories and anecdotes. On the contrary, there are almost too many. But when you start to sift through them all – patterns emerge and you realise you are hearing the same voices, telling the same stories and gradually, almost imperceptibly, forming a hierarchy.

In this particular case it is two voices that dominate above all others – Billy Wilder and Tony Curtis. And between them they have effectively narrated the film's afterlife. They learned what stories worked, what drew laughter and, like any good raconteurs, they honed in on which ones got the best reaction – especially when the subject was Marilyn Monroe.

Almost everyone – whether they've seen the film or not, seemingly – knows the stories about her lateness, the forgotten lines, the drinking and emotional fragility. Those tales have been told so often that they have hardened into fact. But like any well-rehearsed anecdote when you stop to look at them in detail they raise as many questions as they answer. Were things really so simple? Was Monroe truly as difficult as this version of events suggests? Or are we hearing a narrative shaped as much by the pleasure of storytelling (and hindsight) as fact? To get a fuller view, we need other perspectives – including her own – less rehearsed, less refined, and maybe, just maybe, a little closer to the truth.

The Late Marilyn Monroe

The reporters and cameramen clustered impatiently on the runway at Los Angeles International Airport. Trans World Airlines (TWA) flight 91 had touched down, precisely on schedule at 7:00 a.m., Monday 8 July 1958, but the actress they were there for was nowhere to be seen.

Passenger after passenger descended the stairs and made their way past the ever-growing crowd. Still, she didn't appear. The mood amongst the press began to shift – from anticipation to irritation.

It hadn't been that long ago that Marilyn Monroe's well-known delaying tactics were mostly indulged as part of her mystique – an accepted factor of stardom. But seemingly that leniency was now wearing thin.

The studio system and its quirks were unravelling. Just as significantly a very public falling-out with Twentieth Century-Fox Film Corporation – the studio that had supposedly made her – had left its mark. Marilyn had fled Hollywood and spent the last two years on the East Coast. In New York she spoke of personal transformation and time to devote to acting classes, to her health, to her new marriage to the celebrated playwright Arthur Miller and her hopes of starting a family.

However, standing on the tarmac of LAX, the question loomed large: Was Marilyn still a star – or merely the shadow of one? The industry that once adored her now whispered that she was finished. Washed up. Overtaken by younger, hungrier ingenues like Jayne Mansfield, Sheree North and Mamie Van Doren.

These actresses represented as the *Los Angeles Mirror* put it: 'a score of foreign and domestic blondes who fought a war of succession armed with tape measures, their shields bearing the Latin motto, 'Vide mater, tomentum non est.' (Loose translation: 'Look, Ma, no padding.')[1]

1. Our Second Monroe Doctrine, *Los Angeles Mirror*, 9 July 1958, p. 15

And yet, despite everything, they waited.

"She's taking longer than that duck-billed platypus," one reporter muttered, eliciting a round of dry chuckles. The jab was a reference to three peculiar creatures that had recently arrived at the Bronx Zoo, platypuses flown in from Australia as replacements for the late Cecil and Penelope, who had been the last of their kind in North American captivity.

But of more present concern was whether the actress had even been on the plane at all. She had been photographed, hand in hand with her husband, at the airport in New York. Arthur had accompanied her that far but stayed behind at their home in Roxbury, Connecticut, preoccupied with his own serious affairs.

The newshounds shuffled, exchanged uncertain glances and began thumbing through their notes. For all the certainty with which her much anticipated return had been reported, no one could now say for sure where she actually was.

And then, at last, Marilyn Monroe appeared.

A vision in white.

She wore a form-fitting white silk blouse. A belted tight white skirt – *very* tight, as nearly every article would note. No stockings. White heeled shoes. White gloves. Even her hair had been dramatically lightened to a 'sort of white blonde,' specially designed for her new role.[2]

The overall effect of the actress standing at the top of the aircraft stairs in that striking monochrome outfit, was described with near-theatrical flourish. She 'blinked big, sleepy eyes at the world,' one reporter wrote, before beginning her descent 'slowly and wickedly.'[3]

Her lateness, it turned out, had an apparently simple explanation: she had fallen asleep during the flight and hadn't woken when the plane touched down. The task of rousing her and helping her get ready had fallen, as it so often did, to her personal secretary and friend, May Reis. But the real story behind the delay seems to have actually been nerves. It may have been a return to her hometown but it was a day she had been dreading.

The waiting crowd were given fifteen minutes.

---

2. Marilyn Back at Hollywood After Absence of Two Years, *The Shreveport Journal*, 8 July 1958, p. 16
3. Summers, Anthony. *Goddess: The Secret Lives of Marilyn Monroe*, Open Road Media, 2013, p. 238

The reporters asked how it felt to be back in Hollywood. 'It's wonderful to be back,' she said smiling. Like her new co-stars she hadn't had sight of the full script yet but expressed complete faith in the production team: 'All I know is that Billy Wilder is directing. This is good enough for me. I can hold up my end so much better when someone I completely trust is in charge.'[4]

Then she was gone – whisked away in a limousine to the Hotel Bel-Air – her base for the duration of filming.

The coverage the following day was extensive, but beneath the headlines a narrative had already taken root – a relentless cynicism about her reputation that made for irresistible copy.

Jack Smith, columnist for the *Los Angeles Times* captured the underlying tension with a wry remark, noting that Monroe had managed 'the seemingly impossible by arriving half an hour late aboard a Trans World Airlines plane that was on time.'[5]

4. A Look into Movieland, *The Reporter Dispatch*, 22 July 1958, p. 12
5. Marilyn Returns, *Los Angeles Times*, 9 July 1958, p. 3

Part one

Foundations

Chapter One

The Setup

With its thick curtains to block out the Californian sun, dark wooden furniture and piles of books and manuscripts the shared office of Billy Wilder and I.A.L. Diamond wasn't much to look at. Housed at Samuel Goldwyn Studios, the old Pickford-Fairbanks Studios at 1041 North Formosa Avenue, just off Santa Monica Boulevard, it radiated none of the spark that you would expect to see in the place where some of the funniest dialogue in postwar Hollywood movies would be born.

The two men who were usually to be found within those walls didn't necessarily look like the originators of such mirth either. Wilder, ever restless, was prone to pacing – ideas falling from his mouth faster than he could catch them. When he did write his thoughts down, it was in thick black pencil on yellow legal pads.

Diamond – Iz or Izzy to almost everyone – was a more serene presence. Precise, conservatively dressed, brown eyes peeking from behind his glasses, he committed their ideas to his typewriter with efficiency. His wife, Barbara, recalled that at home he sometimes talked to the device to work out the beat of the script. She would later describe Diamond as having a 'perfect ear for the rhythm of American speech.'[1]

The two men had been working together for only about a year but already their pattern was set. They treated screenwriting like a day job. As Wilder relished telling Joseph McBride, they were like 'farkakte bank tellers,' using the Yiddish word for "shitty," when asked, about their routine.[2] Each morning they arrived at the office – usually by nine or

1. Cohan, Steven. *Some Like It Hot (BFI Classics)*, British Film Institute, 2025, p. 39
2. McBride, Joseph. *Billy Wilder: Dancing on the Edge*, Columbia University Press, 2021, p. 384

nine-thirty. They'd read the trades – *Variety* and *The Hollywood Reporter*, gossip about the business, swap thoughts on films they'd recently seen, and talk about their wives – Barbara and Audrey. Then they got to work.

Wilder had been looking for such a partner. A long-standing collaboration with Charles Brackett had ended almost a decade earlier, and a handful of short-lived writing flings had left him adrift. He needed someone sharp, fast and – most importantly – funny as hell.

He had found him, unexpectedly, at the annual Writers Guild of America Awards. The ceremony, as per tradition, was a sparkling cocktail of back patting and backbiting: part industry tribute, part comedy roast. One sketch, by the little-known freelancer, caught Wilder's attention.

Wilder was intrigued and a meeting was arranged. The chemistry was immediate, as both men would later agree.

By the time they connected Diamond had already spent more than a decade working his way through the machinery of Hollywood.

Born as Iţec Domnici in 1920 in Romania, he emigrated with his family to the U.S. at the age of 9. They settled in Brooklyn, where Iţec – soon renamed Isidore – grew up speaking multiple languages and excelling in maths and science.

It was at Columbia University – where he had originally gone to study engineering – that Iz found his calling. He wrote comic sketches for the *Jester*, the campus humour magazine, and penned material for four *Varsity Shows* – those lavish, annual, student written musical revues that had also served as a training ground for the likes of Oscar Hammerstein II.

Then the movies came calling and Diamond took his place as a junior writer in Hollywood, still a relatively small city with a burgeoning main industry. When cinema had first started out it had originally been based in New York, which made sense then as the city was the centre of theatrical and live entertainment. But slowly the entrepreneurs and creatives began to shift west taking over an area that that had originally been farmland, just outside of Los Angeles. The first studio, was likely the Nestor Motion Picture Company, founded in 1909. They set up a permanent base a few years later, on the corner of Sunset Boulevard and Gower Street, and built what's often claimed to be the first proper motion picture stage.

Others followed quickly including the Triangle Film Corporation, and the Famous Players-Lasky Corporation, whose board included a man named

Samuel Goldfish. He later changed his last name to something which would prove more legendary: Goldwyn.

When Iz first arrived Hollywood was, in theory, a writer's town. At Paramount Pictures alone, over 100 writers were under contract – housed in an entire building of their own. Metro-Goldwyn-Mayer (MGM) had one too – long, narrow, and originally called the Scenario Building, then renamed the Writers' Building, as if that gave its residents extra power in the pecking order.

It was a bureaucracy, tasked with feeding the great industrial machine that churned out film after film – up to fifty or more a year, per studio. Big names like F. Scott Fitzgerald, P. G. Wodehouse, Aldous Huxley and Dorothy Parker were imported in, wined and dined, given their own suites, and tasked with turning in a box office hit. Most failed.

Ben Hecht, a former crime reporter from Chicago, who turned around the screenplay for the classic gangster movie, *Scarface* (1932) in less than two weeks, famously described Hollywood's literary ranks as 'for the most part a run of greedy hacks and incompetent thickheads.' Of the thousand or so writers huffing and puffing through the town, in his estimation, fewer than fifty had any real talent. The rest, he argued, were merely deadwood. [3]

The process didn't help. Screenwriting was considered a group activity. A single screenplay might carry half a dozen names, each writer having rewritten, salvaged, or "polished" the lasts. The studios' logic was simple: the more writers, the better the script. Most writers, unsurprisingly, disagreed.

But for newcomers such as Billy Wilder – who arrived at Paramount in the mid 1930s from Europe – creative partnerships offered clear advantages. Wilder later explained that he initially collaborated out of necessity, needing someone who could help navigate the English language and help him with screenplay construction. Over time he came to appreciate partnerships for their own sake.

There were those that stuck it out. And for the ones who persisted, there were perks including a steady pay cheque, a private office, and the possibility of a hit.

Diamond endured. Reliably industrious, he turned in his required pages each week like clockwork, a cog in the larger machine. He passed through

3. Life Among the "Thickheads," *The New York Times*, 27 May 1990, p. 2

many of the commercial studios – a mix of the "Big Five" and the "Little Three" – working at Paramount, then Universal Pictures and Warner Bros. He eventually landed at Twentieth Century-Fox, where he built a reputation as a dependable script writer. His name may not have been top of the billing, but he was steadily employed, and respected – even if his credits were often shared or his work rewritten.

One of his more visible (shared) credits was *Monkey Business* (1952), a Howard Hawks farce starring Cary Grant, Ginger Rogers and Marilyn Monroe. In fact, Diamond's typewriter helped shape several of her early appearances as he also worked on the scripts for *Let's Make It Legal* (1951) and *Love Nest* (1951).

By the mid-1950s, Diamond had grown tired of the studio grind with its endless rewrites and constant compromises. He went freelance, hoping for better scripts and better credit. And then he met Wilder.

Their first collaboration would be *Love in the Afternoon* (1957), a Paris-set romance starring a young Audrey Hepburn and an old Gary Cooper. The film itself was uneven, but the writing partnership behind it sparkled.

By the time they first worked together, Billy Wilder was at the top of his powers: a writer-director with critical acclaim and box office success. But like many in Hollywood, he was also a long way from home.

He had been born on 22 June 1906 and named Samuel for his grandfather.

His early years were spent in the town of Sucha, a province of Galicia – then part of the of the Austro-Hungarian Empire, now part of southern Poland. The region belonged to the Austrian half of the crumbling empire, which would not survive his adolescence.

The young Wilder grew up with his mother, Eugenia (Genia); his father, Max; and an older brother, Wilhelm. Max owned a small chain of railway station cafes and when the family relocated to Kraków he began managing a four-storey hotel and restaurant. But the outbreak of the First World War in 1914 upended everything. Galicia, near the border of the Russian Empire, became a battleground. And when Russian forces invaded, the Wilders fled to Vienna.

The eventual collapse of the empire bought with it hunger, inflation, and an uncertain future. The Allied naval blockade, which continued until 1919, only deepened the hardship. Max lost his work. The family – and everyone around them – struggled.

Despite everything, Samuel finished school and enrolled at the University of Vienna to study law. He lasted just three months.

The courtroom held little appeal. The newsroom, however, was a much more attractive proposition. He turned to journalism and as a sharp observer with a keen ear for human absurdity and a drive that made him prolific – he quickly found his footing. With a wide-ranging set of interests, he published constantly: crossword puzzles, short features, film reviews and celebrity profiles. He even dabbled in sports writing which was then still something of a novelty in European journalism. Sports coverage had only begun to flourish in the early twentieth century, fuelled by the rise of mass market tabloids. By the 1920s, the genre was gaining momentum and he embraced the vogue with gusto.

But more than anything Wilder was obsessed by the United States of America.

And in this he echoed a wider cultural wave sweeping across postwar Europe: *Amerikanismus* – a heady infatuation with American modernity. The 1920s saw the U.S. emerge as a global symbol of speed, glamour and possibility. The Model T. The Charleston. Jazz on every wireless.

Wilder's leanings had deep roots too. His mother, Genia, had lived in New York as a young woman, staying in a Madison Avenue apartment with an uncle who ran a jewellery business. Family legend had it that she once attended a Buffalo Bill's Wild West show at Madison Square Garden – and nicknamed her sons "Billie" and "Willie" in tribute. Wilder would eventually change "Billie" to the more masculine "Billy."

He loved jazz. He was an excellent dancer, was proficient at the Foxtrot and was dedicated to amassing an ever-growing collection of records. He particularly favoured the sounds of Paul Whiteman, the American bandleader who was often referred to as the "King of Jazz."

It was this passion for American music that would, quite unexpectedly, change the course of Wilder's life.

In 1926, Paul Whiteman & His Orchestra – one of the most popular ensembles in the world and among the first to have sold a million records – embarked on an extended European tour. Their entourage consisted of managers, stagehands, family members and 28 musicians including a violinist named Matty Malneck. On 31 March of that year, they set sail from New York aboard the RMS *Berengaria*, a Cunard liner already immortalised in *The Beautiful and Damned*, the 1922 novel by F. Scott Fitzgerald.

After engagements in London at various venues including the Kit-Cat Club, a purpose-built nightclub in the basement of the Capitol

Theatre, Haymarket, the band took a short break before continuing on to the continent, where shows were booked in the Netherlands, France and Germany. Whiteman chose to spend his downtime in Vienna.

Wilder saw his chance. He pitched a profile to a local newspaper and managed to secure an interview. The resulting piece, published on 13 June, was witty, breathless and above all, besotted. Particularly with Whiteman's moustache.

> 'There's that mustache of his again…a splendid, peerless, divine, superb mustache. It alone would have made Paul famous, without a doubt. It is cut quite short and twirled up in the middle, the two ends extend out quite far, and it points upwards towards his nostrils at a sharp angle; the tips have a bit of pomade, which adds an aromatic element to our visual pleasure. That is the mustache of the future. Copyright by Paul Whiteman.'[4]

Charmed by Wilder's enthusiasm as well as amused by his habit of quoting American song lyrics whenever his English faltered Whiteman invited the reporter to show him the nightlife of Vienna. As a man about town Wilder was ideally placed to do so and gave him a good time apparently. When the band continued on to Berlin, Whiteman asked Wilder to come along as a guide, with all expenses paid. He agreed – not letting the tiny detail of having never actually been there before put him off.

This was the Berlin of the Weimar Republic – that brief, brilliant, interlude between the end of the German Empire and the Nazi's rise to power in 1933. Politically fragile but also a golden age of cultural innovation where modern art, Bauhaus architecture, new music, new cinema, new science all flourished. Not to mention the legendary nightlife – hedonistic and unapologetically queer. It was also the most Americanised of all German cities, and it gave Wilder the perfect opportunity for reinvention. The trip was meant to last only three days but he didn't look back. Berlin – restless, modern and utterly decadent became his adopted home and suited him perfectly.

---

4. Isenberg, Noah (Ed). *Billy Wilder on Assignment: Dispatches From Weimar Berlin and Interwar Vienna*, Princeton University Press, 2021, p. 112

The German author Hans Sahl remembered him as 'a slender young man who wore his hat slanted, buried his hands in his pockets and played the American long before we had even discovered America.'[5]

Once again, Wilder earned his keep as a freelance writer. Building on his contributions to Vienna's local newspapers he became a regular fixture in Berlin's booming journalism scene – where forty five morning papers, fourteen evening editions, and at least two lunchtime tabloids jostled for readership. The pay was meagre, but the potential was vast.

He wrote about everything from society figures to oddball trends, but one series in particular captured attention: *"Herr Ober, bitte einen Tänzer!"* ("Waiter, A Dancer, Please!"), a four-part series for the newspaper *Berliner Zeitung am Mittag* which was later reprinted in *Die Bühne.*

The hook was Wilder's short-lived stint as a dancer for hire at Berlin's Eden Hotel, where you could rent a partner by the song. It was a thriving service. For about two months, he had clocked in twice a day: first from 4:30 to 7:00 p.m., in a stiff-collared suit, and then again from 9:30 p.m. to 1:00 a.m. in full tuxedo. He was paid per dance, averaging five marks a day. He even gave Charleston lessons on the side and would often claim to be the first person in Berlin to master that dance.

Though his writing career was thriving, Wilder was always searching for the next move. The growing opportunities represented by cinema, unsurprisingly, soon caught his eye. He only needed a break. One off-repeated origin story – delightfully improbable and almost definitely exaggerated (like so many tales in Wilder's repertoire) involved a chance encounter in a boarding house. As he told it, he was in his small room when a half-dressed stranger burst in begging for sanctuary. The man, who had been caught in a compromising position when his lover's boyfriend returned home early, needed a place to hide. Wilder, already developing a reputation as a ladies' man himself, was happy to oblige. When the grateful fugitive turned out to be a film producer, Wilder seized his chance and pitched some story ideas. As the man fled, he handed over some cash and, apparently, a route into the industry.

Whether it happened quite that way (or at all) is anyone's guess – there's no corroborating account of such an encounter, let alone a matching film

5. Gemünden, Gerd. *A Foreign Affair: Billy Wilder's American Films*, Berghahn Books, 2008, p. 11

credit. But no matter. What is certain is that by 1929, Wilder had found his way into the movie world.

Soon he was working at Universum-Film Aktiengesellschaft, the crown jewel of Weimar cinema. Founded in 1917, UFA became a symbol of German cultural ambition, a home to auteurs and innovators, and a potential serious rival to Hollywood. Having been largely cut off from foreign imports during the First World War, Germany had cultivated a robust domestic film culture. But by the mid-1920s, American movies were flooding back, bringing with them new ideas and stories.

The 1925 Parufamet Agreement formalised the connection in the way that powerful and wealthier parties have a tendency to do. In exchange for a much-needed financial lifeline UFA agreed to reserve seventy five percent of their screening capacity for American films, mostly from Paramount and MGM. In theory, it was a mutual agreement. In practice, it tipped heavily in Hollywood's favour. Still, the overlap between the two would prove significant – especially as Germany's political climate began to shift ominously.

By 1933 the Nazis had seized power, and Berlin was transformed into the nerve centre of the Third Reich. For artists, writers, and intellectuals, especially Jewish ones, the atmosphere swiftly turned from uncertain to unmistakably perilous. Wilder recalled witnessing a brutal scene: SS men beating an elderly Jewish man to death in the street. The moment, he said, was decisive. Like many others with the youth, means and luck to do so, he fled. 'It seemed the wise thing for a Jew to do,' he would later remark.[6]

By March he had arrived in Paris, a hub for the displaced where his neighbours included the actor Peter Lorre and other refugees from UFA and Germany.

There, Wilder began rebuilding. Within months he had co-directed his first feature film, *Mauvaise Graine* (1934). It was a scrappy, guerilla-style production – they had almost no money, no access to sound stages, and had to improvise constantly. Car chases were filmed on the fly, with cameras strapped to the back of trucks. They couldn't afford extras, so Wilder took on a small acting role.

---

6. Lane, Anthony. *Nobody's Perfect: Writings From the New Yorker*, Picador, 2002, p. 716

France had never been his final destination and his focus was already on Hollywood. He pitched an idea to a former UFA producer who had already relocated and found work with Columbia Pictures. The producer liked it and offered Wilder a deal to expand the treatment into a full screenplay. The contract came with a weekly salary – and a ticket to the United States.

In January 1934, Wilder boarded the ocean liner RMS *Aquitania*, bound for New York. A few weeks after that he arrived in Los Angeles – once again starting almost from scratch.

When the film project collapsed, having never moved beyond a first draft, Wilder found himself stranded in Mexicali, Mexico, after his six-month visa expired. Armed only with a birth certificate and passport, he faced rigid immigration quotas for Europeans. In Wilder's telling he charmed the U.S. consul by declaring, "I write movies." The official, a film lover, approved his visa renewal with the instruction: 'Write some good ones.' When Wilder told this story in 1988 at the 60th Academy Awards, he concluded 'I've tried ever since. I certainly didn't want to disappoint that dear man in Mexicali.'[7]

Wilder made it back to the United States (he would become a citizen in 1939) and soon landed a screenwriting contract at Paramount. There, he formed what would become a legendary partnership with Charles Brackett.

7. Hopp, Glenn. *Billy Wilder*, Pocket Essentials, 2001, p. 12

Chapter Two

Rare as Radium

Brackett and Wilder's base of operations was a three-room suite on the ground floor of the Paramount Writers' Building: one room for their secretary, Helen Hernandez; a second dubbed the "Game Room," where Wilder kept his trusty cribbage board at the ready; and the third, a larger room affectionately known as "the Bedroom" – not for any scandalous activities, but for Brackett's cherished midday nap.

From the day they started working together, the difference between the two was striking. Brackett favoured double-breasted suits in conservative tones. Wilder, in contrast, was casual – a pullover, rolled sleeves, no tie kind of guy. One was measured and aloof; the other, intense and always in motion.

As *Liberty* magazine, put it in 1945:

> 'The distinguished Viennese looking gentleman is Charles Brackett of Saratoga Springs, New York. The tough New Yorkerish cherub is Mr Billy Wilder, from Vienna, Austria … Brackett looks like the vice-president of a small-town bank, which he is. Wilder looks like one of the cynical police reporters from *The Front Page*, which he was.'[1]

Their collaboration was fraught but fruitful. Wilder could be hypersensitive to criticism and explosive over perceived slights. Brackett, more stoic, had to learn to adapt. As he wrote in his posthumously published diaries:

1. Idea-a-Minute Men, *Liberty*, 4 May 1945, p. 19

> 'Suggest an idea, have it torn apart and despised. In a few days it would turn up, slightly changed, as Wilder's idea. Once I got adjusted to that way of working, our lives were simpler.'[2]

They bickered but rarely stayed mad for long.

But while their fights were an open secret, *The New York Times* once called them 'the happiest couple in Hollywood,' noting how unusual the partnership was:

> 'These collaborators exercise an astonishing degree of self-government on the Paramount lot. Writers not generally given to soft talk about fellow artists are quick to admit that the Brackett-Wilder setup is rare as radium.'[3]

And for all the volatility the Brackett and Wilder years were remarkable. From the late 1930s through the 1940s, they co-wrote a string of sharp, sophisticated films – works that earned acclaim and professional recognition. At the 14th Academy Awards, which celebrated films from 1941, they were nominated for "Best Writing (Screenplay)" for *Hold Back the Dawn*. That same year Wilder, this time with Thomas Monroe, was also nominated for "Best Writing (Original Story)" for *Ball of Fire*.

But Billy had soon begun once again to stretch himself beyond writing.

It was just that screenwriters, even the very successful ones who were allowed to work on a writing project from beginning to end, were still only cogs in the studio machine. They wrote the scripts but once they passed them over control was lost. Directors could – and often did – change everything. Wilder hated that. He didn't only want to write movies. He wanted to make them. To see his vision all the way through to the screen.

But at that time the Hollywood studio system didn't encourage such evolution and the process remained strictly segmented. Writers wrote. Directors directed. Producers watched the money.

However, change was coming.

---

2. Slide, Anthony, It's the Pictures That Got Small" Charles Brackett on Billy Wilder and Hollywood's Golden Age, Columbia University Press, 2014, p. xvii
3. The Happy Union of Brackett and Wilder, *New York Times*, 18 April 1948, p. X5

Preston Sturges sold his story *The Great McGinty* (1940) to Paramount for $10 in exchange for the ability to also direct it. The following year writer John Huston's directorial debut, *The Maltese Falcon*, made waves. These were examples of screenwriters who'd been granted the reins and had delivered hits. Wilder noticed and prepared for his own turn.

He had already begun closely studying the work of other directors, particularly Howard Hawks, the great master of screwball comedy. After completing the script for *Ball of Fire*, Wilder spent several months on set observing Hawks at work, paying close attention to how he staged scenes and linked them together. What impressed him most was Hawk's technical precisions and his ability to give even individual scenes their own internal structure and momentum. Above all, Wilder came away with lessons that would shape his own filmmaking especially the art of keeping everything simple.

Wilder lobbied the studio heads hard to direct a romantic comedy he had co-written with Brackett. Brackett had his doubts believing Wilder was too volatile, too quick-tempered to manage actors. But the studio was eventually convinced. The result was *The Major and the Minor* (1942), a classic screwball farce with a knowingly absurd premise: Ginger Rogers plays a woman who disguises herself as a pre-teen to buy a cheap train ticket. Naturally, chaos and rather disturbing romantic misunderstandings follow.

Though Wilder had directed before in Europe, *The Major and the Minor* marked his Hollywood debut. But he didn't do it alone.

By his side was editor Doane Harrison – a Paramount veteran since the silent era who brought with him a deep technical expertise that would prove invaluable.

On set, Harrison became for Wilder what his writing partners were on the page: a trusted creative collaborator who instinctively understood him and vice versa. Their partnership spanned more than two decades, ending only with Harrison's death in 1968.

More than anyone, he taught Wilder cutting in camera technique. While it was quite typical for directors to shoot extensive extra "coverage" including wide, over-the-shoulder, and reaction shots which offered flexibility in the editing room, Harrison encouraged Wilder to take a different approach. Every shot was meticulously planned in advance. Every angle was already decided before the camera rolled. Whilst Harrison was ever present on set to make sure there was enough coverage to cut a scene together there would be no unnecessary excess footage and no alternatives. It reduced costs but, more importantly, gave no opportunity for studio executives to re-edit the film behind the director's back.

The method offered Wilder something he prized above all: control. He didn't want studio executives 'fooling with his angles' recalled producer Walter Mirisch.[4]

But it also came with risks. Wilder shot in long, continuous "master scenes" that covered entire sequences in a single take. With no alternate shots to fall back on, if an actor flubbed a line halfway through then the whole scene had to be redone. One mistake could cost an entire morning's work.

As Wilder explained: 'Most people cover themselves – first a wide shot, then a medium, then over-the-shoulder, then close-ups. The actors say the same lines thirty times, from every angle. Me? I overlap one or two speeches, but I shoot knowing exactly how it's going to cut together. I don't cover myself. I just hope it works.'[5]

The *Major and the Minor* was a modest hit – but it was successful enough to grant Wilder more opportunities. Over his career he wrote and directed films that would walk a canny line between box office gold and boundary pushing.

One of his biggest hits came in 1944 with *Double Indemnity*. It was only Wilder's third outing as a Hollywood director, but it marked a turning point – not only for his career, but for American cinema. Based on James M. Cain's crime novel (itself inspired by a real life 1927 case involving a housewife, her lover, and a murdered husband), the film helped define what would be called film noir: morally murky, visually shadowy, and unmistakably stylish.

For *Double Indemnity* the screenplay was co-written with the already well-known crime writer Raymond Chandler. The collaboration would be notoriously difficult. Chandler disliked Wilder's brashness and had little patience for the peculiar compromises and restrictions placed on the script

4. *Nobody's Perfect – The Making of Some Like It Hot* (October Films, 2001)
5. My First Encounter with Billy Wilder, *Kevin Lally on Film,* https://kevinlallyonfilm.com/2023/06/16/my-first-encounter-with-billy-wilder/ accessed 9 June 2025

in the name of morality. Wilder just didn't like Chandler. But despite, or perhaps because of, the tension, the results were electric.

Not for the last time Wilder would have quite a task convincing his leads to sign on. Both Barbara Stanwyck and Fred MacMurray supposedly worried about what playing a femme fatale and a murderer respectively might do to their careers. MacMurray was particularly concerned about playing a character out of his normal range and his ability to take on such a serious role. He even warned Wilder against casting him saying, 'You're making the mistake of your life.'[6] But alongside Edward G. Robinson, as the dogged investigator, their turns as Phyllis Dietrichson and the doomed insurance salesman, Walter Neff, helped make *Double Indemnity* into a sensation. It snagged seven Oscar nominations – including "Best Motion Picture," "Best Director," "Best Screenplay," and "Best Actress" for Stanwyck.

Reunited with Charles Brackett the team (along with co-writer D.M. Marshman Jr.) would next hit another artistic high-water mark with *Sunset Boulevard* (1950) – a darkly glittering and savage tale of faded fame, vanity, and the rot at the heart of Hollywood. It told the story of Norma Desmond, an actress played by the magnificent silent screen star Gloria Swanson and her character's delusional dreams of a comeback. This production earned them their third joint Academy Award – for "Best Story and Screenplay" – but behind the scenes it was the end of the road.

Brackett, the consummate diplomate, recording the dissolution of their partnership with bittersweet clarity in his diary. He recalled Wilder bluntly stating that this would be their last film together, explaining that he wanted to pursue more politically daring material and work with greater independence. Brackett noted that he received this news with a mix of 'consternation and relief,' given how difficult the collaboration had become but that they simply 'resumed writing.'[7]

Wilder, typically more guarded, offered his own version of events: 'Something had worn out and the spark was missing. Besides, it was becoming like a bad marriage.'[8] He rarely dwelled on the split publicly – when

6. Phillips, Gene D. *Some Like It Wilder: The Life and Controversial Films of Billy Wilder*, The University Press of Kentucky, 2010, p. 61
7. Slide, p. 327
8. Ibid, p. 6

pressed, he insisted it was amicable, that they'd remained friends, and that it had simply been time. But the truth was less tidy and the cracks had been forming over the years until they became impossible to ignore.

From there Wilder would move on to new writing partners – Ernest Lehman, Charles Lederer and Harry Kurnitz – and the hits kept coming. However, his relationship with Paramount had also now begun to splutter.

The real rupture came in 1953 with *Stalag 17*, a World War II drama set in a German prisoner-of-war camp. It starred William Holden as one of a group of captured American airmen – one of whom, it turns out, is informing the prison guards about their plans to escape.

The studio loved the film – until it came time to distribute it to the newly reopened post-war German market. The executives requested a small "adjustment" – to change the spy from a German to a Pole. [9] As Kevin Lally related in *Wilder Times: The Life of Billy Wilder*, his response was: 'Fuck you, gentlemen. Haven't you got any shame? You ask me, who lost his family in Auschwitz, to do a mistake like this? Unless somebody apologizes, forget about my contract. Goodbye, Paramount.'[10]

His last film for the studio was to be the romantic comedy, *Sabrina* (1954). The cast was stellar: Audrey Hepburn and Humphrey Bogart included. But the atmosphere on set was anything but harmonious. Wilder found himself in near-constant conflict with Bogart who had been sceptical from the start – dismissing the project as 'a crock of crap.'[11]

Bogart, who was not a particularly easy-going colleague, bristled at both his co-stars and his director. He griped that Hepburn needed too many takes to nail her lines and grumbled about her lack of experience. But his real target was Wilder and, in particular, his practice of not having a completed script by the time filming started.

> 'He's the kind of Prussian German with a riding-crop type of director I don't like to work with … He works with the

9. While Wilder believed his family had died in Auschwitz Concentration Camp later the researcher Andreas Hutter confirmed that his mother had died at Kraków-Płaszów slave labour camp in 1943 and his stepfather, Bernard Siedlisker, in 1942 in Belzec extermination camp. His grandmother, Balbina Baldinger died in the ghetto in Nowy Tag, Krakow. Wilder never learnt their true fates.
10. Lally, Kevin. *Wilder Times: The Life of Billy Wilder*, Henry Holt and Company, Inc, 1996
11. Madsen, Axel. *Billy Wilder*, Indiana University Press, 1969, p. 99

> writer and excludes the actor. I didn't know what the end of the picture would be, as to who gets Sabrina. It irritated me so I went to work on him.'[12]

Wilder, for his part, didn't much care about being liked. On set, he had a reputation for being demanding, controlling and rather cruel. Some called him a monster and a sadist. One colleague memorably described his mind as being 'full of Gillette blue blades.'[13] Typically unrepentant Wilder would pronounce the role of a director as being a cross between 'a policeman, a midwife, a psychoanalyst, a sycophant, and a bastard.'[14]

With *Sabrina* in the can, Wilder's long tenure at Paramount came to an unceremonious end.

What followed was a brief period of professional wandering.

His first major post-Paramount venture came in 1955 with *The Seven Year Itch,* a romantic comedy distributed by Twentieth Century Fox. Wilder co-wrote the screenplay with George Axelrod (who had written the original Broadway hit play) and also, as had now become standard, took on directorial duties.

At the centre of it all was Marilyn Monroe, billed only as "The Girl" – a fantasy figure who becomes the object of desire for a neurotic married man (Tom Ewell) left by his family to boil in his Manhattan apartment during a sweltering summer.

This was Wilder's first time working with Monroe, and he quickly discovered that while she was luminous on the screen she was also occasionally exasperating to work with. Filming ran three weeks over schedule, thanks in no small part, apparently, to Monroe's dependence on her acting coach, Natasha Lytess. Natasha had been mentoring Marilyn since practically the beginning of her career and was a controversial presence on the set. She coached Monroe on nearly every line, much to the irritation of her fellow refugee – Lytess had also fled Europe – Wilder. Never known for his patience, Wilder found the arrangement baffling but ultimately endured it, delivering a huge hit film. Reflecting on the experience, he admitted that

12. Goodman, Ezra. *The Fifty-Year Decline and Fall of Hollywood*, Simon & Schuster, 1961, p. 265
13. Leaming, Barbara. *Marilyn Monroe*, Weidenfeld & Nicholson, 1998, p. 314
14. Lane, p. 711

he never quite knew how Monroe would approach a scene and often had to guide or redirect her performance. Yet he remained deeply admiring of her screen presence, describing her as 'a remarkable person' who was 'much better on the screen than not on the screen.[15]

The following years were busy for Wilder. In 1957 three of his films were released in quick succession: *The Spirit of St Louis* (for Warner Bros.), *Witness for the Prosecution* (United Artists) and *Love in the Afternoon* – his first collaboration with Iz and his first project for Allied Artists Picture Corporation. With an executive team including two brothers – Walter and Harold Mirisch – this company had spent years churning out low-budget B-movies but were now determined to reinvent themselves as serious contenders in first features. To achieve this goal, they had gone hunting for big names – and they got them. In early 1955, Allied had signed a trio of directing heavyweights: William Wyler, John Huston and Billy Wilder.

The appeal to the directors wasn't only creative freedom (although they were also promised plenty of that). Allied Artists offered something even more enticing – stock options. At a time when the U.S. income tax rate on top earners hovered around seventy percent, equity would prove to be an attractive incentive.

Wilder was slated to deliver the flagship film of this new era for Allied but was, unfortunately, unavailable. As was John Huston. And so, the first venture went to Wyler, who began work on *Friendly Persuasion* (1956).

The project looked promising but Wyler was a notorious perfectionist, and the film quickly spun out of financial control. What had begun as a relatively modest $1.5 million production ballooned to more than double that figure when Wyler proved himself to be in no hurry to finish.

As Walter Mirisch recalled:

> 'I saw him make up to fifty and sixty takes of a scene. I saw him reduce actors to tears. I saw actors come up to him and say, "I don't know what to try anymore. What do you want me to do?" Wyler would invariably say, "When I see it, I'll know it." Nothing could hurry him.'[16]

15. Crowe, Cameron. *Conversations with Wilder*, Knopf, 1999, p. 157
16. Mirisch, Walter. *I Thought We Were Making Movies, Not History*, University of Wisconsin Press, 2008, p. 80

Though *Friendly Persuasion* earned some critical praise it failed to make an impact at the box office. Wilder's own contribution, *Love in the Afternoon,* fared little better commercially. Though it came in on budget at a respectable $2 million, it struggled to find an audience – a serious problem in an era when a film's fate depended almost entirely on its initial theatrical run. These were the days before widespread television rights, home videos, DVDs, or streaming after all. Under these more limited commercial circumstances theatrical releases were everything, and a slow start almost always meant a quick death.

Money at Allied Artists grew tight. And by the time John Huston was finally available to begin his project, the coffers had already been drained and his film was shelved. Soon after Allied let the contracts with Wyler, Huston and Wilder lapse.

The crisis wasn't a purely financial one and behind the scenes, the top team were pulling in opposite directions. Some executives, rattled by the losses, wanted to retreat to the familiar territory of B-movies. Others – most notably the Mirisch brothers – recognised that the industry was changing and were still determined to aim higher. So, they left to start their own company.

Chapter Three

Fade Out

Almost since the industry's inception, Americans had flocked to movie houses in extraordinary numbers. Though attendance had begun to slip towards the end of the 1930s, the war years had given it a dramatic second wind. From dipping to around 55 million admissions a week in 1941, a few years later that number had nearly doubled. Wartime, it turned out, was boom time for Hollywood.

There were plenty of reasons for this. With factories running 24-hour shifts and little else on offer during downtime, movies became the obvious escape. Cinemas stayed open late to accommodate workers, and people flooded in – hungry for distraction, comfort and a bit of onscreen glamour. Of course, Hollywood wasn't entirely insulated. The war made its mark – actors were drafted, budgets were trimmed, and story lines changed to reflect a world at conflict.

With peace, in 1945, things began to shift again. Attendance figures, though still strong, started to backslide. It wasn't entirely unexpected. Studio executives like Darryl F. Zanuck of Twentieth Century-Fox had anticipated the dip, but it was no less unsettling when it came. 'When the bottom dropped out of the war-flushed attendance boom,' he observed, 'readjustment towards efficiency became necessary.'[1]

For Zanuck and the other studio moguls this meant cutbacks and a lot more hesitancy when greenlighting new projects.

The makeup of the American moviegoing public was changing too. The core audience was now older, busier and increasingly domesticated. Families with young children weren't heading out to the pictures, instead

1. Solomon, Aubrey. *Twentieth Century-Fox: A Corporate and Financial History*, The Scarecrow Press Inc, 1988, p. 67

they were staying in with the radio. And looming on the horizon was another rival: television.

This particular competition had been slow to fruition. Television (or at least demonstrations of moving silhouette images) may have been introduced to the public as a scientific curiosity by John Logie Baird at Selfridges department store in London in 1925, but decades after that, it was still little more than a futuristic novelty for most Americans. In 1948, *Fortune* magazine estimated that ninety percent of the population had never even seen a TV broadcast. But then, everything changed – and fast.

By 1950, just twelve percent of American households had a television set. A mere ten years later, that figure had soared – and there were forty-six million sets blinking away in American living rooms. In the space of a decade, television had transformed from a novelty to a necessity.

Even so the biggest transformation in postwar Hollywood hadn't come from shifting audience tastes or developing technology, instead it came from the U.S. government.

The Supreme Court had handed down a landmark antitrust ruling (United States v. Paramount Pictures, Inc.,) in 1948, a decision that permanently altered the way the American film industry did business. The Justice Department had been circling for at least a decade, determined to dismantle what it viewed as an illegal monopoly. At the core of the case was vertical integration – a system that gave the studios total control over the life of a film.

It was a model perfected by Paramount mogul Adolph Zukor and had dominated since the silent era. Under this arrangement, studios held the reins on every part of the process. They had everyone including the writers, directors, editors and actors under the then coveted long-term contracts. They ran the processing labs, printed the reels, shipped them out and made sure they landed in their own cinemas. By 1945 the so called "Big Five," also known as "The Majors" – Paramount, MGM, Warner Bros., Twentieth Century Fox and RKO Radio Pictures – controlled seventeen percent of America's picture houses which generated close to half of the nation's total box office revenue.

This system had allowed the studios to impose some deeply unpopular and rather unethical practices. Chief among them was block booking – a tactic that forced cinemas to purchase packages of films, often containing one or two prestige pictures padded with a slate of lower tier offerings.

Worse still was blind bidding, where businesses were expected to commit to screening movies they hadn't even had the chance to preview.

The Paramount Decision determined that these practices were a violation of antitrust laws and the studios were ordered to divest themselves of their chains. They fought the ruling, of course, until the first crack came from RKO. With eccentric business tycoon and film producer Howard Hughes at the helm – and with fewer picture houses than its rivals – they had the least to lose. Hughes split the company into two: RKO Picture Corporation and RKO Theatres.

The move rather undermined the others' claim that such a separation would be unworkable. And soon, another studio, Paramount, followed suit. In 1949, it spun off its picture house operations into a new company: United Paramount Theatres. The rest soon caved as Twentieth Century Fox, Warner Bros., and MGM all sold off their holdings.

Without guaranteed screens, the majors could no longer rely on a built-in marketplace. The film industry shifted from a vertically integrated, top-down model to a more open, competitive one.

This was only the first wave of change. Television broadcasting was developing and fresh challenges were also building overseas. Countries like Britain who were keen to revive their own film industries after the end of the Second World War and reduce the overwhelming dominance of Hollywood – began pushing back. In 1947, the British government imposed a punishing seventy five percent tax on all revenue generated by foreign films. And "foreign," in this context, almost always meant American. The industries in France, Germany and Italy were also starting to find their feet again.

And behind the scenes, even bigger shifts were underway.

A huge change came in 1950 when Lew Wasserman, head of the increasingly influential talent agency Music Corporation of America (MCA) negotiated a new deal for the actor James Stewart.

The plan was that Stewart offered to take no upfront fee for starring in *Winchester 73* (1950). In return, he would receive above-the-title billing and fifty percent of the profits. It was an unprecedented arrangement, but Universal agreed to it as it meant the studio would save on production costs. The actor would earn more money (in this particular case Stewart received $600,000) and pay less tax, since profits were assessed at a lower rate than salaries.

Even as the system was changing so was the audience and the places that people watched films. The number of admissions had fallen to nearly forty million a week and box office revenue dropped by nearly a third. In New York City alone fifty-five cinemas closed between 1948 and 1951. On the other hand, the number of drive-ins, which offered low-cost, car friendly screenings to young families and couples doubled.

The studios also tried to reinvent movies themselves. Widescreen formats arrived with fanfare. So did 3D, Cinerama, Smell-O-Vision, and other short-lived gimmicks – anything to tempt audiences back into their seats. But even with all of this studios still grew more cautious and slashed production schedules, with the number of films released annually dropping by over forty percent.

The system of offering hooks of long-term contracts and the cost of keeping hundreds of staff on year-round payroll – whether or not they were working – no longer made sense and began to be phased out.

And United Artists was one of the clearest signs of what would replace the old ways of working.

Founded in 1919 by four of the most powerful names in early Hollywood – Mary Pickford, her then husband Douglas Fairbanks, Charlie Chaplin and D.W. Griffith – United Artists was, from the start, something of a rebellion. As actors, directors and producers at the birth of the industry they saw the value of being able to control their own films, their own images, and – crucially – their own profits. Together, they decided, they'd be stronger. The studio executives were not amused. As legend has it, one sniffed that this was merely the lunatics taking 'charge of the asylum.'[2]

United Artists had launched as a distributor, offering a crucial platform for independently produced films to reach the public, providing producers with access to their own cinemas or renting out screen time in others not already tied up by the big studios themselves.

These independent producers either had their own assets like the Charlie Chaplin Studios on Sunset Boulevard, or, Mary Pickford's own production company, which was based at the Pickford-Fairbanks Studios on North Formosa Avenue.

---

2. Irving, Laurence. *Designing for the Movies: The Memoirs of Laurence Irving*, Scarecrow Books, 2005, p. 9; Hamilton, Ian. *Writers in Hollywood, 1915-1951*, Heinemann, 1990, p. 15

There is a publicity photograph from 1922 showing the couple standing proudly outside the entrance to their studio. Mary is perched on a ladder beneath a curved wooden sign while Douglas, slightly blurry in the exposure, beams with outstretched arms. You can see that the lot sat on the dusty edge of a largely undeveloped Hollywood, surrounded by dirt roads and open land.

It was here that Fairbanks' 1922 swashbuckling adventure *Robin Hood* was filmed. One of the most expensive movies of its day, with an, at the time, staggering $1 million budget, the production called for a sprawling outdoor set: a detailed recreation of twelfth century Nottingham, complete with an enormous replica of a medieval castle. The stronghold's interior boasted a royal banquet hall said to be the largest inside space in the world at the time – transcending even the grand vestibule at New York's Penn Station. The entire construction sprawled across fifteen acres, with two and a half devoted to the castle alone. A few years later, *The Thief of Bagdad* (1924) would be shot on the same lot, reusing and reimagining parts of the *Robin Hood* set into an exotic fantasy world.

Despite some triumphs United Artists struggled at first. The irony was that while it had no shortage of talent it didn't have enough films. The founding members were still contractually bound to other obligations and slow to deliver new projects. Chaplin in particular, meticulous to a fault, took a long time between releases. As a result, in its first few years, they were able to arrange the distribution of fewer than ten films annually, which was far too little to meet the demands of cinema owners and the public.

To bolster its slate, they began actively courting more independent producers. They offered distribution but also office space and sound stages on the North Formosa lot – now renamed the United Artists Studios.

Samuel Goldwyn was among the first major figure to come aboard, after years of working with a rotating cast of distributors. Joseph Schenck joined the collective, agreeing to deliver six films starring his then-wife, Norma Talmadge. He also brought in his brother-in-law Buster Keaton. Around the same time, Gloria Swanson, one of the era's most powerful actresses, also signed up. And over the years many of these became formal partners including Samuel Goldwyn in 1927 and David O. Selznick shortly after.

And by the late 1940s it had become relatively routine for actors to establish their own production companies, although not always, of course, in conjunction with United Artists. Humphrey Bogart left Warner Bros. to form Santana Productions, focusing mostly on noir films released through Columbia. George Raft, established Star Films, producing titles like *Intrigue* (1947).

But behind the scenes, the collective was struggling. Poor management, internal disputes, high profile exits and a string of undistinguished films began to take their toll. Among the founding members there were also changes too. Mary Pickford retired from acting, although she continued working as a producer. She and Douglas Fairbanks, once Hollywood's iconic golden couple, divorced. Meanwhile Charlie Chaplin became increasingly isolated, controversial and politically embattled. As for D.W. Griffith – well his association with them was only short-lived and hardly covered in glory.

The ownership of the studio lot itself was also unusually complex. Pickford and Fairbanks originally held the deed to the land, while Schenck and Goldwyn owned the buildings and studio facilities. After Schenck left, Goldwyn took over his share. When Fairbanks died in 1939, Mary claimed his portion, making her and Goldwyn essentially joint owners of the land and facilities respectively.

Goldwyn eventually quit the collective (but not the property) and renamed it Samuel Goldwyn Studios, sparking a long-standing dispute with Pickford. By then, its active filming space had shrunk to eleven acres.

Chronically underfunded and struggling against the then still vertically integrated studio giants, United Artists' products faltered. And by the end of the decade, the remaining partners found themselves sinking deeper into debt, losing about $100,000 a week and facing the very real threat of receivership.

Their fortunes changed in 1951 when a group of investors including Arthur B. Krim and Robert Benjamin – two New York entertainment lawyers – approached Pickford and Chaplin with a bold proposition. Having worked closely with film companies through their law firm they had a vision of a rescued United Artists, believing its name, legacy, and distribution infrastructure, would allow it to thrive – but only if run differently.

The consortium intended to take over, covering its overheads and supplying it with content. The deal was that if they turned a profit within three years, they would receive fifty percent ownership with the possibility of then taking full control at a later date.

Pickford was eager to agree. Chaplin was initially reluctant but eventually changed his mind. After premiering his heavily autobiographical film *Limelight* (1952) in London, the British born Chaplin had his U.S. re-entry permit revoked. Facing accusations of communism, financial strain and exhausted from self-inflicted scandal, he chose self-exile in Switzerland and accepted the deal.

With agreements in place the group quickly raised significant funds through loans and began financing bold independent projects and within two years had turned a profit – $313,000 in the first twelve months alone. Two major box office hits, *The African Queen* (1951) and *High Noon* (1952), helped seal their success.

Having met their initial target, they immediately started negotiations to purchase the remaining shares. It took a few years, but they secured the rest – paying Chaplin $1.1 million and Pickford $3 million. In 1957 the new owners took United Artists public, offering $17 million in stocks and debentures for sale.

The new UA continued to function primarily as a financier and distributor by offering access to cinemas and money by purchasing completed films from independent producers for a flat fee.

They continued operations out of the old lot on North Formosa. And, after years of legal wrangling, Samuel Goldwyn had become the sole owner of everything when he bought out Pickford's share – a move that was financially profitable but personally and emotionally devastating for her.

Continuing to offer the lot to independent producers had many advantages and allowed United Artists to be lean, agile, and in tune with the times. This was almost the opposite of the major studios, who were still struggling to adapt to the changing reality.

The big studios had slashed their rosters, released many contract players, but were still burdened by enormous overheads. For example, MGM had its studio facility in Culver City spanning hundreds of acres.

The space had started more modestly: a sixteen-acre lot built in the mid-1910s for Triangle Film Corporation, set up by brothers Harry and Roy Aitken with the film makers D.W Griffith, Thomas Ince and Mack Sennett attached. Their ambitious plan was to supply their own network of cinemas with 200 films a year.

After Triangle Studios failed in 1918 the property's next tenant was Goldwyn Pictures Corporation, who purchased the facility for $325,000.

Goldwyn Pictures would go on to merge with Metro Pictures Corporation and Louis B. Mayer Pictures in 1924 to form Metro-Goldwyn-Mayer. The new company expanded aggressively, growing the lot to 44 acres. The following year, it acquired "Lot Two," located across the street, where construction began on a vast complex of permanent outdoor sets including streets, towns, and façades designed to stand in for any location a script might require. They kept expanding: "Lot Three" was added in 1936, "Lot Four" and "Lot Five" in 1940 and followed by "Lot Six," which was purchased in parcels throughout the next decade.

These vast facilities were symbols of power and prestige and enabled studios to churn out films at scale. But real estate meant maintenance. In contrast independent companies like those working with United Artists had no such burden and they were able to rent out the lots at the bigger studios in any case.

Meanwhile, an entirely new business model was taking shape under Lew Wasserman, head of the Music Corporation of America and a man with a bold, integrated vision for the company. MCA, originally a music talent agency had aggressively expanded into film and television becoming the most powerful agency in the industry, representing screenwriters, directors and actors.

Wasserman pioneered the concept of "packaging:" instead of simply negotiating deals for individual clients, MCA began offering complete, ready-to-go film packages which included a script, director, and stars, all from their own roster. Packaging further shifted power towards agencies and independent producers.

All these changes may have given the independents and smaller studios the opportunity to compete but the downside was that Hollywood lost its safety net. Without the stability of the studio system, the industry would need to become even more risk averse. Each film now, more than ever, had to carry its own weight both commercially and critically.

As a result, safer materials were increasingly sought out like pre-existing novels, hit plays, or remakes of older or obscure properties. Fewer films were made, and the stakes were higher. As Billy Wilder observed: 'Now they make you feel its life or death for a studio. "If you don't hit with this picture we have to dismiss all the secretaries, all the policemen. Everything is going."'[3]

3. Fawell, John. *The Hidden Art of Hollywood: In Defense of the Studio Film Era*, Praeger, 2008, p. 5

Chapter Four

Harold, Walter, and Marvin (and Irving)

After leaving Allied Artists the Mirisch brothers had set up a new company with each holding an equal share of stock and receiving the same salary. Their responsibilities were similarly balanced too: Harold served as President, Walter as Head of Production and Marvin as executive Vice President and Secretary-Treasurer. A fourth brother, Irving, was also an equal shareholder, though he remained uninvolved in day-to-day operations.

From the outset aware of the wider industry problems faced by the established studios, the Mirisch Company prioritised efficiency and their bottom line. As trade magazine *Variety* observed, the company aimed to maintain 'low overhead' while keeping quality high, with nearly all production spending directed toward what appeared on screen. This pledge to efficiency extended to their home base, which was the Samuel Goldwyn Studios. *Business Week* noted that, unlike the major studios, the Mirisches avoided investing in permanent facilities, instead renting office space and sound stages as needed to keep the costs down.[1]

A press release from this time outlined the brothers' vision to –

> 'find the best filmmakers and provide them with the very best story material and most talented associates – enabling the filmmaker to do the thing he most wants to do – concentrate completely on the films, on what appears on the screen and let

1. Kerr, Paul. *"A Small, Effective, Organization," The Mirisch Company, the Package - Unit System and the Production of Some Like it Hot* In Karen McNally (Ed) Billy Wilder, Movie-maker: Critical Essays on the Films, McFarland & Co, 2010, p. 118

> a small, effective organization handle all the other complex matters that are part of making a movie, ranging from negotiating contracts and financing, to persuading actors to work under the Mirisch banner, to arranging pre-production logistics, and perhaps most important, taking the completed film and supervising its merchandising on a coordinated world-wide basis.'[2]

With United Artists agreeing to distribute their films the brothers' next move was to approach Billy Wilder to offer him an initial two-picture deal which was to be a profit sharing "joint production venture."

Under the terms of this agreement, Wilder would be granted complete creative freedom: he had full approval of the crew, story, script, casting, and direction. He would also receive a salary as both writer and director, plus a percentage of the profits.

Wilder was delighted saying: 'All the Mirisch Company asks me is the name of the picture, a vague outline of the story and who's going to be in it. The rest is up to me. You can't get more freedom than that.'[3]

At this time, he was already deep into production on *Witness for the Prosecution*, the bleak, blackly comic courtroom drama set in London's Old Bailey. Based on Agatha Christie's 1953 play, it starred Marlene Dietrich, Charles Laughton, and Elsa Lanchester. But even as Wilder directed that project, conversations were already underway about what would be next.

In the meantime, the Mirisch brothers had moved quickly to establish themselves. Their first two pictures, *Man of the West* and *Fort Massacre*, were chosen for their low production costs and for a fast turnaround. The strategic purpose with these westerns, which were both released in 1958, was said to be primarily to get the phrase "The Mirisch Company Presents" onto screens as soon as possible.

With *Witness for the Prosecution* completed the Wilder/Diamond team would now find themselves under a new kind of pressure. The Mirisch

2. Balio, Tino. *United Artists: The Company That Changed the Film Industry*, University of Wisconsin Press, 1987, p. 165; Kerr, p. 118
3. Wood, Tom. *The Bright Side of Billy Wilder, Primarily*, Doubleday & Company, 1970, p. 179

Company's first two films had actually made little impact, and word around Hollywood was that if this third project didn't deliver, United Artists might pull the plug and end their deal. Expectations may have been high but the trouble was Billy and Iz weren't sure what they were going to tackle next.

They may not have had the next move in place but what they did have was the rhythm of their relationship which had quickly taken hold during their first collaboration.

With Brackett, Wilder had written his great dramas, and the association had been creatively fruitful but often tempestuous. But, under the banner of Ashton Productions, Wilder's partnership with Diamond was totally different and much more democratic. Joseph McBride in Billy Wilder: *Dancing on the Edge* quotes Walter Mirisch who remembered that 'Iz was a man of strong opinions, and Billy had great respect for him … Billy listened to his comments, and they discussed problems while Billy was shooting, or they might make some changes they would both agree upon. In terms of the writing, they were exceedingly collaborative, with a great deal of respect on both sides.[4]

Often, they would act out the sequences themselves to hear if the pace was right – to see if it played. At the end of each day, Iz would go home and type up the results. The next morning, they would go over it again. And when they had no writing commission or no ideas, sometimes they stared at each other in silence, waiting for something to spark.

At first, they toyed with a project for Audrey Hepburn, a film called *My Sister and I*, but that eventually fizzled out. Soon, though, another idea began to form. The spark came from Robert Thoeren, an Austrian-born screenwriter whose life in many ways mirrored Wilder's own. Thoeren had moved to France in the early 1930s before fleeing to Hollywood as Europe grew increasingly dangerous. He was hardly a well-known name and most of his work had been B-pictures, but there was one screenplay, co-written early in his career with Michael Logan, that had kept resurfacing.

The story had already been made into a movie twice. First, in France in 1935 as *Fanfare d'amour* (*Fanfare of Love*). Then again in 1951 as *Fanfaren der Liebe* (*Fanfares of Love*), a film set in post-war West Germany.

It was a simple premise with plenty of potential: two out-of-work musicians, desperate for a gig, disguise themselves to get a job. In *Fanfaren*

---

4. McBride, p. 387

der Liebe, directed by Kurt Hoffmann, that meant Hans and Peter becoming Hansi and Petra to sneak into an all-female band.

Wilder, who had very likely known Thoeren during his years in Berlin, had seen the second version and remembered it vividly if not fondly. But the core idea obviously intrigued him.

He recognised the story itself had the bones of a great comedy even if he had seen little value in the previous versions. They would strip away the tone, the pacing, and much of the plot, keeping only the basic premise as a starting point. Their version would be lighter than the German film and, as Wilder happily admitted, would be filled with far more dirty jokes.

Even so, their film keeps its distance from the original source material. In the opening titles, it is mentioned only briefly – "suggested by a story by R. Thoeren and M. Logan" – tucked beneath the larger credits for Wilder and Diamond. Still, more of *Fanfaren der Liebe* made it into their project than anyone involved typically liked to acknowledge. There was the drag, of course, but also the train journey, the all-female band led by a woman, the glamorous hotel, and the messy romantic entanglements. But once you've seen both films, the echoes are hard to ignore.

For the Mirisches and United Artists this was exactly the sort of project they liked. The fact that the story had already been a hit in Germany – and even spawned a 1953 sequel, *Fanfaren der Ehe (Fanfares of Marriage)*, with Hans and Peter now married to women – made it feel like a fairly safe bet. Walter Mirisch quickly gave his approval and moved fast to secure the rights and the company bought a ten-year option on the screenplay, a bargain in an industry where exciting properties often went for eye-watering sums. But this one wasn't exactly hot – at least, not yet.

Once the rights were secured, the real work could begin.

The ultimate challenge of storytelling is establishing the stakes. Wilder and Diamond already knew their story would also centre on two male musicians disguising themselves as women, but in both the previous versions, the concealment was a choice which the characters could simply abandon whenever they wanted. Nothing truly hung in the balance, and for them that wasn't enough of a motivation.

They asked themselves what could drive two struggling artists to take such an extreme and ongoing action. For sustained (as opposed to merely a farcical interlude for cheap laughs) and credible on screen drag to work in late 1950s America it had to matter. There had to be a "hammerlock." Wilder and Diamond concluded that nothing short of mortal threat would be sufficient. Joe and Jerry had to believe that abandoning their disguises would cost them their lives

The answer arrived, as such things often do, after hours of consideration. The solution was obvious once they found it: the characters would witness a murder. That changed everything. The stakes were now immediate and deadly.

But there was another problem. How could they make the disguises believable without losing the audience's recognition of the actors beneath the wigs? How could they make this work on screen? Iz found the elegant solution – make it a period piece. As he put it: 'when everybody's dress looks eccentric, somebody in drag looks no more peculiar than anyone else.'[5]

Once that decision was made, everything began to fall into place. Even the situation of the murder itself didn't take too long to choose. Wilder had walked into the office one morning grinning. He'd been driving home the night before when the idea struck. He pitched it to Diamond:

> "Chicago. 1929. The St. Valentine's Day Massacre."

It was perfect.

Now the story had teeth. Two broke musicians, accidental witnesses to an actual mob hit, forced to flee for their lives. If they took off their disguises, they were dead. Nothing could be a stronger motivation than that.

The film would also draw on a much older theatrical tradition which went back centuries from Ancient Greek theatre to Shakespeare. By the mid-twentieth century, male characters dressed in women's clothes for potential comedy value had become a familiar plot device. In the short film *Cutey Plays Detective* (1913) the main character disguises himself as a maid. Laurel and Hardy had done it. So had the elastic mouthed Joe E. Brown in *Shut My Big Mouth* (1942), and Cary Grant in Howard Hawks' *I Was a Male War Bride* (1949). Wilder himself had used a suggestion of drag before – in *Stalag 17*, when Sgt Harry Shapiro (Harvey Lembeck)

5. Sikov, Ed. *On Sunset Boulevard: The Life and Times of Billy Wilder*, University Press of Mississippi, 2017, p. 409

fashions a straw wig to pose as Betty Grable during a dance scene with Sgt Stanislaus "Animal" Kuzawa (Robert Strauss).

But there was something deeper going on, too. Placing the film during this period would also draw on Wilder's Weimar experiences and the film culture that he had grown up in: much more open and experimental, especially when it came to gender and sexuality. Drag, Queerness, and non-traditional identities were part of life.

Also setting the film in the late 1920s would add more than mere danger; it brought a rich, visually textured world of prohibition-era America with bootleggers, speakeasies, gangsters, and flappers as backdrops.

Wilder summed up their vision as '*Scarface* meets *Charley's Aunt*,' referencing the wildly popular 1892 stage comedy in which two Oxford students rope a friend into impersonating a rich aunt to chaperone a romantic rendezvous.[6]

The proposed setting would also tap into a wider cultural mood. North America was experiencing a wave of comforting nostalgia for the Roaring Twenties – a decade remembered as freer and more glamorous, filled with jazz, bathtub gin, and carefree rebellion, in stark contrast to the stifling gender expectations of the Eisenhower years, Cold War tensions and atomic-age anxieties.

Whilst it would reach its peak in the mid 1960s Hollywood had already leant into the trend. *Singin' in the Rain* (1952) looked back fondly at the movie industry's transition from silent films to sound, while record labels like Grand Award released *The Roaring 20s Special Edition* albums, featuring jazz-era hits by Enoch Light and the Charleston City All-Stars. The designs of these album covers brimmed with flappers, dancers, and Art Deco flair.

The nostalgic aesthetic reached into celebrity culture too. In 1955, *Screenland* magazine covered a speakeasy-themed party hosted by Debbie Reynolds and Eddie Fisher in their garage, fully decked out in 1920s style. And in June 1958, just weeks before she returned to Hollywood Marilyn Monroe posed for photographer Richard Avedon as actresses from stage and screen who had been famous in previous decades for *LIFE* magazine's forthcoming Christmas edition. Whilst she dazzled as Lillian Russell, Theda Bara and Jean Harlow it was her recreation of Clara Bow in full fringed flapper dress that foreshadowed her next role. The accompanying article, *My Wife Marilyn*, to be penned by Arthur Miller

6. Ibid, p. 416

Chapter Five

"It's just going to be embarrassing."

A memo, dated 17 February 1958, summarising a telephone conversation and now preserved in the Mirisch Company Records at the University of California, Los Angeles (UCLA) Library Special Collections, captures the first crucial moment in the development of this new venture. The call was between Harold Mirisch and Robert Benjamin of United Artists and confirms the official pivot away from *My Sister and I* to a new project then referred to as *Fanfares of Love*.

Wilder would take on triple duty as writer, director, and producer, while Iz would serve as writer and associate producer. This would be one of an eventual eight films in their twelve-picture partnership where he held that credit and a role he shared with Doane Harrison on this particular production.

Together they would oversee practically every aspect of the movie, from the budget, location scouting to logistics, and, most importantly, casting – a complex undertaking which had started almost as soon as scenario planning began.

There are conflicting accounts of who was originally envisaged for each role with everyone involved in the production offering a slightly different version of events. Sorting through them is no easy task, but it is worth trying to separate truth from the layers of myth that have grown up around the process.

The February memo makes it apparent that with the shift in project there would also be a change in casting expectations. Rather than pursuing marquee names like Audrey Hepburn, William Holden or Marlon Brando – the stars initially floated for *My Sister and I* – the plan was now to build the new film around a different kind of ensemble: with actors such as Tony Curtis, Jack Lemmon and Mitzi Gaynor specifically initially mentioned. It was approvingly observed that, as a result of these casting changes, *Fanfares* would therefore be cheaper to produce. The tentative costs were projected to be in the range of $1.8 to $1.9 million, though it was also pointed out that the final figure might climb, especially 'if, in addition to Tony Curtis, we use an important personality in place of Jack Lemmon.'[1]

Those three names may have all been originally floated but the only one that stuck from the start was Tony Curtis. He was considered a safe bet – a known quantity with solid box office appeal. He was also, as Wilder noted, very attractive: 'I was sure Tony was right for it,' he said, 'because he was quite handsome, and when he tells Marilyn that he is one of the Shell Oil family, she has to be able to believe it.'[2]

It was, by all accounts, a fairly straightforward choice although Curtis was initially approached for the role of Jerry that idea was quickly shelved. The more suave, fast-talking Joe (who in the first draft of the script was a clarinet player) was a far better match for Curtis's on-screen persona.

Born Bernard Schwartz in 1925 in New York City, by the late 1950s Curtis had been in Hollywood for a decade and was riding high – a contract with Universal Pictures (initially under the name Anthony Curtis), a string of hit films, a glittering marriage to fellow actor Janet Leigh, a toddler at home (Kelly) and a baby on the way. Professionally, however, he found himself at something of a crossroads. At the age of 33 his name was often mentioned in the same breath as other handsome male leads like Brando, Paul Newman and Montgomery Clift – yet while they were landing meaty, interesting, roles, he was still turning up in what he considered rather run of the mill studio fare that rarely stretched him.

As he put it: 'I'd had some success already, but I had an ego. I wanted more. I wanted to be an outstanding movie actor. *Some Like It Hot* was my chance to show the world what I could do.'[3]

1. Box 1 Folder 12, Mirisch Corporation Records (Collection 1146). UCLA Library Special Collections, Charles E. Young Research Library, University of California, Los Angeles.
2. Curtis, Tony with Barry Paris. *Tony Curtis: The Autobiography*, William Morrow & Co, 1993, p. 159
3. Curtis, Tony with Mark A Vieira. *Some Like It Hot*: Me, Marilyn and the Movie, Virgin Books, 2009, p. 10

Curtis was ready for a change. And working with Wilder was, in every sense, a leap forward. But given the film's central premise, it was also potentially a career risk albeit a calculated one. With some sage encouragement from his agent, MCA's Lew Wasserman, and a chat with Wilder around the scope of the character, Curtis became the first star to officially agree to the film, signing his contract on 7 March 1958.

Attention soon shifted to the other male lead – Jerry. Jack Lemmon's name had already appeared in the February memo, marking him as a contender from the start. And by most accounts, he was always Wilder's first choice for the role but there was some concern about his level of star power.

Born near Boston in 1925, Lemmon was always destined to be a performer, as he put it 'I always "was" an actor, so how could I ever decide to "become" one?'[4] He'd cut his teeth in New York, performing in live TV dramas and radio soap operas. His big break had come courtesy of Columbia Pictures, when he was talent spotted and cast in the romantic comedy *It Should Happen To You* (1954).

Shortly before being given his debut role Lemmon supposedly had a tense meeting with studio head Harry Cohn, who worried that critics might make obvious jokes about the name "Lemmon" in bad reviews. Cohn suggested he change it to "Lennon." Lemmon refused, arguing that in the current political climate, "Lennon" sounded too much like "Lenin" and could spark unwanted associations with communism.

He kept his name, but the studio did not know quite what to do with him. Lemmon believed this lack of pigeonholing may have actually helped his career. As he later explained, he was neither exceptionally handsome nor especially distinctive, but simply 'kind of average,' making him 'easy to identify with.' That versatility allowed him to move comfortably between different kinds of roles, from ordinary working men to professional and leading characters.[5]

But what Lemmon did have was a formidable talent and a relentless drive to push himself. As Wilder said, 'He's the hardest worker in films. Whatever role he attempts, he will research to the bone, worry it to the nub, do the best

4. Baltake, Joe. *Jack Lemmon: His Films and Career*, Columbus Books, 1987, p. 12
5. Ibid, p. 23

possible job – and somehow make his expertise look instinctive.'[6] Wilder had first taken real notice of him after seeing *Operation Mad Ball* (1957). By then, Lemmon had been shuffled through a string of light Columbia comedies and had won a "Best Supporting Actor" Academy Award for *Mister Roberts* (1955). Yet he was still not considered a proven box office draw – something which made United Artists and the Mirisch brothers nervous. Even with Tony Curtis on board, they worried that the film lacked the kind of big name that would guarantee commercial success.

There remains considerable debate about what really happened during this next stage of casting. Names like Bob Hope, Jerry Lewis and Danny Kaye are sometimes mentioned, but no surviving production documents suggest they were ever seriously considered. Anthony Perkins claimed that he had been approached while he was performing *Look Homeward, Angel* on stage on Broadway. 'Billy Wilder stopped by my dressing room,' Perkins recalled, 'and asked if I'd star in a movie with Frank Sinatra.'[7] The actor, however, had already committed to Mel Ferrer's *Green Mansions* (1959) and turned the offer down. There is, again, no solid evidence that Perkins was a genuine contender.

That Sinatra's name came up at all at this point is interesting. As an idea it did make sense. He was one of the biggest stars in America and virtually guaranteed a financial return. He also had a practical connection: his independent company, Kent Productions, worked with United Artists, who would be distributing the film, as per usual.

A lunch in Palm Springs was supposedly arranged where Billy pitched the idea to him. Whilst, by some accounts at least, Sinatra seemed intrigued a follow up meeting which was scheduled for the next week in Los Angeles never materialised.

In the years since, various stories have swirled. Maybe he found the idea of parodying gangsters to be disrespectful to his associates? On the other hand, one persistent theory asserts that Sinatra had cooled on Wilder after *Love in the Afternoon*, a film he reportedly found distasteful – particularly in its premise of a young woman falling for a much older man. If true, the irony would be considerable: the following decade Sinatra, then in his fifties, would go on to marry 21-year-old Mia Farrow.

6. Ibid, p. 23
7. Sikov, p. 410

But whether it was a professional slight or a personal snub, Wilder quipped that Sinatra ghosting him was 'the biggest favour Frank ever did for me.'[8] Known for his unpredictable temperament, Sinatra was unlikely to embrace the discipline Wilder demanded on set. 'He would've done one take,' Wilder said, 'and called it a day.'[9]

And then came Marilyn.

Monroe had caught wind of the project – almost certainly passed along by her agents at MCA who, after all, also represented both Curtis and Wilder. While she didn't know the details, she knew there was a project in the works, and she wanted to be involved with it.

When she reached out to them the team were floored as she hadn't even been under consideration. The initial suggestion, Mitzi Gaynor, would have done a great job. She had the necessary charisma and had just had a decent amount of success in the movie *South Pacific* (1958). But they hadn't considered that they needed a major name for the part as it wasn't a lead woman's role. The female character, as initially envisioned, had been seen more as a narrative device than a fleshed-out persona.

They realised that if Marilyn signed on, that dynamic would need to shift instantly. Her involvement would also eclipse any issues about the star power of the other actors.

Wilder, of course, knew exactly what working with Monroe meant. Their time together on *The Seven Year Itch* had been far from frictionless. Yet as this new project began, he took a pragmatic view. He later acknowledged that she was 'tough to work with,' but believed the results justified the difficulties, describing what ultimately appeared on screen as 'amazing.'[10]

Wilder responded to Monroe's approach with enthusiasm. His typewritten reply letter, dated 17 March 1958, which was sent via her agent in New York, included a three-page synopsis of the developing script. At that point, the female character was named Stella – the transformation to Sugar Kane (Kowalczyk) would come later, the name a nod to Helen Kane, the original "Boop-boop-a-doop" girl who popularised a song which would also be used in the movie – *I Wanna Be Loved By You.*

---

8. Chandler, Charlotte. *Nobody's Perfect: Billy Wilder: A Personal Biography,* Simon & Schuster, 2002, p. 203
9. Sikov, p. 410
10. Rolston, Lorraine. *Some Like It Hot*, York Press, 2000, p. 9

The synopsis sketched a woman also on the run – though not from gangsters, like the male characters, but from her own romantic disappointments. 'Working with a succession of male bands,' Wilder explained, 'Stella has invariably become involved with the saxophone player, and the results have been uniformly unhappy. Heartbroken and fed up, she takes refuge in an all-girl band.'

He wanted her to know that while it was a comedy, it wouldn't be shallow.

He also dropped a few names to sweeten the pitch: Curtis, Lemmon, Sinatra ('great interest from actors,' he noted), as well as many gangster film legends.

And then, in a flourish, he signed off with both affection and in apparent sincerity: 'By all means, keep in mind that I'm dying to work with you again.'

And beneath the formal closing, he scrawled by hand:

'Love, B.W.' [11]

While Wilder was delighted, things were far from settled in the Monroe camp. What he was offering – a ukulele-playing showgirl – was not quite the kind of role Monroe had been looking for. According to some accounts, she was furious. After reading the synopsis, she threw it to the floor in frustration. 'I've played dumb blondes before,' she reportedly snapped 'but never this dumb.'[12] Her main objection was the logic of the character: she couldn't accept that Sugar would be so naive she wouldn't realise that the two "women" she befriended were, in fact, men. It was a stretch Monroe refused to initially accept.

But she may not have had many better options. She had been absent from Hollywood for almost two years, and whispers had already begun that her career might be over. She had been in the business for more than a decade at that point, with her first contract with Twentieth Century Fox signed in the summer of 1946, after a successful screen test.

It was on that day that she first met makeup artist Allan "Whitey" Snyder. The legend has it that Monroe had attempted to do her own makeup, but it

11. Billy Wilder papers, Margaret Herrick Library, Academy of Motion Picture Arts and Sciences.
12. Phillips, p. 213

hadn't gone well. Whitey stepped in to help – marking the beginning of a lifelong professional and personal bond.

At the time, under the leadership of Darryl F. Zanuck, Fox was riding high, having emerged from the war years as a major studio producing expensive, prestige pictures.

It was, in many ways, a promising environment for a young actress to land in.

But Monroe's early film appearances were uneventful. She was cast in minor parts, including *Dangerous Years* (1947) and *Scudda Hoo! Scudda Hay!* (1948), neither of which had much impact. Although Fox had renewed her six-month contract once, they ultimately chose not to extend it further and she was quietly released.

The following year she landed another short-term – this time at Columbia. She was cast in *Ladies of the Chorus* (1948), her first starring role. She was also assigned a drama coach: Natasha Lytess. The two formed a close and, at times, intense working relationship. She would remain her acting mentor for the next eight years before the partnership came to an abrupt, and unexplained, end when Monroe sent a telegram terminating her services and apparently refused all further communication.

Though Columbia ultimately let Monroe go – just as Fox had – she remained undeterred. If Hollywood wasn't quite ready to believe in her star potential, she was determined to prove them wrong.

Friends from the time remember her as fiercely driven. She threw herself into training and committed to serious study. She took classes at the progressive Actors' Laboratory Theatre, focusing on voice, movement and performance. She enrolled in night school at UCLA, studying literature and art appreciation.

To stay afloat during this precarious time. Marilyn returned to modelling – a career she had first begun professionally in 1945 with the Blue Book Agency, one of Los Angeles' most prominent firms. She had been taken on by Emmeline Snively, the agency's head, after completing a three-month course designed to teach prospective models the basics of posture, poise and presentation. Snively had also encouraged her to dye her chestnut hair blonde.

Her original entry into the industry had come almost by chance. While working in a munitions factory as part of the wartime effort, she was spotted by a photographer who saw something compelling in her. What followed was a rapid ascent into the world of pin-up modelling. Going by Norma Jeane Dougherty – she had married her neighbour, the much older James Dougherty, at the age of sixteen in 1942 – she began appearing in magazines and advertising, quickly becoming the agency's most in demand model.

Renowned Hollywood photographer László Willinger later observed that what had struck him most was the dramatic transformation that occurred whenever a camera was pointed at her. In everyday moments she seemed comparatively unremarkable, but in front of the lens she came alive with a distinctive energy and charisma. To Willinger, that ability to transform for the camera was the hallmark of a truly exceptional model.

Born Norma Jeane Mortenson on 1 June 1926 Monroe's early life had been marked by instability and abuse. Her mother, Gladys, plagued by both financial pressures and deteriorating mental health issues, had been unable to provide consistent care. As a child she lived in a mixture of foster homes, an orphanage and with relatives and friends of the family, an experience she reflected on as pivotal to her career choice: Some of my foster families used to send me to the movies to get me out of the house and there I'd sit all day and way into the night. Up in front, there with the screen so big, a little kid all alone, and I loved it.'[13]

Her relationship with James had been, in many ways, a marriage of convenience. It lasted only four years, ending in divorce in late 1946, shortly after she signed her first film contract.

By the close of the decade, although her career as an actress remained precarious, she had begun inching her way up the Hollywood ladder – one small role at a time. These included bit parts in forgettable movies, yes, but also more eye-catching turns like her appearance in *Love Happy* (1949), the final feature film from the Marx Brothers, distributed by United Artists and produced by none other than Mary Pickford – her last film as a producer.

But 1950 was the year things truly began to change when she appeared in two noteworthy films, John Huston's *The Asphalt Jungle* and Joseph L. Mankiewicz's *All About Eve* – both of which gave her a level of exposure she had never experienced before.

13. Meryman, Richard. When you're famous you run into human nature in a raw kind of way, *Great Interviews of the 20th Century*, https://www.theguardian.com/theguardian/2007/sep/14/greatinterviews accessed 1 April 2025

In *All About Eve,* Monroe shared screen time with the formidable Bette Davis. By most accounts, the shoot was nerve-wracking for the young actress: it reportedly took eleven takes to complete one of Monroe's scenes, and when Davis barked at her during one particular take, she was so rattled she left the set to vomit. Still her performance was convincing, and she held her own alongside the cast of seasoned professionals. The film itself was a triumph, going on to earn multiple Academy Award nominations and winning six.

It was enough for Twentieth Century Fox to come calling again and in May she signed a new seven-year contract with the studio, one which was negotiated by her champion (and lover) Johnny Hyde, the then Vice President of the William Morris Agency.

Her employee starting card lists her job title as "actress" with a weekly pay of $500 (a significant increase from the original $75 a week she received a few years earlier). The contract followed the standard studio model of the time: annual options, each with a scheduled raise – so she'd get $750 a week in year two, $1250 in year three, $1500 in year four, and so on, topping out at $3,500 per week by year seven.

It was something she had fought for – but it came at a cost.

While the deal provided immediate financial security and a place on the Fox roster, it gave her virtually no control over the roles she was given. Monroe – like all the other actors in the contract system – was expected to play along while the studio shaped her into a marketable product. For her, that would mean comedies, romances, and light dramas – often fluffy, mostly forgettable.

Films like *As Young As You Feel* (1951), *Let's Make It Legal* (1951) and *We're Not Married* (1952) offered her limited screen time but increasing public attention. The scripts were sometimes thin, though notable writers were involved – I.A.L. Diamond and F. Hugh Herbert among them.

Then came *Monkey Business* which paired her with one of Hollywood's biggest names, Cary Grant, and gave her one of her most high-profile roles to date.

1952 also marked a turning point in her personal and public life. That year, she began dating retired New York Yankees legend Joe DiMaggio. Their romance – and subsequent nine-month long marriage – became headline fodder, feeding the public's growing fascination with the actress.

"It's just going to be embarrassing."

The following year was another breakthrough time. She starred in three major films: *Niagara, How to Marry a Millionaire* and *Gentlemen Prefer Blondes,* as the unforgettable Lorelei Lee, a Technicolor hit that pulled in $5.3 million at the U.S. box office and secured her place in Hollywood royalty. Film historian Aubrey Solomon noted that in 1953, Fox's two greatest assets were CinemaScope and Marilyn Monroe – in that order.

The steady build-up of her career was beginning to pay off. While Fox had been slow to fully capitalise on her potential, they were now enjoying the benefits of having a major new star at a bargain rate, thanks to that fixed term contract. The difference between her status and her rate was so pronounced that while her co-star in *Gentlemen Prefer Blondes*, Jane Russell, received $200,000 Monroe got only $18,000.

There was a scare which threatened to derail her budding career when nude stylised pin up shots she had posed for back in 1949 were leaked. The studio panicked and executives reportedly begged her to deny that the woman in the photos was her. Refusing to be ashamed and declaring that she had done nothing wrong, she went public and took control. In an interview, she explained candidly that she had been broke and desperate at the time. And her honesty struck a chord with *TIME* magazine observing that her willingness to own her past actions only boosted her popularity. Public sympathy grew, and interest in her films soared once more.

On the surface, her popularity may have been in ascension but behind the scenes she found herself increasingly frustrated by the "Marilyn" persona.

She had initially leaned into the blonde stereotype, using her looks, charm, and clever double entendres – which came to be known as "Monroeisms." There were also many publicity stunts: revealing outfits worn in expected places, clothes slipping off. These weren't always accidents, and often were carefully designed scenarios to keep the public's attention.

But over time, the image she had created began to work against her. She disliked the direction her career was taking and felt stuffed into roles that didn't fully utilise her talents. As she got more successful and wanted to take on more serious and varied roles, many people couldn't see past the character. They believed the image was the real her, making it harder to break free.

And, equally as problematically, her contract with Fox left her seriously underpaid compared to her co-stars, something that was very difficult to challenge. The problem was the system led to an imbalance of power. Historically if a player refused an assigned role, they faced suspension without pay – and the studio could tack that extra time onto the end of their contract, prolonging their obligation.

There had been some pushback against this model. A decade earlier, Olivia de Havilland famously challenged Warner Bros., refusing parts she deemed beneath her and undergoing multiple suspensions. In 1944, the landmark De Havilland Law ruled that seven-year contracts couldn't be extended by suspensions.

But change was slow, and most actors – fearing blacklisting or the loss of future work – were reluctant to challenge the powerful commercial studios. A few, however, pushed back against their assigned roles.

Marlon Brando was one of these challengers. In 1954 he had been cast in *The Egyptian* but walked away after the first read-through, citing mental strain. Many believed the real reason was that he didn't like the project and was rebelling against studio control. Fox was forced to postpone production and scramble to find a replacement – then promptly (and unsuccessfully) tried to sue him for $2 million.

Marilyn also began to assert herself. When Fox offered her a role in *The Girl in Pink Tights* opposite a much higher paid Frank Sinatra, she flatly said no. It was a bold move but, given her recent success, a calculated one.

The studio retaliated by placing her on a brief suspension, the first shot in what would become a long standoff.

Monroe switched representation, moving to the powerful MCA. In 1955 her marriage to Joe DiMaggio ended in divorce, with many believing that he had physically abused her. And then, alongside her close friend and collaborator, photographer Milton Greene, she began to push back further. They opened negotiations with Fox, demanding a new contract – one that included better pay and more creative control over her career.

Fox resisted. Their position was simple: Marilyn still had years left on her original contract. They pointed to a revised agreement they had offered her which would have bumped up her pay to $100,000 per picture – but had never been signed. In their view, that omission meant the original contract remained binding.

Marilyn's team countered arguing if a new contract had been introduced, even unsigned, it suggested the previous terms were no longer in effect.

Rather than attempting to sue her Fox, instead, tried to strong-arm her into submission by issuing stern public warnings to attempt to pressurise her into abiding by the terms of the original contract. They withheld a promised bonus for *The Seven Year Itch* – which she had completed after her first suspension was lifted – and even threatened to delay its release. Publicly, they placed the blame for the setbacks squarely on her shoulders. In a calculated move to undermine her and to make her nervous, they began feeding the press stories about younger actresses they were "developing" to take her place.

Despite the surrounding pressures *The Seven Year Itch*, released in the summer of 1955, was a resounding commercial triumph meaning that the studio had little choice but to yield. On 31 December, Monroe signed a new contract which would fundamentally change her standing in Hollywood. The negotiated terms were extraordinary for the era, especially for a woman. She secured approval over scripts, directors, and cinematographers; a $100,000 fee per picture plus a share of the profits; and, crucially, the freedom to make one film per year outside of the studio. The deal also included a $100,000 annual retainer and a weekly allowance during production. This agreement, later described as "instrumental" in the eventual collapse of the studio system, signalled a shift in power: for once, a star was truly calling the shots.

With her new agreement in place, she was also able to formalise a long-gestating dream: Marilyn Monroe Productions. Monroe became president and majority shareholder, while Milton Greene – who had backed her both emotionally and financially throughout her battle with the studio – was vice president with forty nine percent of the shares. Marilyn was enthusiastic about the development stating: 'My Marilyn Monroe Production Company is all set to start things going in a big way. All the legal troubles have been solved. Now it's a matter of finding a good movie, or play, or television story.'[14]

It was a staggering victory. No one had expected her to win – least of all Fox – but she had, and the industry took notice. *TIME* magazine, in

14. Morgan, Michelle. *When Marilyn Met the Queen*: Marilyn Monroe's Life in England, Robinson, 2022, p. 227

its 30 January 1956 issue, summed up with brevity: 'There is persuasive evidence that Marilyn Monroe is a shrewd businesswoman.'[15]

Yet even in victory, the reporting was steeped in sexism. Her defiance had been largely framed as a spiteful tantrum rather than a calculated act of self-determination.

The gossip columns continued to mock her relentlessly and Broadway turned her into parody. In George Axelrod's 1955 play *Will Success Spoil Rock Hunter?,* Jayne Mansfield played a buxom, bubble-headed actress who forms her own production company. The satire was thinly veiled, and the implication obvious: Monroe's ambition was laughable.

Her next project, *Bus Stop* (1956), was the first film under the new contract with Fox and would mark another career turning point. Directed by Joshua Logan, it was also a success, earning her a Golden Globe nomination for "Best Actress in a Motion Picture – Musical or Comedy."

The following project, the troubled, *The Prince and the Showgirl* (1957) was filmed in England and marked the debut independent production of Marilyn Monroe Productions. After that had been completed Marilyn, now married to playwright Arthur Miller, stepped back from making movies, relocating to the East Coast to focus on being a wife and starting a family. The couple divided their time between their New York apartment and a house in Roxbury, Connecticut.

But in August, tragedy struck. Marilyn experienced an ectopic pregnancy that ended in pregnancy loss, almost certainly linked to the long-standing symptoms of endometriosis – a condition where tissue similar to the uterine lining grow outside the uterus. Its cause was, and remains, unknown, but without successful treatment it meant a lifetime of debilitating pain. Knowledge of the condition at the time was incredibly limited and she underwent several surgical procedures, both to ease her suffering and to improve her chances of conceiving again.

Whilst she had stepped away from films she had remained passionately interested in acting, working with Lee Strasberg in New York. It was a move that baffled many and she was again attacked in the press for what was deemed her ridiculous pretentions.

She realised the criticisms had been orchestrated and one editorial in particular stuck with her, bitterly recalling: 'It said: "Marilyn Monroe is a

15. Spoto, Donald. *Marilyn Monroe: The Biography*, HarperCollins, 1993, p. 375

very stupid girl to give up all the wonderful things the movie industry has done for her and go to New York to learn how to act.'"[16]

Marilyn reflected on her decision to leave Hollywood – 'I disappeared,' she said, 'because if people won't listen to you, there's no point talking to people. You're just banging your head against a wall.' Her frustration with the system was palpable: 'They worked me too fast … They rushed me from one picture into another. I never got a chance to learn anything in Hollywood.'[17]

So, when she was offered this new role, it came as something of a conundrum.

On one hand, it was Billy Wilder – her old collaborator, the man who had helped to create one of her most iconic performances in *The Seven Year Itch*, in spite of the problems with the studio. On the other, the part was yet another "dumb blonde" role. For Marilyn, it felt dangerously close to stepping backwards, despite Wilder's assurances that this character would be different.

In the end, her decision to accept was driven largely by practicalities. Marilyn Monroe Productions was faltering. Her partnership with Milton Greene had soured and they had argued over direction, management, and control. Miller also had little patience for Greene and persuaded her to cut ties. Eventually he asked to be bought out for $100,000 – the return of his original investment.

There were also financial pressure. She had not worked for some time which was a problem as she was also currently the primary breadwinner of the family. Miller's screenplay for *The Misfits* (1961) remained stalled, with no clear sense of when it would be completed. Marilyn was reportedly becoming increasingly aware of the strain and told a friend that someone needed to bring money into the house.

It made sense from every perspective. Her agents pushed for it. Twentieth Century Fox approved – even though they wouldn't profit directly as they realised another hit would still increase her market value. Miller also thought the idea was excellent. On 3 April 1958, a meeting of the directors and stakeholders of Marilyn Monroe Productions was held to discuss the

16. Jordan, Elisa. *Hello Norma Jeane: The Marilyn Monroe You Didn't Know*, Applause, 2023, p. 124
17. Ibid, p. 124

issue further. Around the table sat Marilyn, Arthur Miller, and her agents from MCA – Lew Wasserman for the West Coast and Mort Viner for the East. The minutes from that meeting reveal one thing with absolute clarity: the actress was still undecided about what she was going to do.

MCA had officially told Wilder that 'legal technicalities' were holding things up – a polite fiction to avoid any offence. In truth, it seems, Monroe was waiting to see whether Sinatra would actually commit to the project. And then there was the matter of the other co-star. The meeting notes are deliciously, brutally, candid:

'She still doesn't like Curtis.'[18]

Meanwhile, the *Fanfares* production team were also hedging their bets. In a letter dated 18 April, Harold Mirisch wrote to Wilder suggesting Carol Channing as another possible name for the female lead. They were discreetly checking her summer availability – just in case.

But it was an unnecessary back up plan as shortly after, Monroe signed on to the film. A carefully staged photo op captured her smiling beside Walter Mirisch, sealing the deal for the press.

A few days later, Wilder sent her a breezy telegram at home: 'Dear Marilyn: I am genuinely delighted to have you aboard … hope to see both you and Arthur soon in smogsville …'[19]

Yet privately, he was less optimistic. Wilder had previously compared working with her to smoking: 'I knew she was bad for my health, but I couldn't give her up.'[20]

With Curtis and Monroe secured – and Monroe's name providing the box-office reassurance the executives demanded – only one of the film's three key players remained.

Lemmon had been hovering in the wings from the start, kept in the running and in the loop by Wilder. Early in the casting process, Wilder had approached him at Dominick's, a beloved West Hollywood haunt with red-checked tablecloths and heaped plates of pasta. Wilder stopped at his table and quickly outlined the premise. Lemmon immediately agreed to take on

18. Rollyson, Carl. Marilyn Monroe: Day by Day, Bowman and Littlefield, 2014, p. 201
19. Billy Wilder papers, Margaret Herrick Library, Academy of Motion Picture Arts and Sciences.
20. Leaming, p. 303

the role, saying he would do it if he was available, and if not, he would clear his schedule.

There had been silence but then, on 6 May, a few pages of the script arrived at his agent's office at William Morris. It landed like dynamite: 'When I read it, I fell off the couch in hysterics. It was just bloody brilliant.'[21]

The final piece fell perfectly into place when Jack Lemmon officially signed on, as the third billed actor.

Then came the public stirrings and confirmation of the movie's name, when the formidable Louella Parsons – gossip queen of the Hearst empire – announced: 'Marilyn Monroe Set for *Some Like It Hot*,' with the added barb, 'High time Marilyn made a motion picture in Hollywood.'[22]

Prior to this the film had been limping along under the unofficial title *Fanfares of Love* – a holdover from the German film that had inspired the remake. But nobody ever believed that name would survive into actual production.

Back in early March, Harold Mirisch had fired off a clarification note to Rogers & Cowan, the film's publicity representatives and one of the most powerful PR firms in Hollywood at the time. Their only real rival was Arthur P. Jacobs's APJAC Productions and between them the two firms managed the publicity for nearly all of the industry's biggest stars and most high-profile productions. The note from Harold read:

> 'For your information, we have no title on this picture and would prefer not to use the title of FANFARES OF LOVE until such time as we have agreed on a definite title.'[23]

The 'definite title' had been bubbling in the background. It may have been Diamond's idea. Or Wilders. Accounts differ. But, either way, the inspiration likely came from an old English nursery rhyme.

> "Pease porridge hot, pease porridge cold,
> Pease porridge in the pot, nine days old.

21. Widener, Don. *Lemmon: A Biography*, W.H Allen, 1977, p. 166
22. Marilyn Monroe Set for Comedy "Some Like It Hot," *The San Francisco Examiner*, 25 April 1958, p. 25
23. Box 1 Folder 9, Mirisch Corporation Records (Collection 1146). UCLA Library Special Collections, Charles E. Young Research Library, University of California, Los Angeles.

Some like it hot, some like it cold
Some like it in the pot, nine days old."

The problem was that Paramount Pictures had already used *Some Like It Hot* for a 1939 Bob Hope musical – and the title was still under copyright. Worse, those rights were entangled in a pending acquisition by MCA, who were busy buying up old titles for television syndication, part of an early scramble to exploit the growing television market with ready to go content.

Still, a deal was struck and MCA was happy to cooperate – not surprisingly, given how many of its high-profile clients were now involved in the project. The 1939 film was retitled *Rhythm Romance* for its TV release, and Wilder's film got its name. It cost the production a fair bit extra, but it was worth every cent.

The first partial draft of the screenplay went out in early May, and around the same time, Walter Mirisch submitted the official budget to United Artists, a document that has been repeatedly circulated and reproduced in the intervening years and can be found in a number of archives. It makes for fascinating reading!

Billy had secured a payment of $200,000 with a seventeen and a half percent cut after the first million in gross, climbing to twenty percent thereafter. Iz would get $60,000. Monroe (Sugar Kane) locked in $300,000 plus ten percent of the gross – a generous deal paid in instalments with $55,000 due on signing. Curtis (Joe/Josephine/Junior) would earn $100,000 against five percent of the gross, with a $25,000 advance on signing. Lemmon's (Jerry/Daphne) deal matched Curtis's.

There were, of course, plenty of other costs to consider from general staffing, to $34,000 allocated to set design, $99,000 for music, and $17,756 for special effects.

Altogether, the predicted total cost came to $2,373,490 which was a substantial figure for a comedy but by no means exceptional. United Artists approved it, but not without a few raised eyebrows.

Yet, as the script circulated, those budget jitters began to fade. One of the most important voices in the green-lighting process, Robert F. Blumofe – UA's Vice President in charge of production and West Coast operations, and the man whose signature ultimately carried the most weight – was ecstatic.

After reading the first tranche, he gushed: 'I think they are absolutely riotous. If Billy can keep this up, this could be one of the funniest pictures of all time … I'll be waiting for more pages.'[24]

By 9 July, Wilder and Diamond were ready to send out pages 83 to 117, and Blumofe remained enthusiastic once he had read them: 'Very, very funny,' he reported. 'They continue to maintain the quality of the first 82 pages.' The writing team, he noted, had further promised a 'riotous third act.'[25]

That would have to wait. In fact, as was their practice, Wilder and Diamond didn't even plan to have a completed script by the time filming began. This would give the film room to grow organically on set. The writing could adjust to the actors' strengths – or weaknesses – as they revealed themselves. Jack Lemmon recalled Wilder explaining that keeping the last act open helped everyone stay 'sharp and engaged.' [26] Or as Wilder put it: 'The third act is never finally formulated when we begin shooting. Our joke is that if you give the bosses the third act in advance, they can fire you at any time.'[27] Although as Lawrence Maslon pointed out in *Some Like It Hot: The Official 50th Anniversary Companion* (2009) 'it is unlikely that a director like Billy Wilder would have tolerated such improvisation if his screenwriter wasn't also Billy Wilder.[28]

The early drafts show how carefully this balance between planning and organic creativity worked. Whole stretches of dialogue survived almost word for word into the final cut and structurally there are surprisingly few differences between the early versions and the finished film. Most changes were refinements like polishing dialogue, tightening pacing, or occasionally expanding or shrinking a moment for a better payoff. Some early comic set-pieces were dropped altogether, including a scene where Joe and Jerry hide in the ladies' room during the police raid at the speakeasy.

Some elements, however, did evolve. Character names changed – Stella became Sugar, and Joe's clarinet turned into a saxophone. Supporting characters were pruned; a speakeasy waitress named Ginger, later renamed

---

24. Box 1 Folder 15, Mirisch Corporation Records (Collection 1146). UCLA Library Special Collections, Charles E. Young Research Library, University of California, Los Angeles.
25. Ibid.
26. *Nobody's Perfect – The Making of Some Like It Hot* (October Films, 2001)
27. Madsen, p. 43
28. Maslon, Laurence. Some Like It Hot: The Official 50th Anniversary Companion, Pavilion Books, 2009, p. 55

Dixie, was originally important enough that Jerry intended to propose to her. Joe, in a typical bit of con artistry, even tried to scam money out of her by pretending Jerry needed it to buy her a gift. The character was eventually written out entirely.

The pre-production phase was all going well, though not everyone was convinced the endeavour was a good idea. In several interviews, Wilder recalled a conversation with David O. Selznick, the legendary producer of *Gone With the Wind* (1939). Curious about what Wilder was working on, Selznick asked him directly about the project. On hearing the premise, he was alarmed, warning that audiences would reject a comedy involving murder and predicting that it was 'just going to be embarrassing.'[29]

The exact wording shifts slightly in Wilder's different tellings, but the sentiment remained the same – Selznick was convinced it was a terrible idea. Wilder's response, however, was, 'Well, I think I'll try anyway.'[30]

29. Crowe, p. 151
30. Chandler, p. 201

SPOTLIGHT
CHICAGO, 1929. HOLLYWOOD, 1958.

Chicago, 1929

Chicago, once lauded for its pioneering spirit, had undergone a dramatic reputational transformation by the early twentieth century as a nefarious group of organised criminals had woven themselves into the fabric of the city. The kingpin was James "Big Jim" Colosimo. His counterpart, William Hale "Big Bill" Thompson, occupied the mayoral office, which became a cornerstone in their empire. The two ruled over a city full of corruption – an official blind eye turned towards their unsavoury dealings.

When the Volstead Act, the 18th amendment, came into effect on 17 January 1920 it was a pivotal moment in U.S history, as it imposed prohibition on alcohol and heralded the rise of an even more highly profitable criminal enterprise – bootlegging. Chicago, which is situated along Lake Michigan's border, was ideally positioned to capitalise on this trade as it was relatively easy to smuggle liquor from Canada.

Whilst Colosimo showed an uncharacteristic reluctance to venture into this new criminal opportunity, his enforcer and protégé, Johnny Torrio, had no such reservations. Seeing an opening ripe for exploitation, Torrio instructed the notorious Brooklyn enforcer Frankie Yale to erase Colosimo from the equation. The successful hit took place on 11 May 1920.

Yale also introduced Torrio to an audacious young troublemaker, an 18-year-old named Alphonse Gabriel Capone. Infamously known (at least behind his back) as Scarface, Capone had earned his moniker following a violent encounter that left distinctive scars on one side of his face, a testament to his tough early years in New York City.

Torrio and his newly appointed right hand man, took over South Side Chicago. Together, they orchestrated the clandestine production and distribution of illegal liquor in a landscape teeming with illicit bars known as speakeasies. The empire they presided over extended its influence to encompass a network of roadhouses, gambling dens, and brothels.

Amidst this expansion was the ever-present threat of other gangs trying to establish or extend their own domains. Torrio initially navigated this world with finesse – attempting to broker agreements between the rival crime clans.

Despite his conciliatory approach, Torrio found himself locked in a bitter rivalry with Dean O'Banion, the influential leader of the O'Banion mob, which would later morph into the notorious North Side Gang. They proved to be a persistent nuisance, constantly intruding upon the territories Torrio had claimed as his own. O'Banion not only sought to tarnish his rival's reputation but also orchestrated schemes aimed at framing Torrio and Capone for murder. He even dared to double cross them out of a staggering sum of cash, which, of course, exacerbated the tensions between the rival factions.

Torrio, unaccustomed to such affronts called upon Yale once again and O'Banion was fatally shot in his own flower shop on 10 November 1924. Unbeknownst to most, this seemingly legitimate business (he had married florist Viola Kaniff a few years earlier) had served as a front for illicit activities and had become the go-to florist for mob funerals – a grim yet profitable niche, given the frequency of such occasions!

Torrio's retaliatory act proved to be a grave miscalculation. The North Side Gang, under the leadership of replacement George Clarence "Bugs" Moran, now not only wanted to take over the South Side territories but also vowed to settle the score. The ongoing power struggle between the rival gangs surged into what history remembers as the "Beer Wars," a tumultuous period immortalised in headlines and also in blood on the streets. The officially documented casualties which totalled over 700, actually concealed a grimmer reality and the death toll was likely twice as high.

No one was safe – even Torrio and Capone – who were both ambushed and only narrowly escaped death. Fearing for his life, Torrio stepped aside and Capone took over as leader of what now evolved into the "Chicago Outfit." He expanded his dominion through a protection racket which entangled unions and businesses. Behind closed doors, the Outfit oversaw a staggering 10,000 speakeasies – rumoured to bring in between $60-100 million a year. This was not only an indication of the colossal wealth at Capone's fingertips but also allowed him to grease the palms of corrupt officials to the tune of a whispered half a million dollars a month.

But Moran still remained a threat and prevented Capone from gaining total control of the city and expanding his empire even further. Something would need to be done.

The carefully arranged hit unfolded on 14 February 1929. Hidden behind the plain exterior of the S.M.C. Cartage garage at 2122 North Clark Street was the centre of Moran's operations. Across the way, in a rented apartment, men had kept watch for weeks, getting information and waiting for the perfect moment. Once Moran arrived with his men, a signal would be given, and the plan enacted.

That opportunity came on St. Valentine's Day morning – when the spotters reported they had seen Moran and his associates entering the building. Minutes later, a group of men dressed as Chicago police officers appeared at the rear entrance of the garage. Accustomed to routine police intimidation tactics the group inside obediently lined themselves up against the back wall when told to. But these were no ordinary law enforcers. The reality would have dawned on the men when three additional assailants entered through the front door, brandishing lethal weaponry – Thompson submachine guns, colloquially known as Tommy guns or Chicago typewriters, they had been developed in 1918 and rose to prominence in the 1920s as the gangster's weapon of choice. In a hail of over 70 bullets the hitmen soon dispatched their victims. Mob enforcer, Frank Gusenberg, the only one not killed outright, endured a staggering fourteen bullet wounds in the brutal assault. When asked who had shot them, he refused to name names. He died three hours later.

The killers had accomplished their escape using a straightforward tactic: those disguised as police officers ushered the other associates out of the premises. To any onlooker who might have been alerted by the commotion and peered out from their windows, the orchestrated scene would have appeared as though a gunfight had been disrupted by the arrival of the police, and the perpetrators were already under arrest.

Once the bodies were discovered, the massacre dominated headlines, reported in lurid detail and accompanied by graphic photographs that ran uncensored in newspapers for weeks and months. The press revelled in the spectacle, publishing images that left no doubt about the brutality of the attack and cementing Chicago's reputation for bloody violence.

Bugs survived simply because he was not actually there. The operatives tasked with monitoring his arrival had apparently mistakenly identified Albert Weinshank, the gang's bookkeeper, who bore a resemblance to Moran, as the target. In a stroke of fortunate timing, Moran was slightly late to their arranged meeting that morning which led to him witnessing the arrival of the "police," prompting a retreat to evade potential trouble. But despite his lucky escape, the massacre effectively eliminated Moran's North Side Gang as a serious force in the city's underworld. The perpetrators of what came to be known as the St. Valentine's Day Massacre were never officially identified. Capone had a carefully arranged alibi – he was in Florida at the time, accompanied by Miami-Dade County solicitor Robert Taylor – but few doubted who was behind the killings. Moran himself famously remarked, 'Only Capone kills like that.'[1]

While there was no definitive proof of his involvement, Capone was branded "Public Enemy No. 1," and soon faced intensified scrutiny from law enforcement agencies determined to end his influence and clean up the city's image. It would be quite the task.

Hollywood, 1958

The wild energy of the roaring twenties had been cut short by the 1929 stock market crash and the Great Depression. Al Capone was safely behind bars by 1932, and prohibition, which had fuelled so much of the underworld's development, was repealed in 1933. That same year, Chicago began to fully wash away its tarnished reputation with the Century of Progress Exposition, a gleaming celebration of modernity.

Prohibition had not only been a boon to gangster's profit margins, it had also provided contemporary filmmakers with the perfect backdrop: a real-world crisis that brought with it nightclubs, black sedans, bootleg liquor, and the rise of charismatic criminals who would become the stars of these stories. Gangster films had been part of the movies almost since the industry's inception. The oldest surviving American example is thought to be *The Black Hand: True Story of a Recent Occurrence in the Italian Quarter of New York* (1906), though even earlier ones likely existed. But they had really come into their own in the 1920s.

And with the arrival of synchronised sound in 1927, the gangster film transformed once again. Audiences could now hear the sharp, cynical dialogue that came to define the genre, along with the hum of the city, the screech of tyres, and – most memorably – the rapid fire of Tommy guns.

1. Robb, Brian J. *A Brief History of Gangsters*, Running Press, 2014, p. 79

The early 1930s had seen an explosion of gangster films, with Warner Bros. leading the way. That wave is often said to have begun with *Little Caesar* (1931), based on a novel by W.R. Burnett, and starring Edward G. Robinson as Caesar Enrico "Rico" Bandello – a barely disguised Al Capone.

James Cagney burst onto screens in *The Public Enemy*, redefining the gangster as both charming and terrifying. A year later, Paul Muni took the genre even further in *Scarface*, playing Antonio "Tony" Camonte in a brutal, thinly veiled version of Capone's rise to power including the St. Valentine's Day Massacre recreated in chilling bloodless silhouette.

These films, as well as the many others released in that genre, helped forge a new language of American storytelling and were box office smashes.

But then the moral pendulum swung.

The arrival of the Motion Picture Production Code – more commonly known as the Hays Code – changed everything. Named after Will H. Hays, president of the Motion Picture Producers and Distributors of America (MPPDA), it was the industry's answer to growing outrage over both on-screen and off-screen behaviour. Hollywood had long been seen by some as morally suspect, but by the 1920s its casual attitude toward "cinematic sin" had collided with a spate of real-life public scandal – murders, alleged rapes, drug overdoses, and even a supposed death by suicide that was whispered to be murder.

Religious, civic, and political groups, emboldened by their success with the enacting of prohibition, called for stricter regulations. And it was becoming increasingly clear that without decisive intervention, the industry risked a patchwork of state decency laws and even possible federal control.

To protect both profits and reputation, the studios turned to self-regulation. The MPPDA had been established in 1922, with Hays chosen as its head. A former Postmaster General under President Warren G. Harding and ex-chairman of the Republican National Committee, Hays was considered a man of unshakable moral authority. His influence was so strong that the MPPDA soon became known simply as the "Hays Office." Under his guidance, Hollywood adopted a programme of self-censorship, known as "the Formula," a set of recommendations designed to keep filmmakers in line. As Hays himself described the new order, the 'careless, helter-skelter days' of filmmaking were over. He argued that movies executives had come to recognise their responsibilities not only as leaders of a major industry but also as 'custodians' of a powerful medium with significant influence over public morality and education, as well as one of the 'most universal mediums of artistic expression.[2]

A loose set of guidelines known as the "Don'ts" and "Be Carefuls" were introduced. These listed eleven subjects to avoid entirely – profanity, sex perversion, drug use, white slavery, and ridicule of the clergy among them – and twenty-six others to be treated with caution, such as the use of firearms, theft, sympathy for criminals, and representations of women "selling their virtue." Studios largely stuck to the arrangement, and for a while, it all seemed to work. There was no real enforcement mechanism, but everyone understood what might anger local censorship boards and protest groups and avoided aggravating them too much.

However, the understanding soon began breaking down. Writers pushed boundaries and the lure of profit encouraged risk taking. Corresponding mounting pressure from religious and civic groups, the threat of organised boycotts and even government intervention would force Hollywood to act once again. The guidelines were rewritten and expanded into the full "Motion Picture Production Code," designed not only to censor objectionable material but also to uphold "traditional moral values."

Although officially adopted in 1930, the Hays Code wasn't strictly enforced until 1 July 1934, when the Production Code Administration (PCA) was established under the unyielding Joseph Breen. Under his watch, every film script had to be submitted for approval before production, and completed movies could be rejected, ordered to reshoot scenes, or rewritten entirely. Without a PCA certificate of approval, a film could not be shown in any cinemas controlled by the powerful studios, cutting off a major revenue source and the fine for releasing a non-approved film was $25,000 – a huge sum at the time.

Stories were cleaned up, and morality clauses were written into contracts. While there was intermittent resistance, for the next three decades virtually every American film adhered to the Code. That didn't mean they stopped testing it and many filmmakers became skilled at seeing how much they

---

2. Doherty, Thomas. *Hollywood's Censor: Joseph I. Breen & the Production Code Administration*, Columbia University Press, 2009, p. 35

could get away with – pushing boundaries without blatantly breaking the rules.

One of the Codes strictest tenets was that criminals could never be shown sympathetically. This was a direct reaction to the early wave of gangster pictures, which had made outlaws seem dangerously glamorous.

The Code changed all of that of course. And as a result, the output of gangster pictures was slowed and they were replaced with safer fare like musicals, costume dramas, and prestige biographies. When crime stories did appear, they were reshaped to fit the new moral framework. The wild, brash criminals of the "first cycle" were replaced by tamer variations. Stars who had made their names playing outlaws – James Cagney and Edward G. Robinson among them – were recast as G-Men, lawyers, and undercover agents. They still moved through the underworld, but now they were emphatically, and reassuringly, on the side of good.

The gangster himself evolved too, becoming more of a complicated, even tragic, figure. Humphrey Bogart embodied this shift. His performance in *High Sierra* (1941) for many was a turning point, marking the last great gasp of the classic gangster film before the genre transformed into something darker and more sophisticated: film noir.

Noir inherited the crime genre's underworld setting but deepened it, weaving in moral ambiguity, psychological complexity, and a brooding visual style. Influenced by German expressionism and hardboiled fiction, these films were drenched in shadow and fatalism, reflecting a world where good and evil were no longer so clear-cut.

The pre-code gangster, once a genuine menace, began to fade into something else entirely – a myth, a memory, and increasingly, a figure ripe for reimagining, even parody. Wilder and Diamond, with their deep affection for Hollywood's golden age and instinct for satire, wanted to capture the spirit of those old black-and-white classics, with its tough men in fedoras, Tommy guns in hand, trading wisecracks as they navigated the underworld. Authenticity was less important than evoking what audiences remembered from those films. Their versions of gangsters were drawn from the movies, not from reality – closer to a stylised cartoon than to documentary truth.

To achieve this homage, they wanted to cast actors who had defined the genre itself. As Wilder initially explained to Marilyn Monroe, the plan was to fill the film with the great names of the period – Edward G. Robinson, George Raft, James Cagney and Paul Muni.

Wilder understood the shorthand power that casting these actors would carry; they were the backstory. Just as he'd cast silent screen legend Gloria Swanson in *Sunset Boulevard* as a faded icon of the silent era – creating a haunting, meta-textual portrait of decline – he did something similar here.

So, George E. Stone was hired to play Toothpick Charlie, a role that recalled the actor's career as a squealer or henchman in nearly a hundred films dating back to the 1920s. Pat O'Brien appeared as Agent Mulligan, bringing with him a screen history built on trusted roles as priests, cops, and military men. He had often starred alongside Cagney and once quipped that he had worn every possible uniform opposite him.

Even some of Spat's nameless henchmen – "all Harvard men" – came from a world steeped in tough-guy roles. Mike Mazurki, a Ukrainian-American actor and former professional wrestler, had the imposing build and granite face perfect for Hollywood's underworld. After gaining a law degree, Mazurki abandoned the courtroom for the wrestling ring before finding his way to the screen, where he appeared in more than 140 films, almost always as a brainless athlete, thug, or gangster. Beside him was the English born Harry Wilson, who cheerfully dubbed himself 'Hollywood's Ugliest Man.'[3] With his distinctive, heavyset features and gravelly voice, Wilson carved out a career as one of cinema's most reliable accomplices, forever typecast as a brute lurking in the background. As he said:

> 'I've been in Alcatraz, Leavenworth and all the other federal prisons – in pictures – and Sing Sing, San Quentin and most of the state pens, and a lot of foreign jails besides. I've been hanged, electrocuted, shot by firing squads, flogged and forced to walk the plank … I've never had what you'd call a really sympathetic role … I'll leave all that romantic stuff to the pretty boys.'[4]

But there were two actors in particular who apparently topped the production's wish list: Edward G. Robinson and George Raft. With the

---

3. Slide, Anthony. *Hollywood Unknowns: A History of Extras, Bit Players and Stand-Ins*, University Press of Mississippi, 2012, p. 110
4. Ibid, p. 110

possible exception of James Cagney, there were no actors who embodied the gangster genre more completely. There were even specific roles for them. Raft was wanted for the part of Spats Colombo, the local mob boss while Robinson was reportedly envisaged as Little Bonaparte, the hard of hearing head of the national Mafia.

Again, these roles weren't intended as realistic portrayals – instead they were caricatures or at least deliberate homages, to the gangster genre's golden age. Take Spats Colombo. Even the name is theatrical, and the character's appearance followed suit. Colombo was defined by his signature accessory: the eponymous spats – white cloth spatter guards buttoned around the ankle, once worn by fashionable men to protect their footwear from the mud. By the late 1920s, spats had largely gone out of style, allegedly abandoned by the fashion-conscious after King George V stopped wearing them. But in *Some Like It Hot*, they were the perfect touch.

They served a cinematic purpose and Wilder made full use of the effect by shooting some of Raft's entrance scenes from the ground up, letting the spats dominate the frame before revealing the man himself. This happens on multiple occasions from when he gets out of the car in the garage, when he arrives at the Seminole Ritz Hotel and, finally, when he is on the mortuary trolley.

And, crucially, worn over his polished, expensive shoes, they became a visual clue that here was no ordinary thug – that he should be understood as a serious and successful villain. This sartorial choice also echoed the classic gangster films where clothing and flashy possessions were essential markers of standing and power.

The audience had to know, instantly and instinctively, that this was a man you didn't cross. And that's exactly why George Raft would be such a catch.

Born George Ranft to a German family in New York, his route to Hollywood was far from straightforward. He first gained attention as a dancer – a skill taught to him by his mother. Specialising in the Charleston, he performed in clubs across New York and even appeared on Broadway under the name Georgie Raft.

By the mid-1920s, he had taken his act to London, demonstrating both the Charleston and the Black Bottom at the popular and glamorous Florida Club in Mayfair. 'Raft is able to offer up-to-date and authentic versions of these dances,' read one announcement. 'He also will be available to answer questions and give expert advice.'[5] Raft himself commented on his style: 'I could have been the first X-rated dancer ... I was very erotic. I used to caress myself as I danced ... I was more of a stylist, unique. I was never a Fred Astaire or a Gene Kelly, but I was sensuous.'[6]

By 1927, he had made his way to Hollywood, landing small, uncredited, dance roles and bit parts. But his real breakthrough came in *Scarface*, where he played Guino "Little Boy" Rinaldo, the right-hand man to Muni's Tony Camonte. It was in this role that Raft debuted the coin-flipping gesture that would become his signature.

Who came up with the action remains unclear – some credit Raft himself, others point to director Howard Hawks or screenwriter Ben Hecht. Tony Curtis claimed it was a reference to an absent-minded habit of the producer Irving Thalberg. But most agree it was introduced as a way to compensate for Raft's limited acting experience and on-camera nervousness, giving him something to focus on and, in the process, creating an enduring cinematic image.

However, off screen, Raft's real-life connections to the criminal world gave him an air of authenticity. Mobster Benjamin "Bugsy" Siegel was a childhood friend and Raft admitted that he had once wanted to be part of the underworld: 'They were like gods to me,' he said. [7]While he never sank deeply into criminal activity, throughout his life, Raft would continue to socialise with shady characters, resulting in Federal Bureau of Investigation (FBI) interviews, visa denials and a revoked (and later restored) gaming licence for a Las Vegas casino.

This lingering association would also mean that Raft struggled to escape his own mythology. By the late 1950s, he was typecast, underemployed, and – according to many – his own worst enemy. He reportedly had a habit of turning down what would become legendary roles: *High Sierra, The Maltese Falcon*, *Casablanca* (1942), even the role of Walter Neff in *Double Indemnity*. It was such a string of misses that Wilder had once joked: 'When George Raft turned down a part, that's when I knew I was making a good picture.'[8]

5. *Dancing Times*, June 1927, p. 373
6. Yablonsky, Lewis. *George Raft*. McGraw-Hill, 1974, p. 20
7. Weldon Whalen, Robert. *Murder Inc. and the Moral Life: Gangsters And Gangbusters in La Guardia's New York*, Fordham University Press, 2016, p. 25
8. Phillips, p. 214

But when the offer came for *Some Like It Hot,* Raft was eager to accept. Maybe he hadn't heard the jokes Wilder had made at his expense – or maybe he had and simply didn't care. Either way, he saw the value in the part and agreed practically immediately. On 28 May, now in his mid-50s, Raft signed a contract for $5,000 per week, guaranteed for seven weeks.

Raft was secured. Edward G. Robinson, however, proved more elusive.

Robinson's breakout had started with the Broadway production *The Racket* (1927), and with his electrifying turn in *Little Caesar*, he became Hollywood's quintessential gangster. But he was no one-note thug and Robinson had long sought to break free from typecasting. When offered yet another similar role in *Brother Orchid* (1940), he reluctantly accepted but wrote to producer Hal Wallis to make his feelings known. He explained that he did 'not object to doing the genre' but felt that he should not be forever 'circumscribed within these limits' and that he wanted 'the gamut broadened' not out of 'conceit or actor's temperament,' but in order 'to do justice to my capacities, as a whole.'[9]

Robinson succeeded in his evolution, becoming a respected character actor. But the 1950s were not kind. Accused of leftist sympathies during the Hollywood anti-communist and anti-union era, he found himself "greylisted" – not officially banned, but increasingly unwelcome in major studio productions. His career, like many others of that time, went into a steep decline.

Wilder had worked with Robinson before, casting him in *Double Indemnity*. Their collaboration had been a success, and Wilder understood the power of Robinson's presence on screen. To sweeten the offer for this new project, it was said that Wilder even cast his son, Edward G. Robinson Jr. – known as Manny – in the minor role of Johnny Paradise. It was a small but memorable part and Paradise even flips a coin in one scene as Raft walks past, prompting the line: "Where did you pick up that cheap trick?" A clear nod to Raft's own coin-flipping gangster persona.

The reason Robinson didn't ultimately sign on to *Some Like It Hot* remains a persistent bit of Hollywood mythology. One version of events suggests that he walked away the moment he learned George Raft had already been cast.

9. Behlmer, Rudy. *Inside Warner Bros. (1935-1951)*, Weidenfeld & Nicholson, 1987, p. 82

The tension between the two men can be traced back to the early 1940s, during the filming of *Manpower* (1941), a Raoul Walsh directed crime picture that paired them opposite a smouldering Marlene Dietrich. From the beginning, the atmosphere on set was strained. Raft was said to be deeply irritated at receiving only third billing and even more annoyed by what he perceived as Robinson's condescending attempts to "coach" him through scenes.

To make matters worse, both men were reportedly captivated by Dietrich, who was known to inspire intense admiration from her co-stars.

One day during a dispute over a line in the script, Raft verbally lashed out at Robinson, bringing filming to an abrupt standstill. Production was halted for several hours, and the atmosphere on set grew icy as the two men refused to speak off-camera for an entire week.

Later that same month things escalated further until there was a physical altercation. Unfortunately, it timed with the presence of a magazine photographer, who had been sent to the set that very day. The resulting fight was captured in dramatic photos splashed across a May 1941 issue of *LIFE* and picked up by newspapers nationwide.

Warner Bros. lost a full day of shooting and a significant sum of money. The fallout extended beyond bad press with Robinson actually demanding protection from Raft. Roy Obringer, the head of Warner Bros.' legal department, submitted a formal report to their union, the Screen Actors Guild (SAG).

> 'Mr. Robinson became highly nervous ... such nervous condition affected his voice ... and made the same husky so that he was unable to properly and clearly speak his lines ... The position of the Company [became] an extremely difficult one.'[10]

Production on *Manpower* eventually resumed, and the film was completed, but the hostility between Robinson and Raft was said to have lingered. Robinson reportedly swore he would never work with Raft again. Robinson's vow, however, did not hold. The two appeared together in *A Bullet for Joey* (1955), suggesting that time, necessity, or simple professionalism eventually outweighed old grudges. But this subsequent collaboration

10. Ibid, p. 147

does cast scepticism on the idea that lingering resentment was the reason Robinson did not sign on for Wilder's film.

In the end, Nehemiah Persoff, a seasoned character actor, was cast in the role of Little Bonaparte. Persoff may not have carried the mythic stature of Robinson, but he brought an unmistakable onscreen authority. Whether Robinson actively turned down the part or simply never committed remains unclear. It isn't even demonstrable whether he was actually asked. However, some commentators have noted the possible significance of agency politics: Robinson was represented by William Morris, while Persoff was another client of MCA – an arrangement that may have influenced the final casting decision.

There was still one more key piece of secondary casting to lock into place: Osgood Fielding III. And he was perhaps the most complicated character of all, in his own way.

As he was written, Osgood was a walking example of poor taste – a lecherous old man, a wealthy playboy with a trail of ex-wives and a relentless, sleazy manner. In the wrong hands, he could easily come off as grotesque, even repellent.

It was understood that this character needed more than a reliance on comic timing. They wanted an actor who came with built-in goodwill, someone the audience instinctively liked and would continue to like even as the character bothered and blundered his way through scenes. The absurdity had to feel almost harmless, not menacing.

The answer to this casting problem came, by all accounts, as a stroke of serendipity on 18 April 1958. On that day The Dodgers, freshly relocated from Brooklyn after decades of East Coast history, were playing their very first home game to great excitement. Downtown, a 22-car motorcade paraded through streets thronged with fans: Zsa Zsa Gabor gushed in her syndicated column, 'I am delighted about major league baseball coming to Los Angeles – with all those men and that enormous diamond, what woman wouldn't be?'[11]

The team was still waiting for their new ballpark, Dodger Stadium, which wouldn't open until 1962. In the meantime, games were being held at the Los Angeles Memorial Coliseum – a massive venue used for the 1932 Summer Olympics and designed for track meets and football, not baseball.

---

11. *UP,* April 19, 1958

The Coliseum was far from ideal with fans in the upper decks needing binoculars just to see second base. This was an especially big problem in the days before giant video boards – the first demonstration of Jumbotron technology wouldn't happen until the 1980s.

A record crowd of almost 79,000 people filled the stadium that day. *LIFE* magazine wryly observed in its 28 April issue that while the vastness of the Coliseum made it difficult for many spectators to actually see the action on the field many people were there to be seen rather than to watch. Among the celebrities in attendance were Groucho Marx, Jimmy Stewart, Lauren Bacall, Alfred Hitchcock, Jack Lemmon, Edward G. Robinson and, predictably to all who knew him, Billy Wilder.

A lifelong sports enthusiast, Wilder was rarely seen without a transistor radio glued to his ear, even during dinner parties. That day, he sat in the Coliseum stand with Audrey, Iz and Barbara.

And that's when they saw Joe E. Brown.

A baseball fanatic and part-owner of the Pittsburgh Pirates, Brown was the emcee for the opening ceremony. Dressed sharply and grinning ear to ear with his famously enormous mouth, Brown radiated the goofy charm that had made him one of America's most beloved comic actors.

Wilder's reaction was immediate: 'That's the guy,' he said. 'The crazy guy who is old and loony enough looking.'[12]

Brown was perfect. He wasn't lecherous as such – just cheerfully absurd. And he had built his career playing sweet, slightly dim men. His vaudeville background as a tumbler and dancer gave him a lightness that would keep the portrayal from tipping into a grim caricature. And his face, especially that grin, was almost cartoonish in its exaggeration. You couldn't help but laugh with him. The role would also let Brown have fun with his squeaky clean-like characterisation giving a parody of himself, much like Raft and the other actors would do too, but in a different style.

Like the other golden age actors hired for *Some Like It Hot* by the late 1950s Brown's career had slowed down from its peak and his movie career was effectively over. A few years earlier he had co-starred in MGM's lavish Technicolor remake of *Show Boat* (1951) and while he was regularly making television apperances, he was still in need of a new high-profile

12. Castle, Alison (Ed). Billy Wilder's "*Some Like It Hot*," Taschen, 2010, p. 238

project. Osgood offered him such a comeback and Brown accepted, signing on at $5,000 a week with a five-week guarantee.

The principals and main supporting cast were in place, but the writing team still had significant work ahead. Determined to ground the story in detail, they undertook extensive research by contacting the Encyclopaedia Britannica Library Research Service in Chicago, and asking for as comprehensive a report as possible on 'the gangland incident known as the St. Valentine's Day Massacre.'[13]

For the uninitiated, the Britannica Service seems something of a marvel. Marketed to "those devoted to the advancement of learning," it offered expertly compiled dossiers on virtually every conceivable topic (barring professional, medical, or legal advice – as they were keen to make clear). Subscribers received their reports in smartly bound folders, footnoted and annotated, often complete with reading lists. Some topics had already been prepared by their in-house specialists and were available via what was known as "Instant Service." Others required bespoke investigation.

Ordinary subscribers – those enrolled in the Britannica Participation Programme – were permitted a total of 100 reports over ten years but no more than ten per year. Coupons were provided, to be neatly affixed to each request like scholarly postage stamps.

The Britannica Service was a clever workaround for Wilder and Diamond – a way of replicating a provision that those affiliated to the bigger studios had access to: the miracle of research libraries.

At MGM, which had the largest of all studio libraries the research department was housed above the office of the studio manager. At its peak, it was a hive of activity, capable of fielding up to 500 requests each day to access its sprawling archive of over 20,000 books and 250,000 clippings all painstakingly cross-referenced on 80,000 index cards. The collection was so vast it overflowed into three further separate buildings on the lot. Nathalie Bucknall ran the department through the 1950s, followed by Elliott Morgan during the 1960s, and later James J. Earie and Bonnie Rothbart until 1988 – at which point Warner Bros. acquired the entire resource.

---

13. Box 1 Folder 6, Mirisch Corporation Records (Collection 1146). UCLA Library Special Collections, Charles E. Young Research Library, University of California, Los Angeles.

Its holdings were breathtaking in scope: Sears catalogues, vintage menus, nineteenth century travel guides and lovingly kept scrapbooks. There were close ups of architectural details, photographs of costumes, street scenes and even picture files detailing how something as incidental as a Victorian umbrella might have looked.

Ensuring they had similar access to that kind of meticulous research was typical of Wilder and Diamond's working method. Years later, when they were deep into writing *The Private Life of Sherlock Holmes* (1970), Iz would recall reading 'scores of books' – to steep themselves in the tone and manner of Arthur Conan Doyle's original source material. As Diamond confirmed it was 'just to get a feeling for the characters, for the background, so that we were completely familiar with them. Then we could go off in our direction, but in the spirit of what Doyle had written.'[14]

This balancing act between historical accuracy and cinematic licence is evident throughout *Some Like It Hot*, most obviously during its version of the St. Valentine's Day Massacre. While the basic structure of the real event remains – the killing of seven men – there are a few minor differences.

For example, in reality, the massacre took place in the morning but the film moves it to the afternoon. And whereas the real-life killers wore police uniforms to catch their victims off guard, the film dispenses with any disguise. Instead, the attackers charge in, smashing through a chain barrier with their car, making no attempt to hide their purpose.

It's a bolder, more theatrical choice – perfectly in step with the film's heightened, stylised tone.

14. Froug, William. *The Screenwriter Looks at the Screenwriter*, The Macmillan Company, 1972, p. 156

Part Two

Fabric & Facade

Chapter Six

"P.S. I miss you."

The limousine that picked up Marilyn Monroe from LAX had swept her directly to the Hotel Bel-Air, where she would stay during the next few months, when not on location.

Tucked away on Stone Canyon Road in Beverly Hills, the Bel-Air had opened in 1946 with, originally, just sixty-two rooms. The hotel with its white stucco walls, terracotta roof tiles and elegant archways – was all understated luxury. The grounds were lavishly planted, crisscrossed with winding paths, footbridges and famed for its Swan Lake, complete with real swans.

Marilyn had stayed at the Bel-Air several times before, including once whilst recovering from an emergency appendectomy. The pain had begun during the filming of *Monkey Business*, but director Howard Hawks showed little sympathy, insisting she finish before seeking treatment. Only after her final scene was completed was she admitted to the nearby Cedars of Lebanon Hospital for surgery. Even then, she was not left in peace as while still in her hospital bed, Fox required her to pose for publicity photographs. In the images she is shown, fully made-up with her hair perfectly set, reading get-well cards, and exuding a kind of glamour that she can't have possibly been feeling at the time.

But during this 1958 stay, despite her reservations about the project, the circumstances seemed more positive and her suite more spacious – a kitchen, a bedroom, and a private patio with French doors. It was reported that the rooms had been redecorated entirely in white, a deliberate choice meant to echo the style of her New York apartment. A piano had also been placed in the suite and was used to rehearse the film's songs. Music – both playing and listening – had always been a comfort, and she especially loved jazz with Ella Fitzgerald, Frank Sinatra, and Louis Armstrong among her favourites.

With barely any time to settle in, the first event on her schedule was a press reception. Telegrams had been sent out in advance, informing invitees that the night was to: "Welcome Marilyn Monroe back to Hollywood." The reception, jointly hosted by the Mirisch brothers and Wilder, took place in the Rodeo Room of The Beverly Hills Hotel, that grand, old-world palace on Sunset Boulevard.

When the hotel opened its doors in May 1912, Hollywood was practically a remote resort, a pastoral escape for downtown Angelinos – dotted with only the occasional mansion. Among the early luminaries drawn to the area were Rudolph Valentino, Mary Pickford and Douglas Fairbanks, whose legendary mansion and estate, Pickfair, became a symbol of the new elite. Repainted in a cheerful colour during the postwar years, The Beverly Hills Hotel was subsequently dubbed "the Pink Palace" and both the area and the hotel had changed significantly.

On 8 July 1958 it played host to a crowd of around 75 members of the press, many of whom hadn't seen Monroe in the flesh for more than two years. There was genuine anticipation in the air. Jack Lemmon may have been absent – he was still on location in Connecticut, filming *It Happened to Jane* (1959) with Doris Day – but Tony Curtis and George Raft were both also in attendance. Gossip columnist Sheilah Graham, reporting on the reception, playfully remarked on the notoriously fashion-conscious Curtis's outfit: a brown silk foulard jacket and extremely narrow trousers which were said to be slightly under fourteen inches around the ankle. 'I'm told it's the new style …' she added rather doubtfully.[1]

Marilyn arrived at 6:00 p.m., fashionably (and some noted, predictably) late. Wearing a low-cut black cocktail dress, black heels and white gloves she looked spectacular in an outfit that was an almost complete contrast to the one she had worn on her arrival.

She spoke to the press, posed for photographs and greeted her co-stars. There was apparently history between her and Curtis – they had, at least according to him, briefly dated a few years before – but they certainly had little interaction on this night. Curtis later said he was disappointed not to speak with Monroe more before the start of filming.

---

1. Hollywood today, *The Kingston Whig Standard*, 25 July 1958, p. 9

With the reception complete and most of the key cast in town, they moved into the next phase: makeup and wardrobe tests. Or at least that was the plan.

Filming had been scheduled to begin immediately at Goldwyn Studios with the production company signing a deal to use their sound stages for interior shots. The agreement was at a cost of $1,250 per day for studio photography with a minimum 30-day commitment and with a smaller fee during location days.

But there was a problem.

In early July a fire had broken out on one of the sound stages. At the time, the studio was being used for *Porgy and Bess* (1959), a film produced by Samuel Goldwyn – his last before retirement. The production starred Sidney Poitier, Dorothy Dandridge and Sammy Davis Jr., who would all later be regular visitors on the *Some Like It Hot* set.

The blaze tore through the stage, destroying sets and costumes and leaving the space badly damaged and unusable. Rumours quickly spread – some claimed it had been set deliberately; others blamed a careless cigarette. Whatever the cause, the result was the same and production was delayed before it had even begun.

In the following days Marilyn's time would be filled with social calls and encounters from the past as she reacquainted herself with the city. Old friend Sydney Chaplin, son of Charlie, wrote to ask if she could help him secure a part in the film. Emmeline Snively, from the Blue Book Modelling Agency, wrote teasing an idea she wanted to discuss. The press began to follow her movements closely. She was seen at composer Jimmy McHugh's birthday party – arriving late, though not as tardy as Judy Garland, who reportedly turned up five hours after the festivities had begun. She had dinner with producer Joseph Schenck and attended the *Gigi* (1958) premiere at the Hollywood Paramount Theatre, escorted by her hairdresser Sydney Guilaroff. Dressed in a red strappy gown with a black stole and long black gloves, her hair was swept back elegantly. According to some reports of the evening, she went largely unrecognised, which was, once again, spitefully attributed to her prolonged absence from Hollywood.

Yet beneath the public appearances, it was obvious Marilyn arrived already feeling fragile, self-conscious about her body and profoundly lonely.

She told Hedda Hopper that she missed Hugo, her beloved black-and-brown basset hound. He was already a well-known member of the Miller family and Hopper, who had visited them at their New York home, had once described him to her readers as 'the longest and most unwieldy beagle hound I've ever seen.'[2] Marilyn also missed Arthur, and his children, Jane and Bobby, to whom she was very close. Letters she sent them in mid-July also reveal something of her state of mind during those first weeks back in Hollywood.

To Bobby, she wrote that she had been taking ukulele lessons and added poignantly: 'It sometimes gets very lonely here.' Someone had given her a puppy – a golden spaniel named Walter – but she had returned him after discovering he had previously bitten a woman on the throat.[3]

To Jane, whom she affectionately called 'Janie-bones,' she enclosed a newspaper clipping reporting on her arrival and revealed she hadn't been in the 'huge swimming pool' because of an ear infection. 'Nothing serious,' she reassured her. 'But it hurts a little.'

The letter ends – 'P.S. I miss you.'[4]

While she tried to comfort her stepdaughter, Monroe was actually concerned enough about her health to contact Dr Eugen Grabscheid, her doctor in New York. His reply is interesting in that it indicates he believed a previous issue had worsened since she had left home and he requested a blood count and a sinus X-ray.

There was cause to be concerned. Marilyn was prone to infections – both ear and respiratory: bronchitis in 1954; a lung infection during production of *The Seven Year Itch* and pneumonia while filming *Bus Stop* which required hospital stays. Medical examinations in 1956 diagnosed neutropenia, low levels of a white cell type in the blood which leaves people particularly vulnerable to infections and viruses.

Marilyn also met with Jack Hirschberg, brought on as an independent publicity director, and Leon Roth, head of publicity at the Mirisch Company. The subsequent reports described her as cooperative but firm about boundaries. Publicity was not her priority. 'I'm here to make the film,' she reportedly said – echoing remarks she had made many times before. She made it clear to the two men that she would not discuss 'her

2. Marilyn Returning to Hollywood, *Los Angeles Times*, 22 June 1958, p. 99
3. Julien's Auctions, *Property From the Estate of Lee Strasberg*, Lot #320, 17 November 2016 https://bid.juliensauctions.com/lot-details/index/catalog/180/lot/83296/billy-wilder-some-like-it-hot-synopsis-sent-to-marilyn-monroe
4. Ibid

home, her past, [or] her marriage.' The subsequently agreed strategy was deliberately measured: minimal handlers, not too much pressure. Otherwise, as one internal note warned, 'She will become scared and pull the switch.'[5] Whatever they may have promised her in reality there would be constant press attention during the production, something that became a source of extra pressure and stress.

That initial meeting with Marilyn was only one step in a longer publicity campaign, of course. A report dated 20 May had outlined their planned early strategy, much of it centred on her arrival and the initial press reception. One issue raised was the lack of recent photographs – Marilyn had not done a formal portrait session in several years. The "Fabled Enchantress" sitting for *LIFE* magazine that she was scheduled to complete with Richard Avedon before leaving for Hollywood was noted, and it was suggested that another session with him would be arranged. Avedon, one of Marilyn's preferred photographers, was thought ideal for capturing the spirit of the period. But he was unavailable, and in the end, a freelance photographer she had previously worked with, Richard C. Miller, was hired instead.

There was also a more ambitious publicity proposal in the mix: a "Roaring 20s" party on the Goldwyn lot. The plan was that a speakeasy set would be constructed, complete with a live Dixieland band. Props from the film – including machine guns – would be on display, and period cars would be parked outside for added atmosphere. The proposed guest list ran to around 300 names and there were even hopes of booking Paul Whiteman and His Orchestra. And to top it all off Tony Curtis and Jack Lemmon were to arrive in full costume.

It is also very apparent that initially a key part of the early publicity discussions were focused on how to capitalise on the shock effect of the two male actors dressed in women's clothes. Interviews with Billy were proposed to tease their look ahead of the official reveal. One idea, attributed to Wilder and Diamond, suggested staging a *LIFE* magazine photo of Curtis and Lemmon arriving at celebrity hotspot Romanoff's restaurant dressed as their characters.

But concerns emerged had early. On 2 June, Roger Lewis, advertising manager for United Artists, warned of potential backlash, noting the risk

5. Box 1 Folder 9, Mirisch Corporation Records (Collection 1146). UCLA Library Special Collections, Charles E. Young Research Library, University of California, Los Angeles.

that the actors might 'really look like girls,' and fears over how the public might respond.[6]

The more elaborate campaigns were eventually scaled back, and the planned "reveals" seemingly never took place. However, news that costume designer Orry-Kelly would be creating the outfits of all three leading "ladies" was released to the press in advance. Coverage initially took a light, playful tone and referenced current trends for straight lined, rather shapeless dress styles with the writer of the *Hollywood Today* column reporting: 'When they (Jack Lemmon and Tony Curtis) heard that famed designer Orry-Kelly would whip up their costumes, they struck a blow against today's fashions. "No sacks, please," they chorused.'[7]

It was apparent that getting the costumes right, for all the cast, would be essential to the success and feel of the film and Orry-Kelly was the perfect choice.

6. Box 1 Folder 9, Mirisch Corporation Records (Collection 1146). UCLA Library Special Collections, Charles E. Young Research Library, University of California, Los Angeles.
7. Hollywood Today, *The Plain Speaker*, 8 July 1958, p. 19

Chapter Seven

Here Come the Girls

Born in Australia in 1897, as Orry George Kelly he had originally wanted to be an actor and moved to New York to try his luck. A gifted artist he paid the bills painting murals in department stores and nightclubs and by doing sketches of people. Costume and scenery designs for revues followed, and it was during this time he became close to a fellow aspiring star: the vaudeville and variety performer Archibald Leach – later better known as Cary Grant. The two, according to Orry-Kelly at least, had an on-again, off-again relationship for a number of years.

Orry-Kelly eventually moved to Hollywood and, between 1932 and 1944, served as chief costumier at Warner Bros., working on hundreds of films including such classics as *Angels with Dirty Faces* (1938), *Now, Voyager* (1942) and *Casablanca.* A series of disputes with Jack Warner led to his dismissal, after which he moved to Fox.

Then like many of his peers, he went freelance – more by necessity than choice, as studios dismantled their once-vast wardrobe departments. These had been complex machines: ranked designers, supervisors, costumiers, seamstresses, fitters, milliners and more but now, in a bid to cut costs, they had become fragmented.

Over the years he developed a reputation for his ability to make actresses look spectacular, with flattering silhouettes and an instinctive understanding of what worked on camera.

He won many accolades, including multiple Academy Awards for "Best Costume Design" – a category given out for the first time in 1949.

As Orry-Kelly's success grew, he became increasingly selective, taking on fewer roles. *Some Like It Hot*, however, was one he actively wanted. Reflecting later, he acknowledged that he had done 'something I had never done before' by testing for the job, arriving with sketches to present to 'the wily Puck-faced' Billy Wilder.[1]

Whilst he drew inspiration his brief was not bound by strict adherence to the styles of the 1920s. In particular there would be no question of reshaping the lead actress' well-known figure to match the boyish silhouette that had been fashionable at that time – audiences wanted to see Marilyn as Marilyn.

Orry-Kelly later explained his vision for Monroe's wardrobe. Although she played a 'tarty part,' he avoided the usual Hollywood approach, drawing instead of Madeleine Vionnet's designs, whose cuts allowed 'every line of the body to move.' He believed this was far more flattering than the rigid, over-fitted styles often used for screen sex symbols and noted that Monroe fully agreed with the approach.[2]

Outfitting the men presented a different challenge. And with Jack Lemmon not arriving on set until the third week of July there was also an extremely concentrated period of fittings and screen tests to contend with. Later recollections by the cast suggest there was tension from the start. According to Tony Curtis, initial measurements had been done separately – Lemmon's while he was filming in Connecticut, his at Goldwyn Studios. In his version of the story, once they were both on set, the actors were sent to the Western Costume Company, the famous stock house that rented outfits to the industry.

Here, he claimed, they found a disappointing selection. The dresses didn't fit properly, unsurprisingly, as they had been made for women. They looked cheap, were not especially accurate for the period, and, in Curtis's view, unworthy of this particular production. Fashion-conscious and the son of a tailor, he thought they would look poor on camera. Curtis later claimed he went straight to Wilder to object, asking who was designing Marilyn's costumes and insisting he wanted the same person to do theirs. Wilder, he said, agreed to his suggestion.

This narrative, however, doesn't quite align with the documented timeline, as Orry-Kelly had already been commissioned several months earlier to work on their outfits and the appointment already widely reported on. It is possible Curtis's story was a later embellishment – maybe an

1. Orry-Kelly. *Women I've Undressed*, Allen & Unwin, 2016, p. 400
2. Ibid, p. 400

attempt to give himself a bigger pre-production role or perhaps, it was a more coordinated attempt to downplay the early excitement over hiring a top designer to dress two men in drag, especially given that the financial backers had expressed caution to any pre-publicity. Whatever the true story in the finished film Orry-Kelly is only credited as designing "Miss Monroe's gowns."

They would be kitted up with an impressive wardrobe for the woman on the run: including travel outfits for the train, a pair of pyjamas and a nightgown, daytime wear for Florida, a bathing suit, and the evening dresses worn to perform with the band. Their clothes were, in fact, some of the most period-accurate in the film. Still contemporary influences, of course, crept in. Cloche hats and flowing dresses captured the 1920s spirit, but shoes and handbags were unmistakably 1950s in style. In any case Curtis was delighted with the final outcome 'We had custom garter belts and brassieres, shoes that fit us properly, and nice cloche hats and those high collars that Olivia de Havilland used to wear in those early movies. Oh, did I love them!'[3]

Another story that subsequently surfaced is that the wonderful black dress worn by Sugar during the band's rehearsal of *Runnin' Wild* on the train was originally designed for Lemmon but was claimed by Monroe after she saw it and insisted that it would look better on her. This, according to several sources, left Orry-Kelly absolutely furious and forced to design an alternative at short notice. He was reported to have shouted out, 'She took your dress! The bitch has pinched your dress.'[4]

Again, it's a colourful story but one that feels highly improbable. The dress in question – a silk, black, button-down number with a plunging neckline and fringing at the bottom – is so form-fitting that it seems unlikely it was ever meant for anyone but Monroe. Indeed, Curtis said that she was actually sewn into her gowns and was unable to sit down once she was in them. There is a great photo of her on set on a slant board, a contraption which allowed actresses in tight dresses to relax without sitting. By contrast, the black dress worn by Lemmon during the train scenes is far more modest (and much less cliché!). It has a high collar and its loose fit

3. Tony Curtis remembers "Some Like It Hot," Entertainment Weekly, 20 July 2006 https://ew.com/article/2006/07/20/tony-curtis-remembers-some-it-hot/ accessed 1 January 2026
4. Freedland, Michael. Some Like It Cool: Jack Lemmon, Robson Books, 2003, p. 77

is much more in line with the conservative styles worn by his and Curtis's characters throughout the film.

Another oft-told anecdote involves a joint fitting session with the three main actors in the makeup and wardrobe department at Goldwyn, which they initially used whilst their individual dressing rooms were being made ready. In one version of this particular day, while Orry-Kelly was taking their measurements, he supposedly remarked that Curtis had the better backside. According to Laurence Maslon Monroe reportedly responded by opening her blouse and countering: 'He doesn't have tits like these.'[5]

A different version, told by Orry-Kelly himself was that he had merely noted the visual differences between male and female silhouettes on screen with men's backsides appearing smaller – and suggested using satin on the top and crepe on the bottom of her dress to compensate. He considered this a tactful solution, but apparently Marilyn was not appreciative and 'let him have it.'[6]

Whatever the exact truth, it's clear this was a demanding and sometimes tense period. With so much at stake, the preparation – especially for Curtis and Lemmon – was more involved than anything they had experienced before.

Getting the costumes right was only part of the transformation. Hair and makeup were equally as crucial. Behind the scenes, a sizeable, and very experienced, team handled the hairdressing with call sheets listing names like Lillian Lashin, Dotha Hippe, Helene Parrish and Jeanette Marvin. And also credited in the final film were Alice Monte and Agnes Flanagan, a stylist who had worked closely with Marilyn since 1950 and was often called in for her premieres, photo sessions, and public appearances.

Another key member of Marilyn's trusted entourage on set was Sydney Guilaroff, who had worked as chief hairstylist at MGM since the mid-1930s. Renowned for crafting signature looks for stars like Louise Brooks, Guilaroff had worked with Marilyn since *The Asphalt Jungle* and remained involved in nearly all her major projects. On *Some Like It Hot,* he not only styled Marilyn's hair but also reportedly created the wigs for Curtis and Lemmon. And for this he received $4,000.

The make-up team was similarly extensive with Marilyn's personal artist, Whitey Snyder, joining Anthony S Lloyd, Erland (Bud) Bashaw,

5. Maslon, p. 60
6. Orry-Kelly, p. 405

Bunny Armstrong and Virginia Curtis who was responsible for body makeup. But one of the more technically demanding aspects of this work would be Curtis and Lemmon's transformation. The requirements went beyond the run of the mill, as the team also had to develop a reliable beard cover. Both Curtis and Lemmon shaved two or three times a day, but any remaining stubble had to be effectively concealed. Their eyebrows were also plucked to create a more feminine appearance. Hair on other areas of their visible skin was also a potential issue – although while the producers were concerned about the risk of shaving cuts disrupting continuity and delaying filming, Lemmon reportedly only cut his legs shaving once.

To create his female alter ego Curtis worked with Emile LaVigne, a well-respected artist who had trained under the legendary Jack Dawn at MGM and had been part of *The Wizard of Oz* (1939) makeup crew while still an apprentice. Later in his career, LaVigne was made head of makeup for United Artists.

Lemmon worked directly with Harry Ray, a skilled artist and occasional actor who had also been active in the industry since the mid-1930s. Ray would go on to maintain long-standing professional relationships with both the Mirisch Company and Lemmon and even appeared briefly in a speaking role as Dr. Fleischmann in the opening scenes of Wilder's *Avanti!* (1972) as well as doing Jack's makeup for the film.

Despite his significant contributions, Ray was unfortunately not credited for his work on *Some Like It Hot.* Letters from the Mirisch Company Archives reveal an apology from Walter to Harry the following year, explaining that the mistake unfortunately couldn't be corrected because the prints had already been made and distributed. Ray replied graciously, forgiving the oversight.

Alas, the omission extends to the secondary sources as well. There are two well-known photographs of Lemmon and Curtis sitting in makeup chairs during tests. While both images are usually credited as showing Emile LaVigne at work, the artist applying makeup to Lemmon is actually Harry Ray. So, consider him back in the historical record!

The two actors, who had previously known each other only casually, sat side by side, testing looks. Wilder gave some input, but it quickly became obvious that they were taking different approaches. Lemmon threw himself into the process – he treated it as a key aspect of building his character.

'Makeup is vital at times in acting,' he said, 'it certainly was for *Some Like It Hot*.'[7]

For him the lips were particularly important and working with Ray he replicated the 1920s "bee-stung" effect, which was even sometimes slightly altered mid-scene to emphasise his different expressions. Whilst it was effective he also realised that the character ended up looking like a "bad imitation" of his mother, Mildred (known as Millie) – and that her mannerisms found their way into the performance too. Curtis also admitted that he noticed himself channelling his mother, Helen, at times, saying 'I played it like my mother. My mother could be very aloof and out of it: every time I stopped talking, I pursed my lips because they were too thin – that was the female in me. It wasn't any more complicated than that.'[8]

Curtis also complained that finding the right bra wasn't easy – he was, as he put it, a 36-D. Lemmon, meanwhile, found his bra unexpectedly practical. In an interview with the *Daily Mirror*, he claimed it had been an ideal place to stash cigarettes, change and car keys.

Their mid heel shoes were also a particular problem with both men suffering regular muscle cramps. On set, they would swap their footwear for slippers whenever possible and use buckets of ice between takes to relieve the pain.

But one of the biggest trials was preventing the fabric of their dresses from clinging too closely. Two methods used are commonly cited: padding with cotton wool or Kleenex, and a specially designed steel jockstrap intended to smooth out any anatomical distractions. While supposedly effective, the steel device reportedly made using the toilet a complicated ordeal. They had to notify wardrobe beforehand, and undressing was a slow, involved process.

Eventually, Curtis claimed he had devised his own solution – a "relief tube," as he called it. This homemade funnel and hose system ran discreetly around his thigh, hidden inside his silk stocking. When nature called, he simply retrieved the device, used it, then rolled it back into place, claiming: 'It wasn't all that comfortable, but it worked.'[9]

7. Widener, p. 168
8. Maslon, p. 56
9. Sikov, p. 414

Curtis's subsequent apparent ability to get through the day without disruptive bathroom breaks impressed many on set. Nevertheless, when Lemmon caught him using the contraption, he apparently politely declined to adopt one himself.

By the end of July, the wardrobe and makeup team felt they had pushed the transformation as far as possible. But a real-world test was needed.

Curtis tells the story of the day the actors decided to walk into the ladies' room on the studio lot, fully kitted out in their pastel-coloured day dresses with hair and makeup done. Standing in front of the mirror, they chatted casually and touched up their lipstick. It was reported that none of the other women present paid them the slightest bit of attention.

Still another essential element they had to master was movement – how to move more like women. And for this Wilder turned to a consultant.

Barbette had once dazzled audiences, first appearing on stage as part of the act The Alfaretta Sisters. As a drag performer and aerialist Barbette had been admired in both the circus and vaudeville worlds and found particular fame in Europe during the 1920s and 30s, performing at venues like the Moulin Rouge, the Folies Bergère and the London Palladium. Jean Cocteau once wrote of a performance: 'I myself have seen no comparable display of artistry on the stage since Nijinsky.'[10]

By the late 1950s these glory days were over – a career cut short at its peak due to illness and injury. But with that came the opportunity to choreograph, to teach and to consult on a number of Hollywood films.

Barbette taught Curtis and Lemmon a great deal about movement and performing femininity.

For instance: when you sit, don't just plop into a chair – melt into it. Slowly and gracefully.

They were taught to walk with one leg crossing slightly in front of the other, placing each foot where the last had stepped – pointing their feet inward in effect. Push the hips forward. Keep the motion fluid. And tighten the buttocks.

They were also told to sit with their palms facing downwards to avoid flexing the biceps, keeping the arms looking slim.

---

10. Steegmuller, Francis, An Angel, A Flower, A Bird, *The New Yorker*, 20 September 1969 https://www.newyorker.com/magazine/1969/09/27/an-angel-a-flower-a-bird accessed 1 April 2025

Curtis approached the task with athletic discipline as this was something he was used to and good at. Barbette praised his efforts: 'Curtis can be magnificent. Lemmon is hopeless.'[11]

And Lemmon *was* hopeless – but deliberately so. His choice was grounded in character and the reasoning that both personalities shouldn't behave the same way – and why would they? Within the story's timeline, when exactly would they have learned to walk properly in heels, to carry themselves like women? It was plausible that one might be a natural, but both? That was unlikely.

As Joe, Curtis is a womaniser and a gambler, but his secondary character was also modelled on the elegant Grace Kelly. He pursed his lips, swirled his long pearl necklace and moved with controlled confidence.

But as Lemmon saw it, *his* was a very different proposition: goofy, anxious, and terrified. Lemmon listened to Barbette's instructions, absorbed it all, but deliberately avoided perfection. The humour, he believed, came from not quite getting it right. 'I was clumsy, I was an asshole, the shoes were killing me, my ankles were turning.'[12]

Lemmon also acknowledged that there was another layer to navigate. He didn't want to push the performance to an extreme. He was cautious about making the character too feminine – wary of going too far, in his own words, 'like a guy trying to impersonate a gay and overdoing it.'[13]

Beneath this understanding and the concerns raised by the press team and financial backers lay the coded anxiety of needing to reassure the audience that the drag was strictly out of necessity and not preference. After all, this was Eisenhower's America, a conservative time defined by rigid gender roles, sexual hypocrisy and a deeper cultural fear of queerness and gender nonconformity.

Some of the implications of this friction at the heart of the movie came to a head on the day of the comparison test – a screen test designed to evaluate and compare makeup, costumes, and lighting setups. What had felt like a game in the ladies' room was now something very different with the full look, on display, under harsh studio lights, in front of a predominantly male crew.

---

11. Freedland, p. 77
12. Fuller, Nick. *Call Me Bud: Jack Lemmon On Film*, Authors OnLine, 2006, p. 10
13. Gemünden, p. 116

Curtis acknowledged he became overwhelmed. He hesitated, refusing to leave the dressing room at first, and had to be coaxed out. It wasn't only his now feminised appearance he was struggling with. For years he had been fighting to shed his "pretty boy" image – dismissed as little more than a handsome face and a well-built body. He reflected that his time in Hollywood had also been marked by persistent rumours about his sexuality and unwanted attention from men.

Appearing as a woman, Curtis admitted, felt like a direct challenge to his masculinity. In those first moments, he was deeply embarrassed, self-conscious in a way he hadn't fully anticipated when he had taken on the role.

Lemmon, by contrast, embraced the process with infectious enthusiasm. For him, slipping into the costume was like creating a shell and crawling into it – total immersion in character. Or, as some accounts have it, not so much a crawl as a charge. He reportedly grabbed Curtis by the hand and exclaimed: 'Now come on, for Christ's sake, be a woman! You are a woman!' and bounded into the studio.[14]

Curtis soon found his stride, later laughing at how quickly his attitude changed on set. He admitted that, early on, he was not only trying to play a woman but to appear as a conventionally attractive one. Lemmon reportedly told him to focus less on looking perfect and more on the work, reminding him that he was not competing in a beauty pageant.

It was also then that one of the first real strains between Marilyn and the rest of the cast surfaced – an incident many later said set the tone for the entire shoot.

Despite Tony's earlier nerves, they were both ready on time, in full costume and prepared for their call. Marilyn, however, was nowhere to be seen. Though she had already arrived on the lot, she kept everyone waiting for several hours.

Some claimed the delay was triggered by the remark Orry-Kelly had made about her bottom, an offhand comment that reportedly sent her into a spiral of self-consciousness and worry. Whatever the reason, she didn't appear on set until hours after her scheduled call. And because this fell outside standard union hours (9:00 a.m. to 6:00 p.m.), the crew had to be paid "golden time" which was double the usual rate. It was an avoidable

14. Castle, p. 261

expense and, for those involved, an early, an early source of frustration. Before a single scene had been shot, tension was already creeping in.

The following day, the cast and crew gathered to watch the test films – an even more crucial moment than usual during this point of a production, as a final decision had to be made that would determine the entire look of the film – would *Some Like It Hot* be shot in colour or black-and-white?

By some accounts, it was only during this screening that Monroe first realised the film might not be in colour, something that came as rather of a shock. After all it was the golden age of Technicolor, and Monroe, more than almost any other star of the era, was associated with its lush, glamorous palette. She knew exactly how good she looked on colour film, and the thought of giving that up reportedly unsettled her.

The Mirisch Company and United Artists would also have needed some convincing. Colour films dominated the box office and were a commercial expectation rather than a creative choice. They helped distinguish movies from television, which largely remained black-and-white. Compounding the issue (and the financial risk) was that *Some Like It Hot* wasn't offering any other gimmicks either: no widescreen, no 3D, no new visual technologies at all. There were concerns that even with their impressive cast list the audiences just wouldn't come.

But Wilder, its champion, had answers for all the doubters. First, he argued it suited the period the film was set in and that the monochrome palette helped evoke that era. Second, he claimed it would actually help reframe Monroe for audiences – presenting a "new" version of her, as she hadn't been seen in black-and-white for years.

Wilder insisted it was a practical necessity. That the actors needed layers of makeup to conceal their beard shadow. That, in colour, the effect would have looked gaudy, even grotesque. That the available cosmetics were simply not good enough. That black-and-white smoothed everything out, making the illusion more convincing.

Behind his different arguments, Wilder had already made up his mind. He simply disliked colour film and felt that, at the time, the technology still had significant limitations. He argued that colour often distorted the appearance of actors, with skin tone shifting unnaturally. In his view, while some British and Japanese films used colour with subtly, the American tendency to saturate images with heavy, unnatural tones was excessive and, to him, even unpleasant to watch.

To pull off his vision, Wilder had assembled a team of experienced collaborators – people who knew how to work within the black-and-white format and use it to evoke a sense of place and period.

He brought in cinematographer Charles B. Lang Jr., a Paramount veteran with over 100 films to his name, dating back to the 1920s. Lang understood how to light a scene, how to use shadow and contrast as well as how to make everyone, Monroe included, look their absolute best.

Also important to the visual identity of the film were the sets themselves. And Wilder enlisted a design team that included Edward G. Boyle, the Canadian born set director, and Ted Haworth, the film's art director. Haworth, had earned his first screen credit on Alfred Hitchcock's *Strangers on a Train* (1951) and had built a reputation as a master of design for black-and-white filming. The various sets they would create for this new project included the funeral parlour, cigar store, train interiors, hotel lobby, bed rooms, and the magnificent Peacock Room (where Sweet Sue and her Society Syncopators play during their Miami engagement).

Wilder was also as deliberate with his use of music as he was with his visuals. Rather than relying on a traditional orchestral score, he chose period standards and lively jazz-inflected arrangements to root the film firmly in its era.

He brought in two other key team members – Adolph Deutsch, serving as composer and arranger, and Matty Malneck, who oversaw the music as director and supervisor. Whilst Wilder had an encyclopaedic knowledge of the popular songs of the 1920s and 1930s Malneck actually brought with him first hand authenticity. A violinist and former bandleader, he had toured Europe with Paul Whiteman and composed hit tunes of his own including *I'm Thru With Love* (1931) as well as *Stairway to the Stars* (1939), which drifts through *Some Like It Hot* at key moments including when Junior walks Sugar back to the hotel after their date.

Malneck was also tasked with supervising and arranging the music for the on-screen jazz orchestras: first the unnamed band at the speakeasy, then Sweet Sue's ensemble. The Society Syncopator's sound is initially further heard in two distinct styles – first, a stiff, overly polite version with Joe and Jerry attempting to play as delicately and properly as possible, thinking they need to be demure; and then, a livelier, jazzier arrangement that kicks in after Sweet Sue, played by Joan Shawlee, tells everyone to increase the tempo.

The music is deceptively simple, each piece serving a distinct narrative purpose. Wilder had always been adept at weaving songs and dance into his films, using them not only as mere decoration but as an extension of character and mood. A song, like one of his trademark voice-overs, could reveal what a character was thinking or feeling without necessarily stating it outright. As Wilder himself often argued, narration should add something new rather than merely repeat what the audience can already see on screen. His guiding principle was 'show, don't tell,' and his use of music followed much the same philosophy.[15] His use of music followed much the same philosophy.

In *Some Like It Hot* there are three key songs, each allowing us to follow Sugar's inner life more closely than through dialogue alone – Wilder lets the composition speak for her.

The first, *Runnin' Wild* (1922, music by Arthur Harrington Gibbs, lyrics by Joe Grey and Leo Wood), introduces her on the train bound for Florida. Bright and full of promise, it suggests she is heading towards something exciting. The tune then becomes a loose motif throughout the film, fading only when Sugar finally believes she has found love.

The next two songs are performed in The Peacock Room at the Seminole Ritz Hotel, *I Wanna Be Loved By You* (1928, music by Harry Ruby and Herbert Stothart, lyrics by Bert Kalmar), is Sugar's plea for romance – preferably with a bespectacled millionaire. Helen Kane's version, complete with the famous "boop-boop-a-doop," had already cemented it as a song of flirtatious longing, and Monroe uses it here to similar effect.

Finally, *I'm Thru With Love* marks Sugar's lowest point, performed when her dreams of happily ever after are seemingly dashed.

Together, Deutsch, Malneck and Wilder drew on the audience's nostalgia for these melodies, using them to anchor the story and to provide material that perfectly suited the characters. Historical precision, again, wasn't of primary importance; a few songs may have been slightly later than the film's timeline, but they captured exactly the right mood.

15. Rolston, p. 22

The first pre-recording session took place at the end of July and covered a range of background tracks, including the organ music for the funeral parlor and *Sweet Georgia Brown (*1925), which is playing when Mulligan enters the speakeasy, and Monroe's first vocal number for the film, *Runnin' Wild*. By all accounts, Malneck encountered a very different Marilyn from the one seen in the earlier test screening – a focused, punctual professional who arrived ready to work.

Chapter Eight

Goodbye Charlie. Hello Florida.

Samuel Goldwyn Studios would serve as the primary base and its soundstages were reserved for the majority of interior shots, to be filmed later. But for many of the film's early sequences the production company signed an agreement with Loew's Incorporated, the parent company of MGM, to rent space on its lot in Culver City. This sort of arrangement was entirely routine. Studios had been renting their lots to independent producers – and even to rival studios – for years. It was an economical system, after all why build new sets when perfectly good ones already existed?

Every major studio had an area with what was considered the essentials: 'an old-style western town street, a group of odd foreign buildings set around a square, and a row of brownstone houses – the inevitable New York street.'[1] These permanent sets appeared again and again in films, altered as needed with clever dressing, fresh paint, or temporary façades. A single street might serve as Paris one week and New Orleans the next, depending on how it was staged and shot. Even the individual buildings could be adapted to serve different stories by adding or removing elements as needed.

At MGM, the *Some Like It Hot* team took over a space on Lot Two, a sprawling 30-acre site located across from the main lot (Lot One), between Washington and Culver Boulevards on Overland Avenue. Lot Two was home to a mix of storage facilities and long-standing sets, including the "English Home," the "Esther Williams Pool," and the "grand Southern

1. Ramirez, Juan Antonio. *Architecture for the Screen: A Critical Study of Set Design in Hollywood's Golden Age*, McFarland & Company, 2004, p. 103

Mansion" – all of which had appeared repeatedly in productions over the years.

For their purposes, the team specifically contracted three key areas – East Side Street, Fifth Avenue Street (both part of the famed New York Streets standing set) and the Railroad Terminal. The New York Streets section alone covered nearly ten acres and was among the most frequently used parts of the MGM backlot. Though officially "New York," it had previously doubled for London and other locations; now, it would convincingly stand in for late 1920s Chicago.

Archival records reveal fascinating details about how different buildings – both at MGM and Goldwyn – were adapted specifically to their requirements. The "Cigar Store" was completely revamped, both inside and out, while "Warehouse Alley" was given newly aged brickwork to create a more authentically worn, urban feel. In the "garage," an additional brick wall was constructed. The "Music Building," which served as the location of the offices of various music agents including Sig Poliakoff (Billy Gray), underwent some of the most significant changes, with lobby columns removed and new walls added to alter the layout.

The team and cast also made full use of the permanent makeup, wardrobe, and dressing room facilities at MGM. It was to these that the actors reported during the first week of filming, beginning Monday 4 August.

The pivotal moment of the story – the St. Valentine's Day Massacre itself – would be tackled early on, filmed over two days on the Wednesday and Thursday. But, of course, by the time they reach this stage of the movie the audience would have already seen other important establishing shots and plotlines. These were shot out of sequence, combining street scenes with interior work at Goldwyn.

At MGM, the production's opening days were devoted to exterior sequences set around Mozarella's Funeral Parlor.

These included Detective Mulligan questioning Toothpick Charlie, who reveals that Spats is the owner of the speakeasy hidden inside the parlor, passes on the coded entry phrase and gives Mulligan a mourning band; shots of various people entering the parlor through its front doors; and the chaotic aftermath of the raid, with patrons and performers being herded into a police van. Jerry and Joe's escape by jumping through a window and scrambling down a fire escape was also filmed, along with a less frantic – and rather despairing – scene in the alley where they pause to discuss their next move.

The earliest sequence, which was edited into the exciting opening of the film, had actually been shot in mid-July on the streets of downtown Los Angeles. On 15th and 16th of that month the second unit, directed by Richard Talmadge, captured the dramatic nighttime chase.

It begins with a hearse gliding through the city streets, two men seated in the front and two more – played by Mike Mazurki and Harry Wilson – riding in the back beside a coffin. As the wail of sirens grows louder, one of the men pulls back a rear window curtain to reveal a police car rapidly gaining on them. The hearse suddenly accelerates, attempting to lose its pursuers, but a volley of bullets rips through the rear glass panel, narrowly missing everyone inside and shattering the front windshield.

The two henchmen in the back respond quickly, pulling open a silk roof panel to reveal a hidden arsenal. They fire back, and the chase becomes a furious exchange of gunfire. The hearse swerves wildly through the streets, trying to outmanoeuvre the police. At one point, the pursuing car spins out of control and crashes through a fence; its occupants leap out and continue shooting. The hearse itself careens into another car, briefly jolting to a stop, before the driver manages to escape.

Only once the battle ceases do the men in the back of the hearse inspect the coffin. Bullet holes now riddle the wood, and from them a liquid steadily drips. Lifting the lid, they reveal its true cargo – row upon row of bootlegged whiskey bottles, some now smashed and leaking.

A caption then establishes the world of the film: **Chicago, 1929**.

The hearse eventually pulls into the narrow side alley of Mozarella's Funeral Parlor, where a man discreetly lets them in. The coffin is quickly unloaded and carried inside, disappearing into the building's darkened interior.

Meanwhile, primed earlier by Toothpick Charlie, Detective Mulligan makes his move. Notably, he was the first character to speak after the film's extended, high-energy opening sequence – scored largely by the squeal of tyres, the crash of metal, and the rattle of gunfire. Entering through the funeral parlor's front door as part of the advance party for the planned police raid, Mulligan greets the owner, claiming he is there for "the old lady's funeral" and has been sent as a pallbearer.

Mozarella (Tito Vuolo) obliges, guiding the undercover detective to the chapel. The organist, seated dutifully at his instrument, pulls out a specific organ stop which triggers a mechanism to a secret entrance. As the door swings open, the sombre funeral music fades, replaced by a lively, raucous rendition of *Sweet Georgia Brown*.

Mulligan settles into a table in the hidden bar, trying to appear relaxed and inconspicuous. When he requests a drink the waiter responds with practiced fortitude, insisting that no alcohol is served there. Instead, the establishments disguises its liquor as various "coffees," poured discreetly into teacups to maintain the illusion of legitimacy

Spats Colombo, first seen letting the coffin in through the side door, now makes his entrance into the speakeasy, flanked by the four men from the hearse. His trademark spats are immediately drawn to our attention through a clever bit of business – a drunk patron, stumbling too close, spills his cup of "coffee" all over them.

From the moment he appears, everything about the man screams power and danger. We already know from the earlier scene in the alley that he moves freely through the building, and the treatment he receives inside only reinforces his position. The waiter's remark to Mulligan – delivered with a knowing wink – that the table in the corner was set aside only for the "inner circle" makes the hierarchy unmistakable. This is the boss.

Around them the air is thick with laugher and music with dancing girls entertaining the crowd. The atmosphere is lively but rough around the edges: the band members look worn down rather than glamorous, their shabby formalwear hinting at years of hard living.

It's here, in the middle of the song, that we first meet Joe on his saxophone and Jerry hunched over his fiddle. In between ogling the dancers and playing they talk about their plans. It's their first week of steady work after four months of scraping by, and they're set to be paid that night. They have different ideas for the money – Jerry wants to fix a toothache (in the first draft of the screenplay he wanted to buy his girlfriend, Dixie, a diamond ring). Joe, more reckless, has a better idea – go to the dog track tomorrow and bet their entire pay cheque on "Greased Lightning" at ten to one.

Jerry worries about the risks of the situation, but Joe dismisses his concerns with a steam of exaggerated hypotheticals meant to show how unlikely disaster seems.

Reality proves Joe wrong almost immediately when Jerry suddenly notices Mulligan's police badge. Dryly recognising what's going to happen next, he draws Joe's attention to the danger and they pack up their instruments calmly – clearly this isn't their first police raid - and get ready to leave.

This scene does more than establish their banter. Jerry is cautious, pessimistic, always expecting the worst; Joe is hopeful, but his optimism is grounded more in bravado than sense. His wildly unlikely predictions, of course, are an inside joke for the contemporary audience – who already know that the stock market did indeed crash later that same year, Pickford divorced Fairbanks in 1936, and the Dodgers left Brooklyn in 1957. Wilder lets the audience laugh both at Joe's misplaced confidence and at the inevitable chaos the film promises to deliver.

The raid that follows throws Joe and Jerry's lives back into turmoil, ending their brand-new gig in an instant and plunging them back into the grind of scraping for work. Having escaped and now out on the street, they argue about what to do next. Joe, ever the gambler, insists they pawn their overcoats and put the money on "Greased Lightning" after all. Jerry resolutely refuses.

The scene then quickly dissolves to the following day. Joe and Jerry trudge through the streets without their overcoats. It's bitterly cold, and the pair look miserable as they head toward the Music Building, where other out-of-work musicians are gathered outside, stomping their feet against the chill and loitering in the hope of a job. Creating the bleak, wintry atmosphere required careful staging. According to production archives, the "light sleet effect" for a single day of filming – designed to give the impression of a damp, bone-cold Chicago winter – was budgeted at $2,150 with an additional $1,264 in labour costs.

These early scenes firmly establish the setting of late 1920s Chicago: prohibition has made alcohol illegal, powerful gangsters are exploiting it, and for ordinary people (like struggling musicians) times are tough, and jobs are scarce.

Things are bleak but the garage massacre scene is where the stakes are upped and the story veers into darker, more violent territory. Joe and Jerry arrive there almost by chance. They've landed a booking through Poliakoff's agency for a "St. Valentine's Day Dance" at the University of Illinois, Urbana. They will need transport and Joe, ever the charmer, has sweet-talked secretary Nellie Weinmeyer (Barbara Drew) into lending them her car, a Hupmobile Coupe, which they will need to pick up from "Charlie's Garage," where it is being repaired.

Joe and Jerry arrive at the location and are met by the sight of six men, including Toothpick Charlie, casually playing stud poker in the corner. Their instrument cases draw uneasy glances – mistaken, at first, for gun cases. The two musicians explain why they're there, and the tension eases a notch. While the garage attendant is busy filling up Nellie's car, a sleek black Duesenberg Model J comes screeching in. Four men jump out of this brand new expensive looking car, brandishing a mix of sawed-off shotguns and Tommy guns. While Joe and Jerry have managed to hide, everyone else present – including the attendant in the middle of his task – are made to put their hands up in the air and are lined up against the garage wall. Colombo steps out of the car spats first and speaks coldly to Charlie, sarcastically thanking him for the recommendation of his "mortuary" to "some of his friends" before signalling his men to act. In a brutal instant, the seven men are executed. A sudden noise alerts Colombo to the witnesses, and he commands Joe and Jerry out of hiding, telling them in no uncertain terms that they're not going anywhere. When a near-death Charlie tries to reach for the telephone, Colombo grabs a gun and finishes him off. Panic-stricken, Joe and Jerry make a desperate dash from the garage, crashing out into the snowy streets, but not before a few bullets hit Jerry's bass. The "hammerlock" scenario is now set.

Filming for these crucial scenes went smoothly enough – with one notable exception involving George Raft. The trouble came during a scene where Spats delivers a final insult to the bullet-ridden corpse of Charlie – a casual kick to knock the toothpick from his mouth.

Raft supposedly refused. The actor playing Charlie, George E. Stone, was an old friend, and he was deeply uncomfortable doing anything so physically close to his face – especially for such a slight gag. He also reportedly didn't find the scene funny or clever, just crass. Raft attempted a few hesitant tries at kicking the toothpick (which was actually a painted nail) but eventually gave up.

According to legend, Wilder, hoping to demonstrate that the scene was safe, took it upon himself to show how it should be done. Unfortunately, he misjudged the angle and accidentally kicked Stone squarely in the face – hard enough that he had to be taken to hospital. Whether this actually happened is unclear; there's no documented confirmation in the production records unfortunately. But the scene remains in the film, and whosoever's foot is doing the kicking, it looks to be delivered rather cautiously.

For Curtis and Lemmon, the first week's filming ended with another day on MGM's East Side Street set. The focus was wrapping up the massacre sequence. They shot the scenes where Joe and Jerry, reeling from what they've just witnessed, run down the alley, spot the responding police cars, duck into the cigar store, and phone Poliakoff about the job they heard about earlier for which he is unsuccessfully trying to recruit a bass and a saxophone player. Even though they fail to meet virtually every condition from the job – from their appearance and age to the most obvious problem of all – by the end of the scene, their fate is sealed – they're heading to Florida for three weeks.

Chapter Nine

All Aboard!

Meanwhile, over at Goldwyn Studios, rehearsals for the interior train scenes were underway. Things had been running smoothly there and for Marilyn, the 7 August brought with it a piece of good news.

Her return to Hollywood had been characterised by a number of personal worries, including the fact that her husband had found himself entangled in the ongoing House Un-American Activities Committee (HUAC) investigations.

Originally established in 1938 to root out so-called "disloyalty" and "subversive" behaviour, HUAC's focus had tightened in the wave of anti-communist paranoia that swept through America after World War Two. The Committee zeroed in on supposed leftie influence in every corner of public life. The idea that the Soviet Union – shut behind its Iron Curtain – was secretly plotting to turn Americans into communists took hold, and one of the great imagined battlegrounds in that fight was the film industry.

The first public hearings into the industry's supposed communist ties were held in 1947, drawing enormous media attention. There were plenty of "friendly" witnesses, eager to cooperate, including big names like Walt Disney and Jack Warner, who spoke about the dangers of infiltration.

Out of the initial group of people called to testify, eleven "unfriendly witnesses" declared themselves to be opposed to HUAC's methods, arguing that the investigation was unconstitutional. One of them, the German playwright Bertolt Brecht, took the stand, swore he wasn't a communist, artfully dodged most of the Committee's questions and left the country the very next day.

Those that remained were dubbed the "Hollywood Ten" and included screenwriters such as Lester Cole and John Howard Lawson, producer Adrian Scott, and director Edward Dmytryk. Refusing to answer questions, they invoked the First Amendment, insisting the hearings violated their free speech and freedom of association. HUAC disagreed and all ten were convicted of contempt of Congress.

They weren't the only ones to be affected. HUAC's investigations caused enormous damage to the industry, leaving broken friendships, ruined reputations, and an atmosphere of deep mistrust as people were pressured to inform on colleagues.

The studios collaborated with each other, turning it into an industry-wide policy, which they accepted as the price for avoiding further congressional scrutiny. The result was the infamous "blacklist" and its less formal cousin, the "greylist," both of which destroyed careers on a massive scale.

More than 300 people – actors, directors, and writers among them, were eventually barred from working in the motion picture industry, with anyone suspected of communist sympathies becoming essentially un-hireable. Some, like Charlie Chaplin, decided to leave the country and settle in Europe; others, like Dalton Trumbo, wrote under pseudonyms to keep working at all. Some retreated – Edward Dmytryk, eventually returned to the committee, named names, and was allowed to work again – though at the cost of his reputation.

There were ways to "prove" loyalty, but they were often humiliating. Humphrey Bogart was pressured into signing a ghostwritten article for the March 1948 edition of *Photoplay* magazine under the title *I'm No Communist,* and Edward G. Robinson issued similar public statements to ensure he wasn't dragged further into the growing panic.

Arthur Miller, too, was swept up in the hysteria. Investigated by HUAC, he refused to become a "friendly" witness. Pleading political innocence, he said that he knew 'very little about anything except my work and my field' and believed the investigations were creating 'a pall of apprehension and fear.' Miller was given ten days to reconsider his position under threat of a contempt of Congress citation, but he stood firm and publicly announced that he would not cooperate.[1]

In fact, he made this declaration at the very same press conference where he confirmed two other major developments: that he would be marrying

1. Guiles, Fred Lawrence. *Norma Jeane: The Life and Death of Marilyn Monroe*, Granada, 1985, p. 218

Monroe and travelling with her to England where she was filming *The Prince and the Showgirl*.

The Committee were not pleased. Not only had Miller refused to inform on his colleagues, but his play *The Crucible*, which was first performed in 1953, had openly drawn parallels between the Salem witch trials of 1692-1693 and HUAC. Miller was subsequently convicted on two counts of contempt of Congress. He immediately launched an appeal.

Throughout the tribulation, Marilyn was outspoken in her support for him, going so far as to accompany him to his hearing – a brave move, given HUAC's power and the lingering atmosphere of fear it created in Hollywood. Her show of loyalty was all the more remarkable considering it came so soon after her very public dispute with Fox. The case brought with it not only enormous legal expenses but also months of anxiety for both of them.

The dispute was based on the argument that Miller had not been fully informed of the reasons he was required to answer HUAC's questions. On these grounds, his conviction was eventually overturned by a unanimous 9-0 vote, wiping out his 30-day suspended jail sentence and $500 fine.

It was a huge relief when the news came through that the hearing had gone in his favour.

Miller, still at their home in Connecticut when he heard the decision, said he was 'very happy that I have been vindicated, and I just regret that I was put through so much trouble in order to end up where I started – namely, a free American citizen.'[2]

While Miller supposedly celebrated with beer and whisky Marilyn hosted a champagne breakfast in her dressing room. Reporters had quickly descended on the studio, eager to get her reaction. She told them she had never doubted the outcome. 'I am very happy for my husband,' she said, 'but I am even happier for truth and justice that exist in this country.'[3]

It was time to shoot her first scenes, and for that, the production used one of MGM's most recognisable standing sets – the studio's permanent train station. Officially named St. Petersburg Station, it was more commonly known on the lot as "Grand Central Station."

---

2. Playwright Wins Contempt Case, *The Indianapolis Star*, 8 August 1958, p. 35
3. Marilyn's Mate Wins Acquittal, *Los Angeles Times*, 8 August 1958, p. 2

The set included both terminal interiors and exterior track sections and over the decades, it had been the backdrop for countless cinematic arrivals and departures. Judy Garland wandered its platforms yearning for love in *The Clock* (1945). Cary Grant would dash through in it *North by Northwest* (1959). Constructed in 1933, the set enjoyed an impressively long life, with its final appearance coming in 1977 – not in a feature film – but in what would now be called a music video (the term didn't exist at the time) for The Bee Gees' *Stayin' Alive*. It's remarkable to see the difference and the wear and decay that had overtaken the once-grand station set by that time.

By the late 1970's many of MGM's greatest assets had been stripped bare. Earlier that decade costumes, props, and set pieces were practically given away to an outside auction house and sold off piecemeal in what was billed as "the greatest rummage sale in history," which ultimately netted between $8 and $10 million. Lot Two – once the home of bustling snowy streets and the escape route to Florida – was sold off for retail estate development and was fully demolished by the mid-1980s.

However, that was all in the future. In the week beginning 11 August 1958, the train station set was very much still in use and had been transformed into Chicago's bustling terminal. The production team requested several modifications to tailor it for the shoot. The original platforms were resurfaced with fresh concrete, at a cost of $660, while new wooden platforms and footings were constructed for an additional $1,235. The windows were also blacked out to fit the story's timeline, creating the illusion of a late-evening departure for the Florida Limited.

The station scene itself comes a little over twenty-one minutes into the finished film. It's a sharp, brilliantly executed transition. One moment, we're in the cigar store, watching the now terrified gangland crime witnesses on the phone with Poliakoff as Joe slips into a falsetto to secure them the gig in Florida. Then, suddenly, the film dissolves to a rainy train platform, and there they are again – a rear shot of Joe and Jerry, this time dressed in women's clothes. Our first glimpse of them is a tracking shot from behind focusing on their backsides and legs and their difficulty walking in heels.

This transition avoided what Wilder and Diamond saw as one of the main problems with *Fanfaren der Liebe*. In that film, Hans and Peter's transformation is long and detailed. We see it all – the shaving of their chests, makeup application, getting dressed, even lessons on how to walk and behave. In *Some Like It Hot,* none of that happens on screen. We don't know exactly where they got their clothes from. Maybe they were borrowed from the girls in the chorus line (although the outfits look a little too old-fashioned for young, modern, women and also, they were now in police custody after all) or maybe they hocked their evening wear to Sam the Bookie and bought them from their landlady using the proceeds?

Wilder believed there was no need to show the transformation in detail, preferring to cut directly from an idea to its consequence. For this he drew on a technique he particularly associated with the short films of Laurel and Hardy, where events shift abruptly without depicting the intervening steps. Wilder referred to this technique as the power of omission – a jump cut that is funnier, sharper, and far more effective than a literal transition could ever be. The cut forces the audience to immediately accept their new circumstances. Joe and Jerry are no longer Joe and Jerry; they have already become their new selves.

The train platform is also where we meet Sugar Kane for the first time in one of the film's most iconic sequences. She walks alone down the train platform in an elegant, fitted, black coat and feathered cap, ukulele case in one hand, suitcase in the other. Joe and Jerry can only watch in awe as she glides past them – "Will you look at that! Look how she moves! It's just like Jell-O on springs."

The scene was Marilyn's first stretch of actual shooting. She rehearsed the shot, and filming began. But after the first take, Wilder abruptly called "Cut." He disliked the way a background actor passed directly in front of her during the scene. After all this was Sugar Kane's grand entrance, and Wilder decided it had to be hers alone. After a few more takes and the clearing away of unnecessary distractions he was finally satisfied.

But Marilyn wasn't.

After watching the "dailies," the raw footage of the scene she was disappointed. She thought her entrance fell completely flat, and, worse, she felt she was being upstaged by Curtis and Lemmon. Lemmon, reportedly declaring that she wouldn't go back onto the set until the opening scene was reshot.

Wilder later admitted she was absolutely right in her assessment. He praised her 'tremendous sense of joke' and instinct for 'what will work.'[4]

4. Guiles, p. 251

A few days later, a revised work order officially noted the retake and this time it incorporated the more dynamic entrance Monroe had wanted. As she walked along the platform a sudden blast of steam hit her as she passed the train, creating the 'right lead-in for the star of the picture.'[5]

It's a comic beat, but it also highlights one of Monroe's most famous trademarks – her walk, an effect she had been refining for years. Much like how Chaplin built his Little Tramp around his unmistakable shuffle, Monroe built her screen presence around the way she moved. It even earned her the nickname 'the girl with the horizontal walk.'[6]

After the retake Marilyn wasn't needed for the rest of the week, and the focus shifted back to completing remaining exterior details – mainly scenes in the alley and around the funeral parlor. With those sequences finished, shooting at MGM officially wrapped, though it had run slightly over the tentative schedule laid out in the production contract.

The agreement with MGM noted the costs: East Side Street, which included sections of the alley, Brownstone Street, and the garage, was charged at $5,000 for the first day of filming, $2,500 for the second, $1,250 for the third, and $1,000 for each one after that. Fifth Avenue Street was rented by the half-day at $2,500, while the Railroad Terminal set cost $3,000 for the first day and $1,000 for each additional day.

On top of studio fees, there were charges for prop rentals and three trailer dressing rooms – two at $10 per day and one at $5. By the time the production wrapped, the final invoice for all MGM location and equipment rentals totalled a little over $22,000.

After that it was back to Goldwyn for the remaining interior shots of the speakeasy raid that needed to be wrapped before moving onto the next set of scenes. The mood, at least initially, was light-hearted and full of excitement. Diamond said 'There is always that moment of panic when he walks on a sound stage and sees the sets beginning to go up. Good Lord, you think to yourself, they're taking it seriously. They're really going to make this picture!'[7]

---

5. Guiles, p. 226
6. Churchwell, p. 62; Arnold, Eve. *Marilyn Monroe: An Appreciation*, Pan Books, 1989, p. 11
7. United Artists Series 99AN/MCHC 82-046, box 5 folder 14, Wisconsin Center for Film and Theater Research

They were also greeted by a bit of Billy Wilder mischief. Samuel Goldwyn had recently banned smoking on the lot – a precaution introduced after the fire broke out during the filming of *Porgy and Bess*. Wilder, never one to miss a set-up, taped a sign to the door of the soundstage that read:

> 'Come on the Billy Wilder set and smoke your little hearts out.
> *Some Like It Hot!*'[8]

With the production entering its third week the focus was the sequences in the interior sets of the Pullman carriages.

First up, they filmed the scenes where the former Joe and Jerry enter the train's vestibule along with Sweet Sue and Bienstock (Dave Barry).

Joe as "Josephine" is acting strangely. Ever since he first saw Sugar, he's been a little dazed – quiet, even tongue-tied. Jerry, on the other hand, is giddy – throwing himself into the role of "Daphne" – a name he much prefers to the earlier (and more logical) possibility of "Geraldine." In contrast to Joe, he does not speak in falsetto but, instead, raises his voice a pitch.

Jerry has eyes for all the girls and out of their hearing gushes over the experience in gleefully indulgent terms, prompting Joe to caution him against getting carried away and remind him that, for the sake of their cover, they need to practice a little self-restraint.

As they settle in, Jerry tosses his coat over the emergency brake, and Joe rushes to pull it off – ripping one of his friend's false chests in the process. Moments later when they go off to fix the wardrobe malfunction, Jerry almost heads into the men's rest room out of habit, prompting Joe to grab him again tearing the other chest in the process.

The women's rest room scene marks the first time Daphne and Josephine meet Sugar properly.

She's caught mid-swig from a small silver hip flask hidden in her garter, and when she notices them, there's a flicker of guilt. As we'll soon realise, nearly everyone in the film is chasing something they're not supposed to have, especially the prohibited alcohol which almost everyone indulges in, including the other members of the band.

---

8. Morgan, Michelle. *Marilyn Monroe: Private and Undisclosed*, Robinson, 2012, p. 273

Sugar tries to downplay her own private indulgence and insists that she is not truly dependent on drink and claims she could quit whenever she wished – she just doesn't want to.

After Sugar leaves, Joe and Jerry scramble to repair the damaged chest padding. But Jerry's still riding the high of being surrounded by women, especially the beautiful ukulele player, and gets carried away once more. Joe grabs him and shuts him down with a warning.

And with that, Jerry's chest gets torn again.

The first few days of that week's filming went along without much trouble. Wilder and Diamond would have immediately felt perfectly at home at Goldwyn – it was, after all, where their offices were based. Curtis and Lemmon also slipped into an easy routine. Most mornings began with breakfast at the Formosa Café, across the street from the studio.

The Formosa had long been a Hollywood institution. And still is, having been saved from demolition in the early 1990s and beautifully restored in 2017. There had been a restaurant on that corner since at least 1915, but by the mid-1940s it had taken on its now-iconic identity. Famous for the old red Pacific Electric Railway Company trolley car attached to the side of the building, it drew an eclectic mix of Hollywood royalty and underworld figures.

Regulars included some of Hollywood's biggest stars with Clark Gable, Lauren Bacall, and Frank Sinatra among them as well as notorious figures like gangsters Mickey Cohen and Raft's childhood friend Bugsy Siegel. Siegel, had moved to Los Angeles in the early 1930s to develop gambling rackets and extend the Mafia's influence even further. Cohen was such a fixture at the Formosa that he reportedly had his own booth and conducted business right there in the café until his assassination in 1947. A floor safe, now on public display, is said to have belonged to him.

Everyone soon settled into a steady routine on the Goldwyn sound stages, working through the interior train scenes with ease. And by the end of the week, they were ready to shoot the scene where Sweet Sue's band are rehearsing the number *Runnin' Wild.*

Marilyn was singing along to the pre-recorded track, but matching her lip movements to the playback proved tricky. According to Curtis, it took a few tries for everything to line up.

She also had to dance for this sequence and helping her through it was Jack Cole – her long-time choreographer. As the camera rolled, Cole mirrored the entire dance in Marilyn's line of sight, giving her something to follow as she moved through the number. This was also the scene where, mid song, the concealed hip flask slips from Sugar's garter and clinks to the floor. It was supposed to be light but revealing – Sugar would show some alarm and then quickly recover with a guilty smile and a giggle. Wilder had given instructions on how he wanted it played. Marilyn, however, had her own ideas.

She felt it should be a more serious moment, that Sugar would be genuinely frightened. She wasn't only sneaking a drink during prohibition; she was also risking being booted out of the band. Marilyn played it that way, but it wasn't what Wilder was after. They tried again but not only was there a difference in how they perceived the character's reaction it also involved some tricky movements – with Marilyn having to finish the number with her arms raised, then letting the flask slip from her garter at the right time to land at her feet. She struggled with the coordination, and her nerves began to show.

Still unsure, Marilyn walked off to speak privately with her acting coach, Paula Strasberg, who had replaced Natasha Lytess as a constant presence on every set. They talked for nearly twenty minutes while Wilder waited. When they resumed, they finally got the shot.

Jack Cole said that Wilder could be hard on Marilyn, and it's likely he was referring to this particular day. It was tense – both sides holding firm to their views and Wilder struggling with the humiliation of being kept waiting and his vision being questioned. And while they reached a solution, it was the beginning of a power struggle between director and actress that would overshadow much of the shoot.

Curtis also believed this marked a turning point. The atmosphere, he felt, shifted noticeably. Marilyn's punctuality, already inconsistent, worsened. As production records show, she was late the following day – twenty-five minutes behind schedule – then an hour and forty minutes on Monday, and another hour and a half on Tuesday, 26 August.

They were still working on the interior train scenes. The sleeper berths had now been set up, and it was time for everyone to settle in for the night. Sweet Sue takes her sleeping pill and murmurs to Bienstock that the new girls seem a little strange. Joe and Jerry have changed into pyjamas and a nightgown respectively and as they get ready for bed their whispered conversation turns to Sugar.

During this period several scenes from the upcoming party sequence were also blocked and rehearsed – though the main action itself wouldn't be shot until the following week. These included Daphne tumbling into the aisle, a dash for paper cups, the girls from the band making their way toward Upper Seven, and Josephine and Sugar slipping away to the women's rest room.

There, Sugar chips away at a block of ice using the metal end of a jazz brush, balancing the pieces on a cymbal. As she works, she confides in Josephine about her weakness for the wrong kind of man, in particular smooth-talking saxophone players. Joe, in the guise of Junior, will later use the information to his advantage, but in this offhand moment, Sugar begins to come into focus as more than just the glamorous blonde in the band.

Monroe, despite her hesitancy around the role, brings a kind of raw vulnerability that the writers leaned into, and together they built Sugar into a fully realised character with depth

By the end of the film – thanks in large part to the two scenes in the rest room – we actually know more about Sugar than any other character. We learn her real name, her background, her heartbreaks, her age, even her inner state, revealed through the songs she sings. In contrast, Joe and Jerry remain largely blank slates. We never even hear their full names.

We know that Sugar struggles with men and with drink. And that she yearns for something better: But one of her most endearing traits is her honesty about it all. She's remarkably self-aware, unflinchingly candid about her past and her musical limitations. It's this mix of vulnerability and wry humour that makes her so irresistible.

The filming of the scene in the rest room started off smoothly. Wilder was happy with the wide master shot but when they moved in for tighter coverage, things got trickier. Marilyn had some trouble with her lines – perhaps thrown off by the rhythm of the scene or just tired after a long day. Wilder, eager to keep things moving, trimmed a couple of Josephine's short responses to help Monroe through the scene but it ended up requiring several more takes than planned.

It was also around then that observers began commenting on the growing influence of Arthur Miller, who free of his troubles with HUAC had flown to Hollywood to be with his wife. He had been to the set before, but Curtis recalled that particular day clearly as Arthur arrived in a limousine, waited as Marilyn finished, and whisked her away instead of joining the rest of the company for lunch. When they returned, Marilyn went straight back to set, while Miller remained in the car, an unfriendly and condescending presence.

At the start of the following week, filming turned to the scenes surrounding the raucous party in the upper berth. Among them: Daphne sneaking bourbon from Lower Seven, while the other girls – including Olga (Marian Collier) and Emily (Sandra Warner) – gather supplies for the festivities. Their party provisions are makeshift – a hot water bottle to use as a cocktail shaker for their Manhattans, along with a corkscrew, paper cups, vermouth, cherries, salami, cheese and crackers.

The filming schedule hit a snag on Wednesday 27 August, when Marilyn called in sick and while no specific reason was recorded for her illness, her absence forced Wilder to rethink the day's plan.

The production had already begun to drift slightly from its revised timetable – nothing unusual for a film of this scale, but it required some quick adjustments. Wilder pivoted by moving up the shooting of the agent's office scenes, which did not require Monroe's presence.

Here, Joe and Jerry are filmed the day after the raid at the speakeasy, transitioning the story from the snowy exterior scenes, already completed at MGM, into the interior of the Music Building. The sequence follows them as they walk through the corridors, drifting from office to office, trying their luck and searching for work.

One door sign reads "Key Note Musical Agency," followed by another: "Jules Stein, President, Music Corporation of America" – behind which they find only a lone woman drinking from a bottle. It's a quick gag, playing once again on prohibition-era illicit drinking, but it also carries a knowing wink. Many involved, including Wilder himself, had ties to MCA, and this is one more time where he leans into insider humour.

But there's also something more going on beneath the surface. At each door, they're met with the same rejection. On one hand, it's a straightforward way to move the plot along – they're broke, jobless, and desperate (if not yet on the run), much like the other musicians we've already seen milling around outside in the same predicament. But film historians have pointed out that the scene resonates beyond its immediate story function. In 1950s Hollywood, with commercial studios increasingly shifting toward short-term and freelance contracts, many in the industry faced the same uncertainty. For the cast and crew of *Some Like It Hot*, this anxious door-to-door search for work would have felt uncomfortably familiar.

Indeed, it had been very much Jack Lemmon's own experience. In his early years in New York, before he became a star, he lived much like them – poor, determined, and ready to knock on every door he could find. His son, Chris, later wrote in *A Twist of Lemmon* (2006) that his father loved to regale them with stories from those struggling days. He would 'storm the offices of every agent in town' only to be tossed out – quite literally – 'feet first.'[9]

Rejected but still upright Joe and Jerry find themselves in the outer office of the Poliakoff agency, half-heartedly making conversation with Nellie. Still smarting from being stood up by Joe on a recent date she mentions, with pointed casualness and a knowing wink to her colleague, a mysterious job opening in Florida. Her offhand remark sets the wheels in motion once more, leading Joe and Jerry straight to Charlie's Garage – and the beginning of their present troubles.

These scenes completed and with Monroe back on the set, there was musical preparation to tackle before filming could resume. She spent more time under the guidance of Matty Malneck, refining her performance for *I Wanna Be Loved By You*. This session focused on pre-recording the vocals, which she would later lip-sync on camera. The recording of her final big solo, *I'm Thru With Love,* was scheduled for the following week.

The first week of September offered a brief pause before the push to catch up. Monday was Labor Day, so no filming took place, but the days that followed were used to make up for lost time – particularly finishing the party scene in the upper Pullman berth.

This became one of the most memorable scenes in the film. Thirteen women crammed into a tiny train bed, giggling, climbing over each other, passing around cocktails and snacks and all while Daphne gradually relaxes and begins to soak in the experience. It's pure, chaotic fun. Wilder called it his 'homage to the stateroom scene in *A Night at the Opera*,' the Marx Brothers 1935 film in which multiple people pile into Groucho's room in one sequence.[10]

---

9. Lemmon, Chris. *A Twist of Lemmon: A Tribute to My Father*, Algonquin Books, 2006, p. 18
10. Cohan, p. 20

And behind the scenes, the bunk party was chaotic in the best way also. Stills photographer Richard C. Miller remembered Wilder laughing so hard during takes that he sometimes ruined them himself. Laurie Mitchell (Mary Lou) recalled Wilder trying to direct all the women at once, using his hands to point and signal who he was trying to wrangle. Wilder reflected: 'You have to be orderly to shoot disorder. This was the best disorder we ever had.'[11]

The party stands out for more than its humour because it shows the women enjoying each other's company on their own terms, without the presence (or expectations) of men. At the centre of it all is Lemmon's Daphne, simply having fun. There's no scheming or seduction but instead we see someone beginning to experience a new kind of social freedom. As Steven Cohan notes in the 2025 British Film Institute (BFI) Film Classic book about the movie, it's also the point where 'Daphne is already cohabiting with Jerry.'[12] The boundaries between disguise and identity are starting to blur.

Sugar, notably, leaves the party early to get ice and goes off with Josephine, having their own intimate interlude in the rest room.

The next key section of the schedule was a scene between Monroe and Lemmon – their first real two-person interaction of the shoot. Although in the finished film it takes place just before the chaotic party sequence, it was in actuality shot afterwards.

Sugar pops her head through the curtains to thank Daphne for covering for her during rehearsals. As Sugar expresses her gratitude, Sweet Sue appears, weaving unsteadily up the corridor on her way to the women's rest room. To avoid being caught, Sugar quickly jumps into bed, snuggling down beside Daphne until the coast is clear.

It was a long scene with a sustained dialogue between the two. And they did it in one take.

As Maslon points out in the *50th Anniversary Companion* to the film Lemmon, by that point used to the halting rhythm of Marilyn's shooting days was astonished: 'Billy shot it in one. And that was it. And I damn near shit. It was five minutes after eight and we're done.'[13]

---

11. Uproar in an Upper Berth, *Los Angeles Times*, 4 January 1959, p. 110
12. Cohan, p. 22
13. Maslon, p. 72

For this scene Sugar was to wear a black chiffon negligee – something suggestive, but still within the boundaries of what was allowable under the Production Code.

Test shots had been taken, and when Wilder viewed them, he grew uneasy. The negligee, in his opinion, was too sheer to pass the censors. Orry-Kelly was called in and instructed to add more lace to make it less revealing.

Monroe, however, was not pleased. She asked the designer to her dressing room and, with noticeable irritation, demanded to know why her costume had been altered. Orry-Kelly remarked that, in that moment, he realised she was, as he put it, 'an exhibitionist.'[14] Though he always praised how the actress looked in his clothes, he was less enthusiastic about working with her. In later interviews, he summed it up: 'I would rather go to Coney Island and open up a hot dog stand than dress that woman again.'[15]

But while Orry-Kelly dismissed her motivations there was something more layered at play.

The actress' instincts weren't for shock value but because, from Sugar's perspective, there was no threat in an all-woman band and she wanted her character to seem at ease. For Monroe this wasn't about cheap titillation and it made complete sense to use her skin in the same way that you would wear a costume to express some aspect of character.

Monroe had also always been curious about where the boundaries of on-screen censorship lay – and how far she could push them. She'd already started testing these limits in earlier roles and would continue to do so in a nude scene that was cut from *The Misfits*, her final completed film, and in the unfinished *Something's Got to Give* (1962), where she removed a flesh-coloured modesty bikini and swam naked during one scene.

In that sense, she and Wilder were aligned. He too was dedicated to pushing the rules, sneaking innuendo and risqué humour past the censors whenever possible to expose the absurdity of the Hays Code restrictions. He had done this with Monroe before, when her dress is blown up by a subway grate in *The Seven Year Itch* – a scene which had shocked many.

---

14. Orry-Kelly, p. 406
15. TBT: Some Like It Hot (1959), *Frock Flicks* https://frockflicks.com/tbt-some-like-it-hot-1959/ accessed 31 July 2024

He had little patience for such limits to his creativity, dismissing the idea with a curt, 'Censorship is always stupid.'[16]

But, with this particular decision, he decided it would be too much of a risk – too close to the restriction on costumes that revealed "the more intimate parts of the human body." In the end scene she is shown also wearing a black chiffon robe trimmed with fur, although stills exist that demonstrates how revealing the negligee actually was originally.

Over the weekend, the entire production packed up and headed to San Diego, which would stand in for sunny Florida.

For this section of the plot Wilder had decided it would be most efficient to shoot the beach and exterior scenes first before heading back to Goldwyn Studios for the final leg of filming, which would focus on the action inside of the hotel and onboard Osgood's yacht, the *Caledonia II.*

So, nearly 200 people – cast, crew, and a fair number of family members – made the journey south together.

The story called for a sun-drenched resort backdrop for a very good reason. It needed a place that was the complete opposite of poverty-stricken, cold and grim Chicago. The next setting demanded a relative paradise, bathed in luxury and light. Most importantly, it had to be free from gangsters (at least at first) offering a fresh start and a stark contrast to the gritty urban chaos and dangers left behind.

In the 1920s, nowhere would have fitted the bill better than Miami, the epitome of America's burgeoning leisure culture. Publicity campaigns buzzed with catchy slogans like "Miami – Where the Summer Spends the Winter." Roads were laid, land was quickly snapped up, and grand hotels sprang up across the city. As the population (both temporary and permanent residents) soared it transformed into vibrant playgrounds for gamblers, jazz musicians, and wealthy northerners seeking escape.

Large-scale developments fuelled the rise of even more opulent hotels, gambling clubs, and nightclubs, cementing its reputation as a premier resort destination. Though by the decade's end real estate values had plunged again, for a few golden years Miami was the place to be. Later, in the 1930s, the city underwent another remarkable transformation, blossoming into an

16. Biltereyst, Daniel (Ed). *The Screen Censorship Companion: Critical Explorations in the Control of Film and Screen Media*, University of Exeter Press, 2024, p. 146

iconic Art Deco paradise which, thanks to tireless efforts by preservationsists in the 70s and 80s, has been largely saved.

However, when the team were was scouting locations, the majority of buildings were too new for the film's late 1920s setting. And since much of its earlier buildings – including its grand hotels -- had been bulldozed or built over, it left few authentic options for capturing that original glamour.

By contrast, the Hotel del Coronado affectionately known as "The Del," situated on an island across San Diego Bay, had barely changed since it first opened its doors in the late 1880s. A sprawling Victorian beach resort designed by architect James Reid, it had over 400 guest rooms, long wrap around verandas, turrets, towers, and an exterior so ornate it had once been described as 'as snowy white and flamboyant as a wedding cake.' [17]

And it came with its own history. In the 1920s, it had been a popular resort, visited by stars like Charlie Chaplin and Will Rogers. One well-worn legend even claims the then Prince of Wales met Wallis Simpson there. During the Depression and World War Two, business had been kept afloat by the nearby naval base. Postwar, the Del Coronado fell out of fashion and changed hands several times, but its exterior remained largely untouched. It had all the grandeur, charm, and eccentricity they needed and was the perfect Seminole Ritz Hotel. Not only was it visually right it was also logistically perfect too.

Only a couple of hours south of Los Angeles, the Del Coronado also offered easy access, as well as accommodation for much of the production team, either in bungalows or in the actual hotel itself. There was a useful cove nearby, Glorietta Bay, and the only giveaway that it wasn't actually Miami is the faint distant outline of the California hills visible in the film!

But the decision to shoot in San Diego rather than Florida wasn't met with universal approval. In fact, it sparked a minor controversy that made headlines itself.

Robert King High, the Mayor of Miami at the time, took particular offense. Arguing that Florida was being snubbed, he sent a pointed telegram directly to Monroe at the Hotel Bel-Air. The message, reproduced in numerous newspapers, struck a tone that was part flattery and part canny publicity.

---

17. Maslon, p. 102

It playfully compared Monroe and Florida, arguing that both were unique and impossible to duplicate. The Mayor went on to express surprise that a film set in Florida would be shot in California, especially at a time when Hollywood increasingly filmed on location around the world as a matter of routine. He insisted that if the film was going to be set in Florida, audiences deserved the genuine article, urging the production to choose 'the one and only, the original Sunshine State' and 'replace second best imitations with the real thing.'[18]

18. Some Like It Hot (But Not Major), *Miami News*, 3 September 1958, p. 7

Part Three

Under Pressure – Performance & Panic

Chapter Ten

Palm Trees, Sharks and Barking Fish

While the Mayor of Miami may have been disappointed that his city wasn't going to be the filming location, San Diego officials and locals were delighted. For the owners of the Del Coronado specifically, the production brought not just money but renewed glamour and publicity. This association would last for decades, helping turn it into a landmark of movie history which is still honoured today.

The timing was serendipitous too with the company arriving just as the citywide Fiesta del Pacifico, a lively event filled with parades and dancing, began which instantly lifted their spirits.

The first day of location filming, 8 September, was a revelation. After weeks of studio work and a sometimes tense atmosphere, the fresh sea air and beautiful surroundings seemed to have an immediate effect. They began the day with light-hearted material with Lemmon, Monroe, and the girls in the band tossing beach balls around in the sun.

Whilst being in a new environment seemed to reset the mood, problems soon resurfaced – once again around costumes and Monroe's appearance. During one of those early beach sequences, Sugar appears in a fitted black one-piece bathing suit with white trim detailing and compliments Daphne on being so flat chested that clothes hang better on her. According to later reports, the scene sparked an exchange between Monroe and Wilder when he suggested she should consider losing weight. Marilyn reportedly retorted, 'You want your audience to be able to distinguish me from Tony and Jack, don't you? And besides, my husband likes me plump.'[1]

1. Sikov, p. 417

The exact details of the conversation remain unclear but what's undeniable is that her appearance was a constant subject of discussion, both on set and in the press.

There are also strong indications that Monroe herself was deeply affected by these comments, particularly during this period of her life. She had always taken an interest in health and fitness – not unexpectedly for a model and actress in the public eye – but this focus had intensified. She lifted weights, walked, ran, and at times followed strict diets. One such meal plan, given to her that year by Dr. Leon Krohn, who had a private Beverly Hills practice as well as being Chief of Gynaecology at the Cedars of Lebanon Hospital, was a two-page "Calorie Restricted Diet – 1000 calories, 100 grams of protein." The guidelines list limits on sugar and fat and contains suggestions like swapping a slice of bread for a single small boiled potato.[2] Monroe's notebooks from this time also show her tracking food and calories in detail.

She talked to her friends and family about her feelings. In that letter to her stepdaughter Jane, written on her arrival in Hollywood, she had remarked on the help needed to get into her white skirt: 'I almost didn't make it,' she confided. 'But now that I'm busier, I'll start losing weight – you know where.'[3]

Over the coming days, fans and curious onlookers gathered in increasing numbers, eager to catch a glimpse of the stars – especially Monroe. The crowds were enthusiastic, though they brought their own challenges. Wilder found them difficult to manage as they shouted, clapped, and interfered with takes. But when Marilyn asked them to quiet down – simply saying "Sshh" – they listened.

There was even a rumour that a shark had been spotted offshore – production was halted early for the day and an entire afternoon of filming was lost as a result. When questioned, a veteran lifeguard known as "The

2. Julien's Auctions, *Property From the Estate of Lee Strasberg*, Lot #154, 17 November 2016 https://bid.juliensauctions.com/lot-details/index/catalog/180/lot/83039
3. Julien's Auctions, *Property From the Estate of Lee Strasberg*, Lot #321, 17 November 2016 https://bid.juliensauctions.com/lot-details/index/catalog/180/lot/83296/billy-wilder-some-like-it-hot-synopsis-sent-to-marilyn-monroe

Duke of Catalina" dismissed the claim: 'I didn't see a shark,' he said. 'I didn't even see a sardine.'[4] The scare was later determined to be a hoax.

The technical team also faced other logistical challenges as the Californian sun, while beautiful, posed problems for filming. There were concerns that the bright light would overexpose Monroe's platinum blonde hair, and sun burns could clash with continuity. To solve the lighting issues, cinematographer Charles Lang rigged a fine black scrim – a large net-like screen – to diffuse the sunlight.

Still, it was noted in the press that Paula Strasberg avoided the sun completely, and that Monroe herself regularly took shelter between takes, either in a tent or under a large black umbrella. Some coverage seemed to mock their lack of interest in tanning, as though it reflected a broader refusal to fully embrace the setting but also as a way of distancing themselves from the others. However, in an interview published the following year, Monroe outlined her long-standing feelings on the subject of staying out of the sun: 'There's good reasons for doctors to classify sunburns as first, second-, and third-degree burns. That's what a sunburn is – a burn and not a tan. You burn your skin in the process of acquiring that healthy tan.'[5]

Meanwhile, journalists covering the shoot couldn't resist turning their attention back to Monroe's figure. One reporter challenged her to try out the latest craze – hula hooping. While child-sized hoops made from dried vines have existed since Ancient Egyptian times, the modern fad actually originated in Australia. There, bamboo rings were sold in large numbers before the idea was imported to the U.S. and copied by the Wham-O Manufacturing Company of California. Wham-O crafted them out of newly fashionable plastic and they retailed for $1.98.

The country went wild for hooping. Especially in the first part of 1958, millions flew off the shelves, captivating people of all ages. But there was a note of caution – *The Washington Post* warned 'persons of mature years' about potential physical perils, concluding: 'So our earnest advice is to leave the Hula Hoops to those who know how to make them behave;

4. Marilyn Monroe Acts in Some Like It Hot, *San Diego Reader*, 4 September 2003 https://www.sandiegoreader.com/news/2003/sep/04/white-mask-marilyn-monroe-and-hotel-del-coronado/ accessed 26 February 2025
5. Marilyn Monroe: A Champion Sun Dodger Believes Tanning Is For Leather Only, *The Record*, 6 March 1959, p. 30

and these seem to consist exclusively of little girls between the ages of 8 and 10.'[6]

Though the craze was short-lived, it was still very much in full swing while the team were in San Diego. The local newsman who had issued the challenge had hoped to snap 'the photo of the year' – Marilyn with a hula hoop. 'Even if she doesn't know how,' he said with a sly wink, 'I'm sure she would learn fast.' He was told, absolutely not, and left disappointed supposedly 'rolling his hoop in a sad, erratic way.'[7]

Syndicated columnist Erskine Johnson also visited the set and reported on her appearance quipping: 'She not only has a wiggle – she's got a shake.'

While the reporter's cheeky remark may have played into the typical innuendo that so often coloured press coverage of Monroe, it also commented on an obvious physical manifestation of her adoption of a style of acting preparation, particularly those rooted in teaching around relaxation, concentration, and the elimination of fear and self-consciousness that might inhibit performance. These were practices she had learnt in New York under Lee Strasberg's guidance.

Strasberg was director of the Actors Studio, a prestigious but unconventional training ground which had been founded in 1947. It wasn't a formal school, but rather a series of workshops where actors performed intensely. Full membership was only granted through a rigorous audition process, and spaces were limited. Under Strasberg's leadership from 1952, they emphasised techniques drawn from the system of Konstantin Stanislavsky – a Russian director whose ideas evolved into what would become known as "The Method."

Although Monroe was never a formal member – she never auditioned and wasn't part of the official roster – she became deeply involved and took private acting lessons with Lee. At the same time, Paula, his then wife, committed to accompanying her on film sets to reinforce their teachings. In addition, she attended sessions at the studio regularly, often sitting quietly at the back of the room, dressed down and keeping to herself. At first, she barely spoke to anyone. But eventually grew more comfortable and began

6. Conceived in the Fad Crazed 1950s: The Hula Hoop Makes a Comeback, *The Washington Post*, 14 May 1977 https://www.washingtonpost.com/archive/lifestyle/1977/05/15/conceived-in-the-fad-crazed-50s-the-hula-hoop-makes-a-comeback/b0113458-354e-483b-8c32-5c9a6ca56bf1/ accessed 31 October 2022
7. Marilyn Adds Shake To Wiggle, *The Salisbury Post*, 28 September 1958, p. 15

to spend time outside of class with fellow students, many of whom were significantly younger and much less famous. One of the friendships that emerged was with Eli Wallach, with whom she would later work on *The Misfits*.

The approach was intellectual and psychological. It required the actor to closely identify with their character, linking their own emotional memory to the role. Anna Strasberg, Lee's third wife, put it succinctly: 'Lee didn't teach us how to act, but rather how to live on the stage or in front of the camera in the imaginary reality of the play.'[8] Psychoanalysis was encouraged as a tool to aid the process. And in line with their recommendation in February 1955 Monroe began working with Dr. Margaret Hohenberg. She continued with therapy, sometimes with Hohenberg and sometimes with other practitioners, for the rest of her life. Whether it was ultimately helpful or harmful is subject to much debate. Some scholars have suggested it brought painful childhood memories to the surface, exposing vulnerabilities that would have traumatised her further.

The Actors Studio taught several core techniques, most notably breathing exercises and repetition. For Marilyn, it would translate into a personal ritual. Either shortly before a scene, or even during one, she would close her eyes and begin shaking her wrists and arms with intense concentration as a way of preparing herself. She explained that it was a personal method of getting into character and building focus before performing, noting that different actors used different techniques to do similar and this physical routine was simply her own way of doing so. To onlookers, it could appear rather bizarre and unsettling, but for Marilyn, it was an important part of the process.

But for her co-workers it also served as a reminder of her reliance on the Strasbergs, something that not everyone approved of. On set, Marilyn often looked to Paula for advice, particularly during takes. One day, towards the beginning of filming, that dependence had come into full view for the first time. After Wilder called "cut" on a scene, Monroe turned not to him but to Paula, seeking validation. Wilder snapped, "How was it for you, Paula?" – a line dripping with sarcasm. The message was unequivocal: on his set, there was a hierarchy, and feedback came from the director, not an acting coach.

8. Cohen, Lola (Ed). *The Lee Strasberg Notes*, Routledge, 2010, p. xv

Curtis claimed that the Strasbergs were "squeezing" and "abusing" Marilyn. Others on set viewed Paula as controlling. However, Marilyn didn't see it that way. To her, Paula provided stability and reassurance and a vital link to her training, which she credited with helping her develop as an actress, a goal she remained passionately committed to. Strasberg was paid $1,500 a week for her work, and though it was unofficial in the production, it had a real function, and she became Monroe's lifeline during a very difficult time.

Yet it is apparent that the position also came at a personal cost to Strasberg. Away from her home, Paula had rented a house near to Marilyn and to the set, and those she was close to at the time describe her returning each night utterly depleted, burdened by the stress of absorbing not just Monroe's emotional fragility, but also the resentment of a crew who saw her as part of the problem. When Marilyn was late, or when she froze, it was Paula who often became the scapegoat. And her constant presence, seemingly always lingering on the periphery, dressed in black and rarely engaging with others, earned her the derogatory nickname "The Bat," although to Laurence Olivier she was "The Beast."

The next major sequence on the schedule was the beach meeting between Sugar and a mysterious stranger. It opens with Joe, in blazer, yachting cap and thick glasses, claiming a basket chair, grabbing a bucket of seashells and brushing off a child with a clipped "scram," before deliberately causing Sugar to stumble and fall – quite literally – into his life.

Filming the scene highlighted one of the biggest drawbacks of shooting on location – the lack of control over the environment. At the Del Coronardo, the production crew was at the mercy of the nearby naval airbase, with jets roaring overhead every few minutes. The noise was deafening and far too loud for usable audio.

The only solution would be to work around the air traffic, something that was easy enough on relatively short sequences. This particular scene itself was several pages of dialogue – around three uninterrupted minutes between Monroe and Curtis. They rehearsed carefully then waited for a break in the noise. When the jets finally paused, Wilder called "action." Incredibly, they nailed it and the whole sequence was filmed faster than expected.

Joe's "Junior" persona was based on their previous conversation on the train where Sugar revealed the type of man she was hoping to meet.

And she is determined not to miss an opportunity to snag herself such a perfect, young, millionaire who implies his family owns Shell Oil. She's hilariously quite brazen asking which yacht is his, who mixes the cocktails and inviting him to the hotel that night to watch her perform. Sugar, like Joe, is also not above playing a role to get what she wants and changes details about her background and status to impress a stranger – even as they both individually reveal they have no idea about the inner workings of high society.

Junior's disguise is not just in his new outfit, stolen from Bienstock, but also through an accent. Strictly speaking, there would have been no need for Joe to disguise his voice as Sugar had never heard it before, so there was no risk of her recognising him by sound. But the script required a change to help sell the deception, it was felt that a millionaire oil heir with a strong New York accent wouldn't have been very convincing for the characters or the audience.

As an actor who had been the subject of a lot of jokes about his thick accent since the beginning of his career, Curtis was a little sensitive about the subject. But he decided to play it like Cary Grant, an actor whom he had long admired and somebody he could already impersonate. According to one story, he had even asked his wife, Janet, out on their first date some years earlier using Grant's distinctive style of speaking.

There are conflicting stories about how Wilder felt about the impression. Curtis once said the director didn't like it, reportedly telling him, 'If I wanted Cary Grant, I would've hired Cary Grant.'[9] Wilder himself said he was fine with the choice and had even showed the scene to Grant himself, who apparently found it hilarious.

It made sense as a character choice, but it also served a bigger purpose. Curtis was eager to prove he could do more than play the good-looking lead. The impression was a deliberate one to show off his range and comic timing. Reflecting on his decision, Curtis explained: 'I played it saucy. I kicked up my voice a little bit higher … which told you right away: this guy is not English. He is a New Yorker trying to sound English.' [10] To the audience, Joe's disguise is hilariously paper-thin. But to Sugar, it's irresistible.

9. Ibid, p. 85
10. Ibid, p. 84

There were also some deeper, knowing, layers to the inclusion of this impression. 1950s audiences would have immediately recognised the voice as Grant was a huge star by then. But no one in 1929 would have caught the reference. At that time, the British born actor was still performing in New York as Archie Leach, and wouldn't make his Hollywood debut until the early 1930s, when he also changed his name to something more American sounding. It was another knowing nod to the audience, that was also referenced by an update in the shooting script when Jerry says to Joe "And where did you get that phony accent? Nobody talks like that."

Despite these few successful sequences, it soon became apparent that Monroe was struggling again. After a few punctual days, she started arriving late, sometimes hours behind schedule. Those on set suspected she had resumed taking barbiturates to sleep at night – and perhaps even during the day. The pressure of the production was mounting. Arthur Miller had returned home, and without his presence, she seemed even more isolated. And compounding everything, by this time, she may have also realised that there was the possibility she was pregnant again.

On Thursday 11 September she wrote to the poet Norman Rosten, a close friend of hers and Arthur's. The letter still exists and offers a glimpse into her then state of mind. Dictated by Marilyn and typed by her trusted assistant May Reis, it was composed on hotel stationery adorned with a small, printed, illustration of the beach.

The letter expresses a sense of despair and uncertainty, of feeling trapped in a hopeless journey through troubled circumstances, ending with a remark about having 'no phallic symbol to lose.'

Then, a postscript – a reference to the 1933 poem *For Anne Gregory* by Irish poet William Butler Yeats.

> 'Love me for my yellow hair alone.'

At the bottom, she wrote

> 'I would have written this by hand but its trembling'[11]

---

11. Rollyson, p. 205

What makes the letter especially poignant is the personal flourish Marilyn added – a tiny stick figure drawn in ink, seemingly drowning in the ocean, arms raised above the water, with the word "help" scrawled beside it.

The following day, she was late again. The heat was intense, and her delayed arrival meant that little progress could be made. Shooting on the beach in those conditions was already a challenge, so the crew shifted focus to close-up shots of her and Lemmon. Curtis had some time off and had driven a pregnant Janet and their young daughter, Kelly, back to Los Angeles after they had spent some time on set visiting him.

That evening, Marilyn and Arthur spoke on the phone. A letter he wrote to her later that night gives us an indication of their conversation. Addressed to his "Darling Girl," Miller tries to explain his feelings and why he had done certain things. Whilst unclear exactly what he meant by this it is widely believed to be a reference to a painful incident a few years earlier, when he had written in his diary that she was an embarrassment to him. When Monroe discovered the entry, it cut deeply.

Miller, too, was facing his own professional problems. Though he had been working on the screenplay for *The Misfits*, he had recently sent a draft to the director, John Huston, and he currently didn't have any other projects lined up. One of his friends believed he had gone to Hollywood not only to support his wife, but because of a lack of other commitments. Financially dependent on Marilyn, he also reportedly resented the imbalance of power. As Wilder spitefully noted: 'At last I met someone who resented [Monroe] more than I did.'[12]

After their telephone call the night had taken a darker turn when the sleeping pills she had taken – possibly mixed with alcohol – caused a severe reaction. Marilyn became violently ill, vomiting repeatedly. Paula and May found her and deeply concerned, called for medical help and she was rushed to the Cedars of Lebanon Hospital.

While many on set believed it to have been an accidental drug overdose, the exact cause was never confirmed but, in any case, the production company moved quickly to control the narrative. Publicly, they attributed her subsequent absence to "nervous exhaustion," while press statements simply said she was undergoing routine tests. Released

12. Maslon, p. 91

from hospital she took the next few days off flying back to New York to see her own doctor.

With Marilyn unavailable for most of the following week, production in San Diego ground to a halt. As so many scenes revolved around Sugar it wasn't possible to work around her absence. In the end, the only option was to pause and send everyone back to Los Angeles until she was well enough to resume.

There were, rather unsurprisingly, discussions about whether Monroe could be replaced and a few alternative names were even floated. But with a third of the film already in the can and fearful of bad publicity, replacing her would have been hugely disruptive – not to mention expensive. In the end, they decided to wait it out.

The production team scrambled to find ways to use the unexpected schedule change. A few actors who weren't due to film until later were called in early, but there were limits to what could be done as many of the hotel interior sets at Goldwyn Studios weren't yet complete. Fortunately, several scenes set in the Pullman train carriage that didn't involve Sugar were still to be done so filming shifted back to those, including one that didn't make the final cut.

Josephine and Sugar have swapped bunks, and is now sleeping in Upper Two – right above Bienstock. Jerry not aware of the change has planned to continue his conversation with Sugar and the pre party promise of unexpected surprises. With a sleeping Joe lying on his side, back turned, Jerry climbs into the bunk beside him and starts pouring his heart out to "Sugar." He confesses everything – that he's a boy, that he's mad for her – and even pulls off his wig in the dark to reveal his true identity.

Joe, exhausted and fed up, grabs Jerry and starts shaking him. Realising something's gone wrong, Jerry flicks on the light as Joe winds up to slug him. Thinking quickly, Jerry jams his wig back on to shift back into his female persona and avoid being hit.

Even after Marilyn returned to set, filming the Pullman scenes continued but it was obvious she wasn't back to full strength. Studio records show she arrived late every single day of the week beginning 22 September.

Still, they managed to push through. And on screen, her performance didn't seem to unduly suffer and at the end of that challenging period, Paula wrote a note to May Reis, who was back in New York: 'This week was a most difficult one for Marilyn. But I saw the rushes and they were extraordinary.'[13]

During the following week, most of the cast and crew returned to San Diego for three days of pickup shots. The production was now very behind schedule, and there was pressure to move quickly and stay on track. Marilyn returned as well, now accompanied by Miller, who remained on set throughout the rest of the shoot.

One of the key scenes still to be filmed was the before and aftermath of Sugar's and Junior's assignation. She's still wearing the Orry-Kelly gown described as "nude soufflé draped on the bias." It's the dress she wears during her performance of *I Wanna Be Loved By You*, played to a packed house of around 200 people – including Osgood, who is patiently waiting for Daphne to accept the invitation to join him on his yacht. Orry-Kelly had designed Sugar's dress to be especially daring, dyed to match her skin tone, with a sheer silk bodice, her breasts outlined in sequins and a small heart shaped detail cut out on one buttock. It was so revealing that cinematographer Charles Lang had to use net scrims, black cardboard, and a narrowed spotlight beam to cast strategic shadows and keep it within the Production Code's limits. It's stunning but also serves to set her apart from the rest of the Society Syncopators, who are wearing matching black, sparkly evening dresses with long earrings and necklaces.

Whilst the musical sequence would not be filmed until mid-October at Goldwyn they shot the aftermath of the performance after Joe has convinced Jerry to ensure Osgood is nowhere near the *Caledonia*. He has plans of his own. Sugar runs down to meet Junior, is taken aboard the yacht and then returned to the shore after their date. Although in the film the final sequence is meant to take place just before dawn, it was actually shot in full daylight, in order to keep on schedule. To create the illusion of early morning, the crew filmed on the shaded side of the hotel, used reflectors and artificial lights to soften the brightness, and then further adjusted the footage in post-production to mimic the cool, muted tones of pre-dawn light.

They also shot the scene where Joe scales the side of the building, trying to sneak back into his room without being spotted in his millionaire

---

13. Julien's Auctions, *Hollywood Legends*, Lot #469, 31 March 2012 https://bid.juliensauctions.com/lot-details/index/catalog/68/lot/25725/marilyn-monroe-related-letter

disguise. Originally concerned about insurance, Wilder had planned to use a stunt double for the climb, but Curtis proved eager to do it himself. After demonstrating he could safely manage the ascent, Wilder gave him the green light to perform it on camera.

Later that same week, Curtis pulled off another stunt – jumping off the pier and driving the motorboat in reverse. Wilder, impressed by Curtis's determination and physical agility, told him, 'Bill Holden was the best guy for stunts – until you came along.'[14]

Coming from Wilder, it was no small compliment. He rarely offered personal praise, at least to Curtis, who said he often felt like an outsider on set – overshadowed by Monroe's star power and Lemmon's easy camaraderie with the director.

So, when the director finally acknowledged him, it meant more than recognition for a well-executed feat it was a much-needed validation of his skills.

Pick-up shots continued throughout the week, and thrillingly, we get a rare behind-the-scenes glimpse of the production thanks to a 90-second news reel filmed at the time. It's short but striking – and well worth tracking down online.

The footage, which only re-surfaced in the late 1990s, captures Monroe and Lemmon joyfully running out of the sea and across the beach. In another shot, Joe E. Brown lounges on the hotel veranda alongside the group of "millionaires" in their rocking chairs. He is notably the youngest among them. Les Webb, a bellman at the hotel, remembered that during filming, a real guest had unknowingly sat down in one of the rockers. Wilder had to politely ask him to move so they could continue shooting.

But behind the scenes, the previous tensions were still simmering.

According to Curtis, Monroe was now barely speaking to him. Paula was watching over her more closely than ever. Miller, now a near-constant presence on the set, rarely left her side and made sure Marilyn kept her distance from the others. Audrey Wilder recalled that one evening she had invited the main cast to a party, to mark the end of location filming. Audrey went to Marilyn's bungalow to bring her along, and at first, she was ready to come. But as soon as Arthur appeared, Marilyn abruptly said, "I have to go," and left with him instead.

14. Curtis & Vieira, p. 43

But while stories from the set often cast Miller and Strasberg as controlling influences, it's important to remember that Marilyn didn't necessarily need shielding – nor was she helpless. Friends noted that she didn't like large parties – often keeping to herself at social gatherings by clearing ashtrays of reading a book. It was clear that she didn't like to converse with strangers, something she addressed to journalist Liza Wilson in 1952 saying: 'I guess there are several reasons I feel more comfortable not saying anything, because I feel they'll only misunderstand me. When I feel a lack of contact with a person, I can't talk with him and still be completely myself.'[15]

It's also possible that Monroe was the one protective of Miller, rather than the other way around. His presence on set often caused tension. Crew members found him aloof, and his habit of weighing in on matters that didn't concern him had irritated many. The sense of superiority he was said to carry apparently didn't sit well. The gulf between him and the team had been observed right from the beginning of production, most notably at a lavish dinner thrown by Harold Mirisch at his Beverly Hills home. Disappointingly to many of the 80 guests present the Millers didn't show up till very late in the evening many hours after the party had started. While Marilyn was immediately forgiven, Walter said that she had 'captivated everybody' that night – Arthur had made a less favourable impression. According to several people there, he cornered Wilder and Diamond and began offering unsolicited advice on cowriting. With an arm slung around each of them, he began lecturing, 'The difference between comedy and tragedy …'[16]

Billy and Iz, unimpressed they tried not to show their discomfort, but Marilyn had noticed.

15. Morgan, *When Marilyn Met the Queen*, p. 137
16. Sikov, p. 411

Chapter Eleven

Take 47 – Bourbon, Breakdown and the Method Divide

With all the exterior shots finished, it was time to leave San Diego behind and return to Goldwyn for the final stretch of filming. The next phase, which included all interior scenes in the hotel as well as the yacht, would be crucial. And since much of the remaining work revolved around Sugar's storyline, Monroe's presence would be essential for nearly every setup.

Marilyn's need for extra takes had been frustrating, but still, so far, manageable. Now, things started to unravel even further. Her hesitation before scenes grew worse. Her lateness – already a pattern – became more extreme.

There was gossip about a Thermos she carried with her everywhere. Diamond recollected that after each scene, Marilyn would call, "May! Coffee!" and Reis, would bring her the flask. Iz claimed it contained vermouth. Others whispered it was vodka and orange juice. Tony Curtis later said 'I know she was drinking champagne out of coffee mugs when we were doing that scene [on the train].'[1] No one really knew but the rumours had begun that she was drinking to deal with her anxiety.

Whatever was in it, the Thermos, in particular, seems to have become a symbol of the mounting delays. But the truth is, drinking on set wasn't especially unusual in Hollywood at the time and many stars had reputations

---

1. *Some Like It Hot: Tony Curtis looks back,*' Entertainment Weekly, 25 May 2001 https://ew.com/article/2001/05/25/some-it-hot-tony-curtis-looks-back/ accessed 1 January 2026

for far worse. Spencer Tracy and Errol Flynn, to name only two, were infamous for disappearing on alcohol binges, shutting down productions for days or even weeks. By comparison, reports of Monroe's behaviour – if even accurate – were mild. But after decades of studios indulging their star's whims there was far less tolerance than before – and for a woman, even less.

However, her habit of arriving late on set was, undeniably, a far more serious issue. Many of her previous directors had found it disruptive, and Wilder was no exception. Marilyn knew she had this problem, and over the years had offered various explanations. One of the most revealing supposedly came in a flash of introspection: 'It makes something in me happy to be late. People are waiting for me. People are eager to see me. I remember all the years I was unwanted, all the hundreds of times nobody wanted to see the little servant girl, Norma Jeane – not even her mother. And I feel a queer sensation in punishing the people who are wanting me now. But it's not them I'm really punishing. It's the long-ago people who didn't want Norma Jeane. The later I am, the happier she grows. To me, it's remarkable that I get there at all.'[2]

She offered a glibber explanation in 1959 to journalist Bill Foster: 'It's not really me that's late. It's the others who are always in such a hurry. Seriously, I don't know why. If I knew, I'd get over it.'[3]

Whatever the reasons the uncertainty around Marilyn's arrival and starting times threw off the shooting schedule and slowly wore down morale even further.

Walter Mirisch later explained how her behaviour came to dominate his daily routine. He would routinely check with the studio gate guard each morning to see whether Monroe had arrived, as she was usually scheduled for early calls in order to be ready for a nine o'clock start. However, she was often still in her dressing room well into the morning, leaving everyone else on set waiting for her.

Monroe's unpredictableness became so routine that it became necessary to find increasingly creative ways to kill time. Wilder tried to make the best of it: 'We didn't waste those hours,' he once jokingly remarked. 'We played

---

2. Taylor, Roger G. *Marilyn on Marilyn*, Virgin Books, 1984, p. 114
3. Morgan, *When Marilyn Met the Queen*, p. 79

poker. I managed to read *War and Peace, Les Misérables,* and *Hawaii* and we all got wonderful suntans.'[4]

Others found their own diversions. Betting pools sprang up over how many takes Marilyn would require to get through a scene. A piano was also brought onto the soundstage much to Lemmon's delight. He had taught himself to play by ear as a child and kept up the practice throughout his life. Even whilst studying at Harvard, he'd sneak off to play. After the war, where he had served briefly as a Navy signal officer, he moved to New York. He made a meagre living playing in the dark for silent films at a well-known Manhattan spot – a quirky mix of beer garden, restaurant, vaudeville stage, and movie house. He had earned a meagre $13 a week, picking up extra work to stay afloat while waiting for his big break.

Wilder enjoyed listening, even if he could not always follow the tune. Lemmon recalled that when he played music Wilder liked, he would sometimes join in, but his timing and pitch were constantly off.

On Monday 6 October the plan was to film the scene where Sugar stops by Josephine and Daphne's room to invite them for a swim – followed by the lively chase back through the hotel corridors – Sugar eager to share the news of meeting Junior on the beach, and a suspicious Daphne determined to catch Joe in his latest deception. The sequence ends with them bursting into the hotel room, hearing *Runnin' Wild* being sung from the bathroom, and discovering Josephine lounging in a tub full of bubbles.

But everything quickly went off course. Marilyn was late, and by midday, word spread through the crew that she was unwell, feverish and not in condition to film. Still, Wilder, asked her to come on to set anyway and she managed to get through part of the scene.

However, the next day, she was too sick to continue. With a temperature of 102 degrees, Marilyn was diagnosed with a viral infection and ordered to rest. A studio press release confirmed her illness, and production was forced to pause once again. The bubble bath scene, in particular, couldn't be completed without her as matching the foam from one shot to the next was a continuity nightmare, making it impossible to shoot around her absence.

When Marilyn returned, they were finally able to finish the sequence in the bathroom. However, what should have been a straightforward shoot

4. Zolotow, Maurice. *Billy Wilder In Hollywood*, Pavilion, 1977, p. 270

ended up consuming the entire day as she struggled badly with her lines, particularly during the close-ups.

Curtis described the painful pattern – she'd miss a line, get upset, and start crying. Then her makeup artist, Whitey, would be called in to fix her face. They'd reset and try again but the same thing would happen. Mistakes, tears, more makeup, and another retake. It didn't seem that she was trying to derail the shoot – more like she was stuck in a loop, tormenting herself with every misstep.

She also became increasingly preoccupied with minor details, especially her appearance. A crew member recalled how she would suddenly complain about her eyebrows or lipstick – seemingly anything that might delay shooting.

Cinematographer Jack Cardiff, who had worked with Monroe on *The Prince and the Showgirl*, would have recognised the signs. He had observed that on a regular basis as her makeup was completed, she would begin to retreat inward, overcome by panic. Just before stepping onto set, she might suddenly decide to call someone in New York. Whitey would warn her, 'That might take you an hour, and they're waiting on set,' but Marilyn would insist on making the call anyway.[5]

Whitey described the constant fear she had with being watched. He believed this was one of the things she struggled with most. It was especially noticeable during close-ups, when the focus on her face felt, to her, like too much attention all at once.

Wilder echoed this assessment. He believed that Monroe was simultaneously intimidated by and drawn to the camera, suggesting that her nervousness contributed to the repeated mistakes. Yet he also felt she possessed an effortless screen presence that came through regardless of what she did, calling it a quality of which she was 'not even aware.'[6]

To ease her fears Monroe focused on her process. She often said the reason she needed so many takes wasn't because she couldn't do it, but because she was easing into the role – finding the truth of it. 'I'll go a bit further on the next try,' she would say.[7]

---

5. Cardiff, Jack. *Magic Hour*, Faber and Faber, 1996, p. 202
6. Crowe, p. 164
7. Spoto, p. 443

At one point Wilder grew impatient and asked Monroe to speed things up. She calmly responded that, as a disciple of Stanislavsky, she needed to fully connect with her character. Wilder, exasperated shot back 'could you contact her a little faster?'[8]

Still, even Wilder, for all his grumbling, knew she had something unique. 'You have to go with Monroe,' he said, 'even if other actors suffer, because when Monroe is on the screen, the audience cannot keep their eyes off her.'[9]

The repetition of scenes often meant that as Marilyn became more expressive and grounded, the actors around her became more fatigued. The longer it went on, the more it took out of them.

Lemmon took a philosophical view, recognising that Wilder would ultimately use whichever take best served Monroe's performance. He understood that multiple takes were often required, sometimes many and sometimes only a few, depending on her mood. Accepting this early on, he decided not to let the unpredictability affect him, concluding that it would only harm his own performance if he did. He reportedly told Walter Mirisch that his 'worst nightmare' was that they would do their fiftieth take and that would be the one Marilyn would finally get right and he would 'screw it up.'[10]

Over that weekend a small party was held at Curtis's house with some of the cast and a few select friends (but not Marilyn and Arthur). During dinner, Wilder's back suddenly went out. A doctor was called, and he was given an anti-inflammatory shot. The general consensus was that the strain of working with Monroe had finally caught up with him.

Wilder admitted he had begun struggling with sleep and that stress was wearing him down. His back issues worsened to the point that he began walking with a cane. Audrey, speaking somewhat tongue in cheek, suggested that at this point he even needed help from a therapist simply to get up in the morning.

Monroe's volatility was also a constant challenge. Wilder described how he never knew what each day on set would bring or how she would behave in a given scene. He noted that she could be cooperative or difficult, and

8. Zolotow, p. 262
9. Ibid, p. 262
10. Mirisch, p. 101

that tensions sometimes escalated before a single shot had been completed, leaving the production in a constant state of uncertainty.

As Lemmon told Michael Parkinson, the British chat show host, in the 1980s – she put up a distance between herself and everyone else 'a glass window' and wouldn't let anyone else in. He believed that it was because she had been hurt before and that he hadn't let it bother him.[11]

Marilyn herself was well aware that she wasn't exactly a calming or sociable presence on set. Jack Cardiff had once described her as having 'an aura of blank remoteness, of being in another world,' a quality that made her feel distant, even to those trying to connect with her through simple conversation.[12]

But she had her own reasoning for the way she appeared to others. In an interview with Hedda Hopper, Monroe explained that she didn't consider herself experienced enough to move easily before casual conversations and demanding dramatic scenes. For her, staying in character, required sustained focus, and she preferred to return to her dressing room between takes to concentrate on what came next and keep her mind 'in one channel.'

She also acknowledged admiring actors who could switch seamlessly in that way and that she feared some would mistakenly view her as 'high hat' or attention-seeking because she could not work that way. In reality, she explained her focus was on giving the best performance she could.[13]

Interestingly, despite her reputation for disrupting production, she seemed most at ease in the ensemble scenes, particularly with the women in the band. Curtis noted that she came alive in those group settings.

And, despite attempts to frame it otherwise (much was made in the press of false stories that she had a stipulation that she would be the only blonde in the production), Marilyn formed similar bonds with others in the cast. She apparently gave Barbara Drew a heart-shaped gold pin that she had admired one day on set, and they remained friendly after filming wrapped. Allen Breneman, who played the Seminole Ritz's bellhop intent on seducing Josephine, remembered being introduced to her on his first

11. Fuller, p. 10
12. Cardiff, p. 201
13. Marilyn Returning to Hollywood, *Los Angeles Times*, 22 June 1958, p. 99

day, recalling that she 'was very polite' and 'charismatic.'[14] Joani Hannon, who played the drummer in the Society Syncopators, recalled a moment between takes when Monroe stood beside her kit and said softly, 'I just love the drums. I wish you'd teach me to play.'[15] Hannon, starstruck, found her to be unexpectedly sweet and down-to-earth. Penny McGuiggan, the trumpet player, remembered Monroe as 'adorable; very, very charismatic.' [16] Even Curtis had to admit that she 'went out of her way to make those girls comfortable. I would see them huddled off set, whispering and giggling.'[17]

And Marilyn's lateness had a fiscal silver lining for many of the supporting cast. 'I was originally contracted for two weeks,' McGuiggan said, 'but that went up to four months.'[18]

The next week was devoted to two of the film's elaborate musical sequences – where Sugar performs *I Wanna Be Loved By You* and then, later, *I'm Thru With Love.* The vocals had been pre-recorded, and her performance was to be lip synced.

But before they could return to filming the close-ups, Monroe fell ill again and the production team were forced to turn their attention to other parts of the script. Curtis and Lemmon filmed several scenes, including the point where Joe, in his hotel room, speaks to Sugar on the phone and kicks a box containing white orchids and a diamond bracelet – originally given to Daphne by Osgood – across the hallway.

On Wednesday 15 October, Monroe was officially marked absent due to illness and she didn't return for the rest of the week. Her repeated no shows had started to stir gossip. One rumour, in particular, had been circulating for some time – that she was pregnant. These whisperings were a real concern for the producers, who worried about how the timing of a pregnancy might impact the production schedule as well as the continuity of the sections that had already been filmed.

---

14. Heritage Auctions, Lot #1123, 11 December 2018 https://entertainment.ha.com/itm/movie-tv-memorabilia/some-like-it-hot-shooting-script-and-production-materials-from-the-collection-of-bellhop-allen-breneman/a/997052-1123
15. Rolle, Elisa. *Queer Places: Pacific Time Zone* (California – 90230 to 92999): *Retracing the steps of LGBTQ people around the world*, 2016
16. Morgan, *Private and Undisclosed*, p. 274
17. Curtis and Viera, p. 96
18. Ibid, p. 274

Initial speculation had further flared up after her hospitalisation in September and gained more traction when it was revealed that her doctor there had been Dr. Leon Krohn, its Chief of Gynaecology. One reporter even noted, 'Perhaps no other question crops up so frequently. Hardly a day melts into night that some columnist doesn't drop this tidbit into his word mill: La Monroe is going to be a mama! What makes this so recurrent? Is America laboring under a mother complex, as some psychiatrists claim? Or is it suffering a Monroe complex?'[19]

For the press, the pieces seemed to fit together perfectly, and they eagerly pursued the pregnancy angle. Hedda Hopper even called Curtis at home over that weekend and asked him directly. Curtis confirmed that while he didn't know the details, in his opinion 'Marilyn's tits are enlarged.'[20]

Later, he claimed that the only reason he had been so indiscreet was because Hopper had threatened to publicly expose his philandering unless he spilled the beans. Whatever the truth, the damage was done – and it would only add more tension to an already strained set.

The following Monday, Marilyn arrived on time but stayed in her dressing room. Then came the big blow. She was given a copy of that day's *Los Angeles Times* which carried Hopper's story, featuring the claim that Marilyn's closest friends believed she was pregnant. It ended with a particularly devastating line: 'If true, I hope she'll be able to carry this baby.'[21]

The piece hit Marilyn hard. Curtis told of her reacting with fury – shouting obscenities about Hopper and whoever was the source for the rumour. For Marilyn, privacy was deeply important, and it would have felt like a particularly stinging betrayal.

Her half-sister, Berniece, would later reflect that Marilyn saw anyone who spoke to the press, even well-meaningly, as disloyal. The fact that these kinds of stories were often attributed to unnamed "close friends" only made it worse. She couldn't be sure who was talking, or what might be said next. It left her feeling isolated, and more suspicious of those around her. It wasn't even the first time that pregnancy rumours had swirled – in 1957 when filming in London Miller had been forced

19. Clipping in author's collection dated 24 September 1958
20. Curtis & Vieira, p. 158
21. Mitzi Gaynor and Niven Will Costar, *Los Angeles Times*, 20 October 1958, p. 78

to dismiss similar claims as 'absolute rubbish' and assured the press that 'there is no baby on the way.[22]

And it was under these circumstances that the most-legendary problems on set began to happen in earnest – most famously during two scenes that have since entered Hollywood lore.

The first of these came during a short, seemingly simple line, "It's me - Sugar," delivered through a closed door to Josephine, who's in bed, with Daphne standing nearby. Sugar has come to tell her friends about her wonderful date on the yacht and her plans to see Junior again.

There are several accounts of what happened that day. Curtis recalled that, at the first cue, Marilyn didn't say anything at all. Wilder added that all anyone could hear was the soft, repetitive sound of her snapping her fingers, almost frozen with fear. When she did speak, the timing was off. Sometimes she was too late. Other times, she forgot the line entirely. Now and then, she got the words wrong: "It's Sugar. Me" or "Sugar, it's me."

The takes stacked up – into the twenties, then thirties, then beyond. Each time, Curtis and Lemmon had to reset and repeat their parts, waiting for Monroe to come in on cue. Wilder attempted to reassure her, interpreting her difficulty as nerves, but she responded with confusion, questioning what there was to worry about.

Eventually, the prop department stepped in. A cue card was made and lightly taped against the door to prompt her. But even with the line written out for her, she still struggled. Frustration grew – both hers and everyone else's. Her mood swung between sadness and bursts of anger.

In the end, it took a little under fifty takes to get the scene right.

The other legendary difficult sequence was the "Where's that bourbon?" line, where Sugar, who has now learnt that Junior is leaving for South America for an arranged marriage as part of a merger with a Venezuelan oil company, despondently enters their bedroom, rifles through a few drawers without finding the bottle, says the line, and then walks over to where Joe and Jerry have been hastily packing their suitcases.

But here, too, she had real trouble getting the line right. She kept stumbling over it, forcing multiple retakes. After each attempt, she would leave the room, shake out her hands to relax her fingers, and then come back to try again. Takes climbed into the fifties and beyond.

---

22. Morgan, *When Marilyn Met the Queen*, p. 137

The other's frustration was almost unbearable.

Cue cards were placed inside the drawer to help her with her lines. At one point, when Wilder offered direction, Monroe asked not to be spoken to, explaining that it would interfere with how she intended to approach the scene. Lemmon later recalled that Wilder was left momentarily speechless, visibly stunned by the interaction, before quietly shaking his head and returning to the camera set up.

In the end, it took over eighty takes, according to Wilder. She couldn't get it right, but she kept trying and never gave up.

So, what was going on?

It was no secret that Marilyn had already been struggling during the shoot. She was also known for going through many takes before she felt a scene was right, using the repetition to settle into a rhythm. But now the sting of the Hedda Hopper piece still hung in the air, and some thought she was simply worn down, emotionally as well as physically. Whilst all of this is undoubtedly true there's another theory – that these particular scenes represented the peak of the power struggle between Monroe and Wilder.

Some commentators have speculated that she was, at least in part, sabotaging takes intentionally as a form of resistance – a way to assert control over how she was being directed. Diamond believed she was abusing her power, arguing that having reached the top she was, in effect, paying the world back for all the difficult experiences she had endured.

Others point to the fact that she and Wilder had fundamentally different ideas about how her character should be played, and the subsequent tension surfaced in subtle, and sometimes not-so-subtle, ways on set.

It's a standard bit of a seasoned actor's toolkit to have a technique to avoid giving a performance they don't believe in. Orson Welles, for example, was known to undermine lines he disliked by delivering them so quickly or quietly they were unusable in the final cut. One story tells of Welles doing thirty-six takes of a scene, subtly ruining each one. Only when the director refused to back down did the actor finally give a clean take.

And added to that it is one of the central beliefs of Method Acting that the actor must work from within, shaping a performance out of personal truth rather than simply following instructions. It gives the performer a certain inner authority, especially over emotion, and encourages them to trust their own instincts, even if that means resisting the director's reading of a scene.

Monroe was also fiercely determined. She had an unwavering sense of what she needed from a director and insisted on being treated with respect.

One of the turning points in her evolution as an actress came with *Bus Stop*, directed by Joshua Logan. It was the first film she chose under her new, hard won, contract with Fox, and was a project that was intended to mark her transition to a serious performer.

Logan initially wasn't convinced at all about Monroe's participation and didn't even believe she had the ability to act. He admitted in his autobiography that when the venture was initially pitched to him, he had little interest, assuming Marilyn was just another pretty face without substance.

He recalled that Monroe was routinely treated as the butt of jokes within Hollywood, that she was typecast as a 'beautifully formed but stupid blonde.' Before accepting the job, Logan sought the opinion of Lee Strasberg who responded with unequivocal endorsement. Strasberg told him that, among the hundreds of performers he had worked with 'there are only two that stand out way above the rest. Number one is Marlon Brando and the second is Marilyn Monroe.'[23]

Strasberg's assurances convinced Logan to take the project on, and what he discovered surprised him. Not only did Marilyn possess real talent, but she was also deeply committed to her craft. She studied hard to master an Ozark accent, contributed meaningfully to costume and character decisions, and showed up focused and engaged. He had anticipated her lateness and anxiety but made a conscious decision not to let either frustrate him. He came to see Marilyn as one of the great talents of her generation, describing her performance as both vulnerable and luminous.

Even when ill, Marilyn had pushed herself to deliver. During *Bus Stop* she had fallen seriously sick with a respiratory infection and had to be hospitalised. But when she returned to set, she continued with the same dedication. And subsequently, the role of Chérie, earned her acclaim and helped redefine her public image. Her work with Logan revealed what she was capable of when she felt safe and respected and it also deeply shaped how she expected to be treated moving forward.

That experience stood in sharp contrast to the next major project. When Laurence Olivier signed on to direct and star opposite her in *The Prince and the Showgirl,* he too reached out – this time to both Lee Strasberg and

23. Logan, Joshua. *Movie Stars, Real People, and Me*, Delacorte Press, 1978, p. 43

Logan to get a better understanding of how to work with her. Logan, with Marilyn's consent, replied with candid advice. He emphasised that she was unlike any actress he had ever encountered but cautioned Olivier not to allow Paula Strasberg to interfere during rehearsals or filming. He made it clear – keep Paula in the dressing room – before concluding that she was 'worth all the trouble.'[24]

He also advised Olivier not to dictate line readings or micromanage her performance – explaining that Marilyn needed time to discover the emotional truth of her scenes, and that process couldn't be rushed. Logan clarified that if she didn't respond to direction, it may be because she didn't fully understand or agree with it, not because she was being difficult. That her hesitations and forgetfulness were often rooted in self-frustration and not rebellion.

Strasberg echoed similar guidance but also pointing out that Marilyn hadn't come from the stage and wouldn't respond well to rigid theatrical direction. That she needed emotional cues, not orders. But Olivier, who clearly read the letter many times and even underlined passages, ultimately dismissed most of the advice.

From the very beginning, she sensed his condescension. She said she felt he was treating the role, and her, as beneath him. That impression was reinforced at their first table read, where Olivier pointedly remarked to the group on how alien her acting style was compared to their more traditional approach. Marilyn was stunned by the snobbery. It rattled her and put her on edge immediately.

What made this all worse was the context – it was Marilyn's project, her production company's film and he had been her choice of co-star and director. She had fought hard for the autonomy to make her own creative choices. Having Olivier dismiss and undermine her on her own set felt like a betrayal.

The result was a far less collaborative working relationship than she'd had with Logan. Where she had previously been punctual and engaged, she now arrived late and often retreated into herself. Tensions ran high. Still, despite the turmoil, her performance was subtle and nuanced and ultimately better received than the Shakespearean actor's own. Critics noted that it was Monroe, not Olivier, who brought real warmth.

---

24. Guiles, p. 227

Each director seemed to draw out a different version of Monroe, and Wilder was no exception.

The difficulties with the "Sugar" and "Bourbon" scenes in particular can be understood as epitomising the underlying tension between Monroe and Wilder. And after so many takes, the final cut shows Marilyn playing it with her back to the camera. Wilder could have spared everyone the ordeal and dubbed the line after. When, many years later, fellow director Cameron Crowe asked him why he didn't, Wilder simply shrugged and said, 'Maybe I was just stupid.'[25]

Or possibly he was trying to break her or prove a point. Wilder, known for his caustic wit and intolerance for inefficiency, had little patience for what he considered unnecessary difficulty. His opinion of Marilyn had become increasingly negative. He later described her in extremely harsh terms and suggested that his experiences working with her were far more difficult than he ever publicly revealed, insisting that the full extent of it would likely never be known or even believed.

Whatever the full truth, the atmosphere on set had become oppressive. Marilyn's inconsistencies continued, and Wilder, grappling with severe back pain, even had to take a day off midweek. Tensions mounted. Wilder had become the enemy in her eyes, and because she tended to see people in extremes, either to be fully trusted or deeply distrusted, their worsening relationship would become another major obstacle. Paula Strasberg was deeply disheartened by what she witnessed on Wilder's set. 'Why can't they handle her the way Josh Logan did?' she asked. 'He showed her respect, and Marilyn felt it.'[26]

She started calling him "Mr. Wilder," a dig that echoed a similar tactic she had used with Olivier, whom she mockingly referred to as "Mister Sir" after he had issued a demeaning direction to her to 'be sexy.'[27]

For some it might seem childish, but these were some of the few ways she could assert herself at a time when she often felt powerless.

The mood infected the entire set. According to Barbara Diamond, who witnessed much of the production firsthand, the environment became so fraught that it actively hindered her ability to perform. Barbara noted that

25. Crowe, p. 159; Maslon, p. 84
26. Strasberg, *Susan. Marilyn and Me*, Doubleday, 1992, p. 138
27. Cardiff, p. 209

Wilder, Lemmon, and Curtis could all be harsh, and their combined attitude only increased Marilyn's anxiety.

Arthur eventually stepped in. Concerned for her health, he confirmed to Wilder that she was pregnant and urged him to ease the pressure. He told Wilder that Marilyn was under too much strain – her days were too long, the workload too intense, and the stress too unbearable. Wilder said he sympathised but felt compelled to explain the underlying issue: it wasn't the scheduled hours that were the problem. It was how those hours were being used.

Wilder pointed out that Marilyn often didn't arrive until well into the day, and even once there, she would spend hours in hair, makeup, and preparation before filming could begin. By the time she was ready, most of the day was already gone. If she began earlier, he said, they could finish earlier, but that simply wasn't happening. In fact, it wasn't uncommon for her to be difficult to coax from her dressing room altogether. According to one story, she often pushed back, telling crew members to "drop dead" or "fuck off" when they tried to get her on set.[28]

It was a difficult and delicate situation. Miller was right to be worried. Marilyn's health was fragile, and her emotional state increasingly tense. Yet the production was backed into a corner – they couldn't move forward without her, and some of the most crucial sequences of the entire film were next on the schedule: date night!

There were two sequences to be filmed. One was the playful, romantic one aboard the yacht with Sugar and Junior; the other was the wildly comic night between Daphne and Osgood. In the latter, Osgood enthusiastically suggests a night out at a roadhouse with an energetic Cuban band where they can dance late into the night.

Over the course of three scenes, we see an attitude change towards Osgood, from dismissal of this "dirty old man" and bored resignation, to starting to get into the spirit of things. By the end of the night, Daphne has completely taken control over Jerry and the transformation is complete. The chairs are stacked on tables, the restaurant is long closed, and Osgood has indeed kept his promise – the band is blindfolded. Daphne is dancing with real enthusiasm now, swept up in the feeling of being chased and admired as well as the rhythm of the music, *La cumparsita.* That same piece of

28. Sikov, p. 417

music had also been used by Wilder in *Sunset Boulevard,* underscoring Norma Desmond's lonely New Year's Eve tango with William Holden's Joe Gillis.

As Lemmon prepared for the dance scenes with Joe E. Brown, he supposedly found himself being coached by none other than George Raft. When it became obvious that the young dance instructor Wilder had hired wasn't quite up to the job, Raft reportedly stepped in and personally taught both Lemmon and Brown how to tango. While this may have just been a story fed to the press it is apparent that, despite his reputation as hard-edged, both on-screen and off, Raft had proved himself to be surprisingly genial on this particular set.

The film cleverly intercuts the night of dancing with the scenes between Sugar and Junior on the yacht. Wilder used swish pans to transition between the two parallel dates, giving the sequences a sense of shared rhythm.

The *Caledonia II* set was one of the more elaborate constructions on the soundstage. The production team built a full promenade deck, even installing a shallow pool of water beside it to enhance the illusion. On another part of the stage, they constructed the yacht's interior salon, creating the distinct spaces required for the key scenes.

Filming the promenade deck sequence, when they first board the boat, was relatively uncomplicated. The scene itself was brief and executed efficiently, captured in a single long tracking shot. No close-ups were needed, which helped keep everything to time.

What makes the scene particularly intriguing, however, is through a glimpse into Monroe's preparation process. One of the surviving pieces of ephemera from this shoot was her "prompt book" – a bound folio compiled with her scenes and lines typed out separately from the full screenplay. This document became a working journal of sorts, filled with annotations.

Though not every scene is marked, many pages are filled with underlined words, circled passages and acting notes scribbled in the margins. Some markings have faded with time or are partially illegible, while others remain vivid.

In preparation for the scene when they first board the yacht, for example, she jotted down notes like 'Alice in Wonderland' and 'she sees Coney Island,' suggesting the action should feel dreamlike and full of wonder for

Sugar. At the top of one page, she wrote a guiding mantra: 'All I have to do is trust the moment.'[29]

Next, Sugar and Junior move into the salon, which had been ingeniously constructed with breakaway walls to allow the camera full freedom of movement during filming. Interestingly, they began with the main seduction scene, which surprised some of the crew. It was well known that Marilyn needed time to ease into emotionally significant moments, so starting with such a pivotal, intimate scene seemed counterintuitive. But from a practical standpoint, it made sense. She was actually present on set and given her tendency to leave midway through the day and not return, it was wise to capture such an important scene while they had the opportunity and everyone still had energy.

Curtis offered a more cynical perspective. He claimed that Wilder scheduled that scene for that particular day because Arthur Miller wasn't on set. Without her husband there, Marilyn might feel less inhibited and more willing to engage in the romantic mood without discomfort. It would have also helped that the set had been cleared of all but the essential crew. Even a visiting journalist from *TIME* magazine was politely asked to leave.

Curtis claimed that before heading to set, she invited him into her dressing room to share a glass of champagne. He also alleged they kissed when they were alone and that Monroe became physically provocative with him during filming, was aware of his arousal, and encouraged it. He described her as sexually assertive and enjoying the power she held over him.

There was a great deal at stake with this particular scene – not only in terms of performance but also in navigating the boundaries of the Production Code. Even though censorship was loosening, filmmakers still had to tread carefully. Wilder and Diamond knew that this scene needed to be genuinely sexy, but also clever enough to elude the censors. Originally, the scene was envisaged with the conventional dynamic of a man seducing a woman, with Joe's character attempting to compromise Sugar but in the end a more innovative approach was taken.

They reversed the power dynamic entirely. Instead of Junior being the aggressor, he pretended to be impotent, "harmless" – after a brief initial

---

29. Cohan, p. 68

kiss – allowing Sugar to become the initiator. In her prompt book, Monroe noted that Sugar took Junior's comment about impotence as a 'personal affront.' This flipped the sexual script but also gave Joe a way to manipulate her emotions and her defences through false vulnerability. As Maslon described Wilder's last minute inspiration: 'It must be better to be subdued, seduced, and screwed by Marilyn Monroe – what could be better? So we switched this thing around … Now we set it up, it was just like picking oranges, you know.'[30]

To imply intimacy without violating the Code, Wilder relied on visual innuendo. Two subtle but unmistakable clues communicated what was happening. The first was Junior's glasses fogging up. Wilder had initially hoped Curtis would become so genuinely flustered that the lenses would steam up on their own, but when that didn't happen, the prop man had to simulate the effect with grey paint. The second visual indication was Junior's leg lifting into the air in a movement of comic ecstasy. Curtis claimed the leg raise was his idea, an impromptu suggestion to Diamond, who encouraged him to try it. Wilder, however, insisted it had been part of the original directions.

Regardless of its origin, the leg gesture perfectly underscored the scene's comic sensuality and the implication of sex. Wilder later reflected that he 'always played an honest game with the censors,' arguing that sex in his films was only used when it was 'dramatic or it is funny,' and noted that the censors ultimately accepted the humour of the scene on the yacht.[31]

Over the next few days, filming continued in the salon, though progress was frequently disrupted by Marilyn's lateness and absences. Despite these delays, Curtis remembered that she nailed their first scene together in the initial sequence. However, as the date went on there were more issues. She needed several takes of the scene where he handed her a glass of champagne. The prop man had to constantly refill and reseal the bottle, then rinse and dry the glass between each take.

And the scene where he chews on a cold pheasant leg and tells the story of the fate of his fiancée, "Nellie," at the Grand Canyon, proved problematic too. For practicality and visual appeal, they used a chicken

30. Maslon, p. 121
31. Malone, Aubrey. *The Defiant One: A Biography of Tony Curtis*, McFarlane & Company, 2013, p. 85

leg, as it was realised that real pheasant wouldn't have held up well under the hot studio lights. Unfortunately for him, Marilyn kept stopping and restarting during takes, requiring the scene to be shot over and over. By the time they finally got the shot, Curtis was visibly unwell and he later said he felt physically sick by the end of the process and was so affected by the experience that he avoided eating chicken for a considerable period afterwards.

Despite some progress the *Los Angeles Times* article clearly was still impacting her mood, and the pregnancy itself was also taking a toll. Over the weekend, she checked into the Cedars of Lebanon Hospital. Records show she was charged for a room on 24 and 25 October, along with lab tests, pharmacy receipts, and a series of follow up telephone calls.

That following Monday, she wrote another letter to Norman Rosten thanking him for his kind wishes while expressing sadness about their continued separation. She described feeling emotionally unsettled and creatively blocked in such a gloomy environment. Finally, she noted that Miller was weaker 'from holding me up' and that she needed 'something to hold on to.'[32]

Meanwhile, the Mirisch Corporation were also becoming increasingly anxious, though their concern had little to do with Marilyn's well-being. Their focus was on the costs and delays that her illnesses and then pregnancy had caused and the extra filming days the project would now need. In a letter to Robert Blumofe, dated 28 October, Harold outlined mounting pressures as the budget for completing the film rose to $2.6 million and was showing every likelihood of increasing further.

> 'I know you are just as concerned about *Some Like It Hot* as we are and so there will be no surprises when the final cost comes in, I want you to know that as of today Marilyn Monroe has been out because of so-called illnesses for a total of twelve days and has been late on the set for a total of thirty-five hours, which, in essence, comes to an additional five days delay.

32. Summers, p. 242

> A small part of this illness is covered by insurance, but the rest of it is on account of pregnancy and other things which you are very much familiar with.'[33]

That very same day Marilyn failed to report to work again, prompting a formal suspension of filming. Marvin Mirisch issued telegrams to the cast to inform them that production had been temporarily suspended due to Monroe's illness.

Monroe returned to the set on 30 October though her lateness continued, an issue that persisted into the following week. In the press, Miller tried to strike an optimistic tone, saying, 'I think Marilyn will be able to finish the picture without any more trouble. As soon as it's over, we'll head back to New York.'[34]

But several scenes still needed to be completed, particularly some close-ups, along with reshoots for the hallway and phone conversation sequences. One of these were her reactions during the phone call in which Sugar learns that Junior is leaving to get married. In the final cut, it's still faintly apparent that Monroe, in places, is reading her lines off something out of frame. Despite efforts to conceal it, the workaround couldn't be fully hidden.

It wasn't only Monroe who faced difficulties on set, tensions simmered between Curtis and Wilder as well, something Curtis attributed to Wilder's approach to directing which 'scared the shit' out of him. He summed up their dynamic 'I didn't avoid Billy, but I kept my distance.'[35]

Wilder, never one to hold back a quip, often took aim at Curtis's appearance – especially the snug "Continental" trousers he favoured at the time. At one point, he joked that Curtis looked 'as though someone had dipped him in India ink up to his waist.'[36] The two simply weren't clicking.

In an effort to lighten the mood, Curtis organised a prank while rehearsing the sequence that takes place during the dinner of the 10th Annual Friends of the Italian Opera. Instead of Johnny Paradise leaping out of the birthday cake to execute Spats and his henchman as the script demanded, a topless woman sprung out instead and ran straight to Wilder,

---

33. United Artists Series 99AN/MCHC 82-046, box 5 folder 14, Wisconsin Center for Film and Theater Research.
34. Marilyn Returns; Mum About Stork, *Independent*, 30 October 1958, p. 10
35. Hall of Fame. Tony Curtis: Survivor, *Empire*, December 2001, p. 110
36. Sikov, p. 412

planting a kiss on him. Wilder, predictably, was far from amused with more wasted time on set.

Around this time, Curtis also received confirmation that his original vocal performance as Josephine wouldn't be used in the final cut. The issue was that he couldn't maintain his high-pitched voice for very long and it was felt the resulting uneven performance wouldn't be convincing enough for the audience to believe that anyone would fall for his disguise. Rather than risk undermining the illusion, the filmmakers decided to dub over his lines.

They brought in veteran voice actor Paul Frees, known as the man of a thousand voices, who, not only re-recorded Josephine's dialogue but also provided the voice for Tito Vuolo's character, Mozarella, the funeral director. On 1 November, Curtis signed a contract granting permission for this change. Given the already tense relationship between him and Wilder, it's no surprise that he wasn't particularly happy about the decision.

It marked a low point for Curtis, both professionally and personally. Frustrated by the problems during filming and increasingly alienated, he decided to watch the most recently completed sequences hoping to get a sense of how the film was coming together, particularly the yacht scenes. On that day the screening room was packed with cast, crew, studio staff, and people from other productions also viewing the rushes.

As the footage rolled, Curtis grew more and more agitated. Wilder, he felt, had deliberately selected takes that flattered Marilyn – showing her at her most radiant and controlled – while choosing shots of him where he looked visibly tired, washed out, and disengaged.

Adding to the discomfort, Curtis recalled hearing crude remarks from the back of the room, jokes aimed at Marilyn's body, made openly and loudly. While it's doubtful that he felt especially protective of her, the tone of the comments seemed to implicate him as well. They cast him as passive, weak, or effeminate – whispers that had followed him for years in Hollywood and had already caused him significant unpleasantness.

When the screening ended and the lights came up, Curtis got up to leave. As he went out, someone shouted the question: 'What's it like kissing Marilyn?' Curtis didn't pause to reflect on the wisdom of his response. 'What do you think it was like, buddy? Like kissing Hitler,' he snapped, and slammed the door behind him.[37]

---

37. Curtis & Vieira, p. 187

Over the years, Curtis gave conflicting accounts of what happened that day. At first, he flat-out denied even saying the controversial comment: 'Never happened. Never fucking happened.'[38] Later, he softened, calling it ironic – 'Come on. Kissing the most desirable woman in the world and being asked repeatedly what it was like – it began to annoy me. What was I supposed to say, that it was like skiing down a snow-covered mountain and floating to earth on gossamer wings?'[39] Eventually, though, he conceded that he had said it, although not seriously: 'I figured a question that stupid deserved a stupid answer,' he said in one interview.[40]

Lemmon, who was also present at the screening, confirmed what actually happened: 'When we watched the rushes of that scene, Tony said something which he really didn't mean,' Lemmon recalled. 'If I were him, I might have said the same thing. But when the lights went up, Tony stood and said, "It's like kissing Hitler." I turned to someone next to me and said, "Jesus, he didn't really just say that, did he?" And the guy said, "Yeah, he said it."'[41]

The remark soon leaked to the press and inevitably found its way back to Marilyn. She rarely spoke publicly about Curtis, but in what would become one of her final interviews, with Richard Meryman for *LIFE* magazine, she addressed the controversy directly. Rather than responding with anger, she suggested that any discomfort reflected his feelings rather than hers, that it was 'his problem.'[42]

There's also an undated, handwritten note from Monroe that adds an extra sting of wit (if it indeed actually refers to Curtis): 'There is only one way he could comment on my sexuality, and I'm afraid he has never had the opportunity.'[43]

Fortunately for everyone involved, the production was nearing its end. They were down to the last few scenes, including the motorboat escape sequence, a process shot completed entirely in the studio, where Joe

38. Castle, p. 278
39. Malone, p. 86
40. Curtis, Tony with Peter Golenbock. *American Prince: My Autobiography*, Virgin Books, 2008, p. 214
41. Munn, Michael. *Tony Curtis: Nobody's Perfect,* JR Books, 2011, p. 156
42. Marilyn on Marilyn: Conversation with Life Associate Editor Richard Meryman, *LIFE*, 3 August 1962
43. Julien's Auctions, *Property From the Estate of Lee Strasberg*, Lot #418, 17 November 2016 https://bid.juliensauctions.com/lot-details/index/catalog/180/lot/83303

confesses that he is exactly like all the other saxophone players who have hurt her before.

Marilyn's last big scene was performing *I'm Thru With Love.* Whereas last time Sugar was in the Peacock Room she was wearing a nude-coloured gown and in an exuberant, hopeful, mood, now she is in sheer black. This dress with its shimmering butterfly appliqués and fine beaded fringe created by vertical rows of jet-like beads and sequins catching the light, is absolutely stunning. Legend has it that it was also so tight she had to be lifted onto the piano for the performance. The screenplay sets the scene simply: "Sugar perches on top of the piano, bathed in a spotlight. She is a little drunk, and more than a little blue, and she sings the lyrics with heartbreaking conviction." This is also the scene where Joe kisses her. He forgets, or perhaps no longer cares, that he's dressed as a woman or that having witnessed a second mob massacre he is on the run once again. In that instant, Joe drops the act, showing he's ready to be honest, even if it means revealing himself at the worst possible time. Being forced to live as Josephine, even temporarily, has transformed him, it seems.

While Sweet Sue is speechless in shock at this apparent lesbian kiss. Sugar realises the truth – Josephine is also Junior, and neither of them are who she thought they were. Still, she doesn't hesitate to follow him to the waiting motorboat.

Whilst Marilyn wrapped filming on 7 November shortly after she was rushed to the Cedars of Lebanon Hospital. She remained in Los Angeles for the next week, first in hospital, then back at the Hotel Bel-Air, under strict bed rest and cared for by Dr. Krohn. The reason was reported as pregnancy-related complications.

She had originally been scheduled to return to the studio for publicity photos but now she was not only forbidden to travel onto set – she was also visibly pregnant and therefore physically different to how she was at the beginning of filming. The production still needed imagery for promotions and publicity so a stand-in was used. Sandra Warner, who played Emily ("toodle-oo!") in the film and had a similar body type, posed in her place with Marilyn's face added through – not always well done – photo retouching.

As soon as she was able, Monroe returned to New York. It was a high-risk pregnancy, and her doctors there ordered her to rest, along with instructions to stop drinking and to avoid any unprescribed medications.

In mid-December, the news her friends and family had been fearing arrived – Monroe had experienced a miscarriage.

Messages of sympathy soon followed. One of the most personal came from *Some Like It Hot's* publicist, Jack Hirschberg, who wrote: 'Dear Marilyn, I was terribly saddened to read that you had lost your baby. I remember our chat about children and know how extremely disappointed you must have been.'[44]

For the rest of the cast, only a handful of scenes remained.

One was the end of the final motorboat sequence after Sugar and Joe kiss passionately. As they drift out of frame the spotlight shifts to Osgood and Daphne for the film's famous closing exchange.

Another scenario took place in Spats' hotel room, where a henchman reveals that Little Bonaparte is upset about the murder of Toothpick Charlie as, "they used to be choir boys together," before they spot Joe and Jerry trying to climb down the side of the and escape detection.

With these completed without incident final photography for all wrapped on 12 November.

Curtis summed up the feeling: 'And now no more wigs. No more falsies. No more fucking high heels. Elation. And then – a drop.'[45]

---

44. Julien's Auctions, *Hollywood Legends 2013,* Lot #1059, 5 April 2013 https://bid.juliensauctions.com/lot-details/index/catalog/120/lot/52138/marilyn-monroe-letters-to-and-about
45. Curtis & Vieira, p. 192

Part Four

Creating A Classic

Chapter Twelve

Stitching the Final Cut

That may have been the end for the actors, but for the production team it was only the start of the next phase. Once shooting was complete, work shifted immediately to editing, spurred on by the push for a March 1959 release. With preview screenings set for the end of January, the schedule was tight.

But for Wilder, it wouldn't have been much of a worry. He had planned his shots with such precision that there was almost nothing to trim. He worked closely with his trusted collaborators – Doane Harrison and editor Arthur Schmidt, who as a team kept the process moving smoothly.

Wilder aimed for edits that were nearly invisible with each cut flowing seamlessly into the next to preserve narrative clarity and emotional rhythm. But unlike many directors who relied solely on simple cuts, Wilder often brought a more stylised touch. He favoured elegant dissolves that lent a dreamy, fluid quality to transitions, or theatrical wipes that moved across the screen like a stage curtain closing.

Photographer Richard Miller, who witnessed the process up close, was in awe of the speed with which they assembled the film. It was, he acknowledged, something he'd never seen any other director manage.

The location of the first preview was The Bay Theatre in Pacific Palisades, Los Angeles. Designed by S. Charles Lee and built in the late 1940s, the Bay was a sleek example of Streamline Moderne architecture. Its exterior featured smooth, sweeping curves and a striking vertical marquee that rose high above the entrance, designed to catch the attention of passersby and draw them in. Inside, was simple but capacious, with a 1,100-seat auditorium and a modest lobby, both reflecting the same aesthetic as the outside.

The Bay was often used for "Major Studio Previews," where the audience would turn up without knowing what film they were about to see. The screenings were part of the production testing process and viewers would be asked to fill out short comment cards afterwards, giving their honest reactions to help gauge whether any changes were needed before release.

For the first *Some Like It Hot* showing, the crowd also included Billy and Audrey, Iz and Barbara, Jack Lemmon and his then girlfriend (later wife) Felicia Farr along with several Mirisch Company executives. It wasn't packed, but there was a solid turnout. Unfortunately, the reaction was far from what anyone had hoped. Audrey later recalled that the audience reaction was extremely muted, with only a couple of friends laughing. Barbara was even more blunt in her assessment, describing it as one of the worst preview screenings she had ever experienced.

Several explanations have been offered for why the first screening was received with such a resounding thud. According to Audrey it was because people were unsure whether laughter was appropriate, and they were unsure on how to respond to what they had just seen.

Barbara agreed with the assessment, pointing out that aside from the lively opening titles, the first few minutes offered no indication that the film was meant to be a comedy. Indeed, it jumps from the credits, straight into the back of a hearse and then onto a nearly four-minute sequence with no dialogue whatsoever. And with Marilyn Monroe not appearing until slightly over twenty minutes in, audiences were left trying to make sense of a film that opened like a gangster picture and then suddenly offered two men in drag. Lemmon later recollected how strong the reaction was for some audience members, noting that a number of parents removed their children from the screening. He remembered people expressing shock and discomfort, muttering that the film was disgusting.

The Mirisch brothers wasted no time in offering their suggestions – they wanted changes and fast. More Marilyn, they insisted. Make a tighter edit and cut the running time by ten or fifteen minutes.

Accounts of Wilder's reaction that evening differ. At first, he seemed to have been stunned and reportedly told them he would make the requested changes. Some recall him lashing out, brusque with anyone who tried to offer comfort. Yet others remember a more vulnerable side. Michael Caine shared that the legendary Irving "Swifty" Lazar, who was Iz's agent, told him that Wilder slipped away to a nearby Hamburger Hamlet after the screening, overwhelmed by disappointment, where he sat and broke down in tears.

In the end, Wilder made only one minor cut, removing a single scene – the one on the train where Jerry climbs into bed with Joe, mistaking him for Sugar. Wilder had been uneasy about the sequence for a while, feeling it was unnecessary and slowed the pace. Curtis, ever blunt, claimed it was cut because it showed 'one man humping another.'[1]

The alteration had to be made quickly as another showing had already been scheduled. 'If you can't change the picture change the audience,' as Audrey quipped.[2] This time, the screening took place at The Village Theatre in Westwood, close to the UCLA campus, and from the start, the atmosphere was entirely different. Whereas the Bay had drawn an older, more affluent, family-oriented crowd, the Village Theatre brought in college students who were savvier, sharper and more attuned to risqué comedy. And crucially, they were let in on the joke from the very beginning. Instead of the usual on-screen card declaring "The Management is proud to present a major studio feature preview," the new version changed the last section to: "a minor studio feature preview." It was a small tweak, but it helped to ensure that people knew it was going to be a comedy.

Satisfied with the results and determined to make no more changes – Wilder also faced the crucial step of submitting the film to the Production Code Administration, a process he approached with some apprehension.

Wilder had already stopped submitting his scripts to the PCA in advance, even though the rules technically required it. Other than his stance on censorship not submitting a complete script also suited his and Diamond's working style – Wilder disliked locking in a script too early, treating it instead as a living document that evolved right up until the last day of shooting. Dialogue could be rewritten at any time; scenes could shift entirely so why restrict himself unnecessarily?

And for years, he had also played what he called a cat-and-mouse game with the PCA, first with Joseph Breen and, after Breen's retirement, with Geoffrey Shurlock who was Director between 1954 and the late 1960s when the Code was retired and replaced by the Motion Picture Association of America (MPAA) rating system. His skill at using suggestion rather than confrontation was one he credited to director Ernst Lubitsch, who

1. *Nobody's Perfect – The Making of Some Like It Hot* (October Films, 2001)
2. Castle, p. 292

had taught him how to get past the censors by allowing the audience's imagination to do the work. As Wilder put it, 'I learned from Lubitsch that the scene between two lovers the next morning tells you much more about their sexual behaviour than actually showing them having sex – and it pushes the story forward.'[3]

He may have been operating at the fringes of censorship but this was also smart film making. The slow erosion of the Production Code had been happening for years. Otto Preminger's *The Moon Is Blue* (1953) had been released without the PCA's official seal and, rather awkwardly, it still made money. The message was unambiguous – the PCA no longer held the power it once did.

Television had changed the game too. With sponsors steering clear of anything even slightly controversial, there was an opportunity for new movies to stand out by being more daring. Audiences were changing also. By 1957, a survey showed that seventy-two percent of American moviegoers were under thirty. They wanted stories that felt more grown-up, sharper, funnier, and bolder. Social tastes were shifting, and so were box office realities.

Even so *Some Like It Hot* pushed the boundaries more than most – especially with regards to sexual content, which wasn't graphic, but the innuendos were constant. The characters joked about sex, referenced past experiences, and spoke with a frankness that felt different, especially for women.

The women in Sweet Sue's band are brash, bold and love dirty jokes. At one stage, Sue even prompts Bienstock to remind them to tone down their language in front of Josephine and Daphne.

Sugar is presented as someone with a frank, unguarded approach to relationships, openly acknowledging a history of romances with saxophone with various bands over the last few years. She makes no attempt to disguise her past and reflects a more modern, independent attitude toward love and personal freedom in a way that makes Josephine and Daphne's prim, cautious ideas about how women behave seem almost quaint.

Which made Marilyn Monroe an even more perfect choice for the part.

Monroe spent much of her career negotiating the image that she had built up around her. A paradox – sexually experienced yet naive, sophisticated

3. Biltereyst, p. 146

yet innocent. She embodied both sex and wholesomeness at once – a duality often seen in portrayals of women of the period, especially in films and advertising. And her heightened femininity was, in its own way, as exaggerated as the men in drag.

She may have pushed back against the label of "sex symbol," but she also understood the opportunities it created. In what would be her final interview, she reflected on the inherent contradictions of this position. She argued that sexuality was most appealing when natural and spontaneous. Whilst she disliked being reduced to a symbol or 'a thing,' she joked that if she had to represent something, she would 'rather have it sex' than many of the alternatives.[4]

Still, the film's themes are not all subversive. Underneath the jokes and the boldness, some more traditional ideas remain. *Some Like It Hot* hints at the permissive 1960s but has its roots in a more conventional attitude towards love and marriage.

Sugar, for all her sexual confidence, is sad. She drinks to forget her repeated past abuses by men and dreams of one with money who'll take care of her. She wants romance, yes – but also marriage, or at least a future that feels secure.

This rather less than romantic ideal is also reiterated by Jerry, who himself has known a lot of financial insecurity and an uncertain future. This is a film about survival of various types after all. Asked by Joe why a man would marry a man, he answers: "Security." Then he jokes about annulments and alimony. For him love, not surprising considering the hardships he has endured, is less important than survival and protection.

Wilder was genuinely surprised when the PCA gave its official approval in February 1959 without the pushback many had expected.

However, within weeks, other moral watchdogs were making disapproving noises. Several of the state censor boards raised their own objections. The Kansas board took issue with the scenes on the yacht (and insisted on removing part of it), while in Memphis, the film was only allowed to be shown if it was labelled "Adults Only."

But none made more fuss than the National Legion of Decency. Founded in 1934, they produced ratings that were designed to guide Catholic audiences on what was considered morally acceptable, and historically a

4. Rolston, p. 62

negative rating could seriously damage a film's chances at the box office. Some in the industry may have dismissed the system as out of step or overly dramatic, but it still held real influence.

After learning of the PCA's approval the Legion's executive secretary, the Very Reverend Monsignor Thomas F. Little, fired off a strongly worded letter to Shurlock, accusing him of being far too lenient. He informed Shurlock that the Legion had given the film a "B" rating: "Morally Objectionable in Part for All," and listed several complaints. They said the content was offensive. The costumes, dialogue, and situations were called grossly suggestive. And they didn't hold back – going so far as to call parts of the film 'outright smut.'[5]

Shurlock, writing back to Little, stood by their decision. He pointed out that there had been no backlash from early previews, in fact, the film had received nothing but praise.

He acknowledged that the subject matter came with certain 'dangers,' but argued that drag for plot purposes had long been part of theatrical tradition – going back to *As You Like It* and *Twelfth Night*, and even earlier.

He ended on a dry note: 'We are of course not defending the two exaggerated costumes worn by the leading lady; but we gathered these were not your major concern.'[6]

5. Motion Picture Association of America Production Code Administration records, Margaret Herrick Library, Academy of Motion Picture Arts and Sciences.
6. Ibid.

Chapter Thirteen

Creating a Legend

At the same time as the moral controversy had been brewing, the publicity machine was already in motion. Anticipation for Wilder's latest film was building – and it needed to as there was a lot riding on its success.

Not only the eventual \$2.8 million cost, which was no small figure for the time but not particularly unusual (and certainly not proportional to all the press related fuss around it), but also the reputations of several major Hollywood players and businesses.

Like most movies of the era, *Some Like It Hot* would have to earn back its investment quickly. The industry relied on "front-loading" where most of a film's profits came in the first few weeks, before audience interest typically began to drop off. For a production that had gone over budget, those early days at the box office were especially vital and a slow start could spell disaster.

The studio and publicity teams pulled out every trick in the book – bold posters, carefully planted gossip, and just enough scandal to keep people talking.

One of the main tools in the team's arsenal was the classic two-minute theatrical trailer – shown to targeted audiences. The trailer integrated clips from the film with lively orchestral versions of featured songs playing underneath. The voiceover tied everything together in that familiar breathless Hollywood style, full of over-the-top hyperbole and dramatic flair:

"You've never laughed more at sex – or a picture about it!"

"Not since *Scarface* so much action. Not since the Marx Brothers so much comedy. Not since *The Seven Year Itch* so much Marilyn!"

Subtle it wasn't, but they knew exactly what they were doing, with the bold sexual content – and Monroe – front and centre in how the film was being pitched.

As the trailer came to a close, audiences were given another nudge: "Hear Marilyn sing the fabulous songs of the Roaring Twenties!"

This was a reference not only to within the movie but also to the official United Artists soundtrack album which was released concurrently. Whilst these albums were good cross promotions at the time soundtrack records weren't seen as major money-makers in their own right, their real value was to boost admissions.

At one point, there had even been plans to give *Some Like It Hot* its own theme song – a decision that went directly against Billy Wilder's instincts. He made no secret of his opinion – he thought title songs were tacky and unnecessary. But at the time, theme songs were expected. Studios liked them, and more often than not, they got their way.

So, composer Matty Malneck flew to New York to record the number with Marilyn. The result – simply titled *Some Like It Hot* – was released as a single and included on the soundtrack album. But it never actually made it into the final cut of the film.

Lemmon also used the platform to build his own musical ambitions – releasing *A Twist of Lemmon* (1958), an album of pop standards and jazz as well as *Jack Lemmon Sings and Plays Music From Some Like It Hot* through Epic Records the following year.

The cover notes for his second album promised broad appeal: "No matter what one's taste in popular music, Jack Lemmon is sure to please both those who like it hot and those who like it smooth, and he offers, moreover, a splendid souvenir of a delightful movie."

Another major part of the publicity push would come through advertising. Nearly $126,000 was spent across eight key cities – including New York, Los Angeles, and Chicago – with ads placed in multiple newspapers in each market. Another $47,000 was earmarked for radio and television spots.

But one print advert, in particular, got people talking.

The ad featured a cheeky caption: "*Marilyn Monroe and Her Bosom Companions – Tony Curtis and Jack Lemmon.*" It was all in keeping with the film's playful tone, but not everyone found it amusing. *The Washington Star*, a staunchly conservative paper, refused to run the advert unless the word "bosom" was removed and the space was left blank.

The minor scandal made the news, and the fuss over a single word brought the film even more attention.

Internally the marketing campaign also caused a few headaches, particularly from Tony Curtis.

He took issue with how his name appeared in some of the advertising.

He felt it was a violation of the "equal prominence" clause in his contract and had his lawyers contact the Mirisch Company to raise the matter formally.

They consulted their advertising team, who responded with practiced diplomacy and cutting sarcasm:

> 'As I understand your position, you are objecting to the fact that Mr Curtis' name appears on two lines, that is, his first name on one line and his last name on the second. In our opinion, and by our I mean the opinion of experienced advertising men who have spent their professional lives in this aspect of the business, this method of printing a name does not in any way detract from its prominence. At least it is not possible, we believe, to argue that one method creates a greater aura of prominence than the other.'[1]

Curtis hadn't just activated his lawyers he also reportedly raised the issue with Wilder himself – who was, predictably, less than sympathetic. Wilder is said to have curtly retorted: 'The trouble with you, Tony, is that you're only interested in little pants and big billing.'[2]

Ultimately, though, the film's most powerful marketing tool wasn't crafted in a studio office or dreamed up by a publicity team. Not officially, anyway. It was Marilyn – and the way that she was presented in the media.

The so-called "battle of wills" between Monroe and Wilder had been gleefully reported on throughout production and well after the cameras stopped rolling. The press framed it as a clash of temperaments – the sharp, disciplined director versus the troubled and unpredictable star who brought

1. United Artists Series 99AN/MCHC 82-046, box 5 folder 14, Wisconsin Center for Film and Theater Research.
2. Sikov, p. 412

her private turmoil onto the set. There was some truth in it, of course, but the coverage of her behaviour and tension was certainly exaggerated for effect.

Gossip columnists had a field day riffing on the long tradition of reporting on "difficult to work with" actresses. Marilyn was portrayed as unreliable, constantly late, demanding endless retakes, and slowing down production. Wilder, by contrast, was presented as the steady hand, a professional trying to get his film made against overwhelming odds. This courtesy was extended to him despite the well-publicised conflicts with other writers and actors, including Humphrey Bogart, that had been a consistent feature of his career.

Once again, Monroe found herself the subject of constant commentary – at the centre of a media storm every bit as unkind as the one she had weathered during her disputes with Fox.

Two pieces in particular stood out, both filed after production had finished, and neither did anyone involved any favours.

The first article appeared in *TIME* magazine on 17 November 1958. Written in a sarcastic tone, it questions whether 'type-cast sexpot' Monroe could retain her appeal while pregnant and attempting to 'rise to higher levels of intellect?'. The piece claimed that her love scenes with Curtis lacked warmth and including a colourful Wilder analogy comparing her to a Swiss clock which you 'have to shake a little – not just any old way – but just so.' Curtis was also mocked, portrayed as a relatively unsophisticated actor still dazzled by the prospect of acting a love scene opposite Monroe.[3]

The second appeared in *Parade* magazine on 7 December, under the leading headline *How much time and trouble is Marilyn Monroe?* To journalist Lloyd Shearer, who had been a frequent visitor to the set, Wilder openly admitted his frustrations with Monroe's lateness, illnesses, reliance on acting coaches and the production delays that followed. Yet he also emphasised that these difficulties were outweighed by the unique and 'indefinable magic' she bought to the screen, something he believed no other actress could replicate. To illustrate the point, he contrasted her with his actress aunt in Vienna 'She always comes to the set on time.

3. Cast of Characters, *TIME*, 17 November 1958, p. 74

She knows her lines perfectly .. At the box office she is worth fourteen cents.'

Harold Mirisch also chimed in, estimating that Marilyn had delayed production by about two weeks and pushed the budget almost to breaking point. '[T]o answer your question. Just how much Marilyn is worth in time, trouble and money? We'll have to wait until the picture is released to find that out.'

But the bit that reportedly stung Marilyn the most came at the end of the piece. An unnamed actor – identified only as someone involved with the film – was quoted as saying: 'Marilyn is a dear, sweet, sincere, adorable girl. I hope she settles down with Arthur Miller and has a half dozen children. I know she has made a wonderful wife, and she will make an even more wonderful mother. But a great actress she ain't.'[4]

The frequency and unprofessionalism of these pieces prompted Joe Wolhandler, vice president of the publicity firm Rogers & Cowan, who were handling the film, to intervene. He wrote to reassure Marilyn, pointing specifically to the *TIME* piece, which he described as 'in a class by itself for unmitigated nastiness and inaccuracy.'

He added that the agency didn't believe anyone involved had been quoted correctly and had asked *TIME* for a retraction – though, as he admitted, 'knowing them, I don't know if we will get it.'[5]

It all left a sour taste that only deepened over the following year as Wilder continued to stoke the fire with a series of interviews reflecting on their time working together.

The most brutal of these interviews was published on 10 February in the *New York Herald Tribune*. In a column by Joe Hyams, pointedly titled *Film Director Asks Purple Heart After Two Pictures With Marilyn* – Wilder let loose again, in typically misogynistic fashion.

He joked that his health had improved after finishing work with Monroe, noting that he was eating better, sleeping properly for the first time in months, and no longer wanted to take out his frustrations on his wife. When asked if he would consider working with her again, he jested that he had

4. How Much Time and Trouble is Marilyn Monroe Worth, *Paradė*, 7 December 1958, pp. 20-21
5. Rollyson, Carl *Marilyn Monroe: Day by Day*, Bowman and Littlefield, 2014, p. 209

discussed it with his physical and mental health professionals, who advised him against it.

After reading the *Herald Tribune* piece Monroe apparently phoned gossip columnist Earl Wilson to give her response, pushing back against claims about her on-set temperament by suggesting that it was often the director's who got to behave erratically. Wilson also reported that she felt the production had come at a personal cost during a difficult period in her life. Separately Augusta, Miller's mother, blamed Wilder more directly allegedly that she had been made to repeatedly run up stairs in extreme heat while already unwell.

Whether that was true – or even fair – is impossible to say. Curtis, in one of his memoirs, dismissed the charge entirely. He wrote that the set never reached temperatures above eighty degrees and that she, in his opinion, hadn't done anything physically demanding enough to cause such harm.

But the real feud turned out to be between Miller and Wilder. Miller insisted, loudly and publicly, that Marilyn's pregnancy loss had been brought on by overwork during filming.

To Miller, Wilder was a cold, sarcastic dictator – quick with a wisecrack but slow to show any empathy. Miller believed Marilyn had given a remarkable performance under enormous pressure, and he couldn't understand how Wilder could continue mocking her in the press. Years later, when asked by German filmmaker Volker Schlöndorff what he thought of Wilder, Miller didn't hesitate. 'He was a bastard,' he said.[6]

Wilder, in turn, was baffled by Miller's unwavering defence. He saw Monroe's behaviour as, at best, disruptive and, at worst, completely unprofessional. And he couldn't quite believe Miller's refusal to acknowledge it, especially as a fellow artist.

The tension between them soon boiled over into what was gleefully dubbed a "telegram war."

On 11 February 1959, at exactly 9:28 a.m., Miller fired the first shot, via Western Union. He refused, he said, to let Wilder's 'vicious attack' on his wife go unanswered. That she had started filming with a severe throat infection against specialist advice. That Wilder had been informed by her physician that she was pregnant and medically unable to work full days, yet had ignored this during production and, worse, failed to

6. Phillips, p. 222

mention it in his public criticisms. Monroe, Miller insisted, had continued filming out of professional responsibility – to the studio, the cast and to Wilder himself. For Wilder now to mock her in the press, he argued, was contemptible. [7]

Wilder's reply was characteristically sharp. The rumours of Monroe's unreliability, he maintained, had been circulating since the earliest days of the shoot, and reporters from London, Paris and Berlin had pressed him for comment. He had deflected them, even lied to protect her. The interview that angered Miller, he claimed, had actually softened what might have been far harsher conclusions. While expressing sorrow over her pregnancy loss, Wilder firmly rejected any suggestion that overwork or mistreatment had caused it. On the contrary, he wrote, the production had indulged her at every turn. Had Miller endured what he had, Wilder concluded acidly, he might have 'thrown her out on her can, thermos bottle and all, to avoid a nervous breakdown. I did the braver thing. I had a nervous breakdown.' [8]

Miller's anger hadn't been satiated by just sending messages to Wilder. He also wired Joe Hyams, the journalist behind the *Herald Tribune* piece that had published Wilder's pointed remarks, accusing him of warping the truth for the sake of a good story. [9]

Arthur still wasn't finished. The following day, 12 February, he sent another furious telegram to Wilder. The fact that others might have criticised her, he argued, did not excuse Wilder from doing so publicly. Whatever the difficulties, she had done her job – and done it superbly. And to belittle this achievement with a joke was not merely unfair but improper, especially coming from the man that benefited most from it. [10]

Wilder responded again, this time adopting exaggerated humility to hasten a truce. In the interest of 'burying the hatchet,' he declared Monroe a unique and blameless personality and himself the villain. Concluding 'in the immortal words of Joe E. Brown – "Nobody is Perfect."'[11]

---

7. Billy Wilder papers, Margaret Herrick Library, Academy of Motion Picture Arts and Sciences.
8. Ibid.
9. Ibid.
10. Ibid.
11. Ibid.

A few months later the temperature between the two had cooled. Wilder sent Miller a final telegram in a markedly lighter tone, expressing hope that they had made peace and urging him to read a glowing review of the film that he had enclosed. He signed off with his best to Marilyn.[12] And with that, the so-called "telegram war" fizzled out. But the damage lingered and neither man ever seemingly forgave the other.

12. Ibid.

Chapter Fourteen

Premieres and the First Run

Small, select screenings came first – the usual Hollywood way of testing the waters. After the initial previews but before the big, glittering premieres, *Some Like It Hot* was released to industry insiders whilst also giving many of the cast the opportunity to see it for the first time in full.

One such evening was 25 February 1959, at the Screen Directors Guild on Sunset Boulevard. After the screening, Paul Nathan, a producer with Hal Wallis Productions, dashed off a note to Walter Mirisch, full of delight: 'It's hysterically funny, wildly dirty and will probably make millions of dollars. If it doesn't, then I think we all ought to give up.'[1]

Elsewhere, the promotional machine was doing its usual slightly absurd work. Various newspapers announced a contest to find Monroe look-a-likes – promising prizes that included "a voluptuous evening gown" and an all-expenses trip to the gala opening of the film in New York City complete with guaranteed newsreel and TV coverage of the winners' arrival. All the entrants needed to do was send a photograph, along with their name, age, address, weight, height, and hair colour. A panel of three "businessmen" (of course) would choose the winner. The eventual victors were said to have had a great couple of days but were left rather disappointed as they did not actually get to meet Monroe.

Meanwhile, the House of James salons struck an exclusive deal with United Artists to promote "The Cocktail Soufflé," billed as the new hairstyle of the year as, 'worn by Marilyn Monroe.'[2]

The film rolled out nationwide in March, with the first of several glittering premieres held, fittingly, in Chicago. And on the 19th of the

1. Box 1 Folder 6, Mirisch Corporation Records (Collection 1146). UCLA Library Special Collections, Charles E. Young Research Library, University of California, Los Angeles.
2. Advert, *The Indianapolis Star*, 30 March 1959, p. 8

month, the crowds at the United Artists Theatre buzzed with anticipation, elevated by the promise of Monroe's appearance. For Marilyn it marked the first and only Chicago premiere of her career, and for the city, it was a major event. Still, the *Chicago Tribune* couldn't resist a jab, suggesting she'd only agreed to attend after being falsely told that Monroe Street was named in her honour.

Marilyn was to arrive the day before the premiere, accompanied by her press agent, her secretary, and Kenneth Battelle – better known as the "Hairdresser of the Stars." Mr. Kenneth had trained at various beauty schools before launching his career in Manhattan, first at Helena Rubinstein's salon on 52nd and Fifth Avenue, and later rising to head hairdresser at Lilly Daché's prestigious salon on East 56th Street. Over time, he built a clientele of some of the most prominent women in America, including Jacqueline Kennedy.

Marilyn had begun seeing Mr. Kenneth after the designer Norman Norell recommended him, hoping to undo the damage her hair had suffered from excessive bleaching and perming. He succeeded, and from then on became her trusted stylist whenever she was on the East Coast.

Monroe arrived in Chicago to a flurry of media attention, a mob scene as Mr. Kenneth described it later. Marilyn, he recalled, didn't fuss much over clothes or jewellery. Before leaving New York, she had bought three simple silk shift dresses (white, black, and tan) from Jax on 57th and 5th, borrowed a mink from Maximilian, and threw on two strings of pearls.

Emery Hutchinson of the *Chicago Daily News* noted that she stepped off her American Airlines flight at Midway Airport 'sporting light beige-colored hair and a full-length mink to match.'[3] Reporters immediately peppered her with questions, including a predictable one about her weight. With great self-control, she smiled and replied, 'Activity takes care of the poundage.'[4]

From the airport, she made her way to the Ambassador East Hotel, where a press luncheon had been arranged in her honour – an event beautifully captured by photographer Manfred Kreiner.

---

3. This Week in history, *Chicago Sun Time*, 5 August 2020, https://chicago.suntimes.com/2020/8/5/21356077/this-week-in-history-marilyn-monroe-chicago-some-like-it-hot accessed 1 February 2025
4. Ibid

Now dressed in the white shift, things didn't get off to a smooth start as a nervous photographer accidentally spilled a drink all over her. One journalist praised her poise, noting that she 'remained calm, showed no anger, didn't act like the great star she was.'[5] But Mr. Kenneth remembered the outcome quite different: 'You could see everything,' he later said. He urged her to put on underwear but she refused, insisting it left lines. Laughing, she supposedly added, 'Jean Harlow didn't wear underwear either.' According to him, he then dashed to the hotel drugstore and returned with powdered milk of magnesia, twenty percent peroxide, and spirits of ammonia, an old-school formula for decolouring hair and told her to go back to her room and 'bleach it.'[6]

The press, as usual, also couldn't resist commenting on her punctuality, with reports once again suggesting that she was late. But, this time, that particular criticism was met with a firm defence. Mae Tinee of the *Chicago Tribune* pushed back against the criticism, arguing that the charge of her lateness – on this occasion at least – was unfair. She noted that Monroe arrived only a short time after the scheduled start and pointed out that a press agent had mistakenly directed her to Ambassador West rather than the Ambassador East hotel. In Tinee's view, the delay was insignificant, and she remarked that she had frequently 'waited longer than that for lesser stars.'[7]

The next day marked the grand premiere. Newspaper ads blared with excitement: "In Person! Marilyn Monroe On Stage! One Appearance Only at 12 Noon!" And the promise of seeing her in the flesh drew thousands of fans into the streets.

Mr. Kenneth recalled the chaos vividly He said that as he, Marilyn, and a publicity man that had been sent to accompany them by the studio approached the theatre, their car was surrounded by thousands of screaming fans. People climbed onto the vehicle, tried to force their way inside, and rocked it from side to side. He locked the doors as the crowd pressed in around them. And as they did Marilyn became increasingly distressed as was everyone else in the car. They eventually reached the theatre entrance

5. Rollyson, p. 215
6. Longo, Giuseppe. *Kenneth: Shear Elegance*, Schiffer Publishing, 2020, p. 76
7. They All Came Running to See Marilyn, *Chicago Tribune*, 29 March 1959, p. 143

after their driver slowly forced the car through the crowd, arriving, in his words 'in a state of near collapse.'[8]

After the Chicago premiere, Marilyn returned to New York ahead of the next major event to be held at Loew's State Theatre at 1540 Broadway.

Originally opened in August 1921, Loew's had a rich history, once hosting vaudeville acts alongside second-run films, those already successful elsewhere and brought back for wider audiences. Vaudeville came to an end there in the late 1940s, and from then on, Loew's began competing for first-run releases and major film premieres.

It had recently closed for a year-long renovation, fully modernising to meet the demands of the evolving movie industry. The upgrades included compatibility with CinemaScope and VistaVision wide-screen formats, and a new interior colour scheme of sophisticated beige and gold which gave the venue a fresh, upscale feel.

The gala event on Saturday, 28 March 1959, marked both the New York premiere of *Some Like It Hot* and the grand reopening of the refurbished cinema. Invitations were issued – a folded ticket which opened to reveal photographs of Josephine and Daphne lying down and gazing up at a playful 3D pop-up insert of Sugar playing her ukulele. Guests were instructed to dress formally, black tie only, for the 6:30 p.m. start.

On the night, Marilyn arrived arm-in-arm with a tuxedoed Arthur Miller, turning heads in a shimmering silver-toned evening gown and a lavish ermine coat. Though radiant, she seemed a touch anxious. During brief radio and television interviews outside, she stammered occasionally, her confidence faltering slightly, perhaps uncertain how the film would be received, overwhelmed by the enormous crowd that had gathered or maybe just not too keen on seeing it again.

There is no public record of what she truly thought of the film but privately, there was talk of her disappointment, of her being "in despair" after seeing a preview.

As usual Norman Rosten was there to reassure her.

> 'About the movie – don't jump! Look at it this way: it is a completely enjoyable film, full of fun and YOU. It is not a starring vehicle for you because the story is simply not

8. Longo, p. 76

> set up that way … BUT … nothing could really destroy your wonderful quality that gives the film the one touch of "seriousness" (humanity) it needs for any sort of balance. It will not hurt you one little bit, and let everyone be more watchful the next time."[9]

Miller reportedly found it charming – delightful, even. But for Marilyn, everything was far more complicated and was tainted by her experiences while filming. Nevertheless, she had done the promotion, appeared at two major premieres – once alone, and in New York alongside other stars, including George Raft.

Tony Curtis, however, was noticeably absent at any of the events. Officially, he cited scheduling conflicts, but his personal life was also marked by turmoil. His father had a heart attack and passed away shortly after filming ended in November, and then his second daughter, Jamie Lee, was born a few days later. Curtis admitted he had fallen into a deep depression and said he was barely keeping up with what was happening with the film as he had already moved onto his next project. However, he also acknowledged that taking on the role had ultimately been beneficial, as it helped him establish himself as a major player and let to roles that both accommodated and expanded his talent.

Whilst the previews, premieres and early trade reviews had been largely positive within the production team there was still an undercurrent of anxiety. Diamond recalled that the film's first week felt underwhelming, and Walter admitted he had also been concerned.

Yet the box office numbers told a very different story. By late March and based on returns from only six major cities, *Variety* had already ranked *Some Like It Hot* as the third highest-grossing film in the United States. Harold wrote to Marilyn in New York to update her: 'You know, of course, that the picture is doing tremendous business, and you should be very happy.'[10]

---

9. Rollyson, p. 211
10. Julien's Auctions, *Hollywood Legends 2013,* Lot #771, 5 April 2013 https://bid.juliensauctions.com/lot-details/index/catalog/90/lot/38912/marilyn-monroe-received-some-like-it-hot-note

Word of mouth spread quickly, and as the film reached more auditoriums, its momentum only grew. When it opened at Grauman's Chinese Theatre in Hollywood on 8 April, it stayed for an extraordinary nine-week run, which was almost unheard of at the time. A relieved Diamond called it 'one of those rare phenomena in the picture business – it just kept building.'[11] Soon the film had climbed to number one at the box office, holding the top position for several weeks and even reclaiming it after briefly slipping down.

It was a remarkable achievement – made all the more impressive given the fierce competition that year which also saw the release of the blockbuster *Ben-Hur*, *Compulsion*, and *The Long, Hot Summer*, along with popular comedies like *Auntie Mame* and *The Shaggy Dog*. By the end of the year, *Some like It Hot* was on track to become one of the highest grossing pictures for United Artists, with the exception of *Around the World in Eighty Days* (1956), starring David Niven.

With *Some Like It Hot* fully launched in the U.S., it was time to head across the Atlantic for the European leg of the publicity tour, which included stops in thirteen cities. The film faced strict age restrictions in many countries – except in France, where it was awarded an "all audiences" certificate.

The Hollywood delegation to Europe was an impressive one – the Wilders, the Diamonds, several members of the Mirisch family, and Jack Lemmon. They made the journey in true style aboard the SS *United States*, the sleek, state-of-the-art ocean liner that, at the time, symbolised the height of transatlantic glamour.

There's a wonderful story from that voyage. Among the *United States'* other illustrious passengers were the Duke and Duchess of Windsor. *Some Like It Hot* was screened in the ship's cinema, and midway through, the royal pair apparently tried to slip out early to avoid the crowd. But a steward stopped them with a firm, 'You don't want to miss this.' According to Diamond, the Duke and Duchess obediently sat back down. At dinner that evening, the delegation from America were seated near to the Windsors. A companion leaned towards the royal pair and whispered, 'I think one of the actors from that picture is at the next

11. Curtis & Vieira, p. 1

table.' 'The one I liked?' asked the Duke loudly. 'No, dear,' replied the Duchess, 'the other one.'[12]

When they docked at the Southampton Ocean Terminal on 14 May, Wilder seemed in high spirits from the experience: 'It went down great,' he told reporters with a grin. 'They tell me it's the first time the Duke has ever sat through a two-hour film.' When Lemmon was asked how it was to work with Marilyn, he gave a perfect, diplomatic reply: 'Divine. What do you think?'[13] Wilder later noted that Jack was 'incapable of saying anything mean or unpleasant about anyone. He's compassionate. He'll always find a way of saying something nice about other people.'[14]

Wilder planned to stay on in England for a few days, telling journalists he wanted to 'take in the galleries.' He acknowledged being a collector of modern art. 'My wife lets me spend a mere few hundred pounds on paintings,' he said. 'Anything more valuable, we go into conference – and that may mean talking her out of a pair of earrings.'[15]

His passion for art, in fact, went far beyond a casual hobby. With his habit of treating himself to a new painting each time he finished a movie Wilder would go on to amass one of the most extensive private collections in Hollywood, once calling it a "sickness" and confessing he didn't know how to stop himself. To celebrate his considerable earnings from this project, he had bought pieces by Paul Klee, one of his favourite artists.

That same evening, the London Pavilion in Piccadilly Circus hosted the film's gala premiere, described by one newspaper as full of 'gimmicks, glamorous guests and gaiety.'[16] Entry was by invitation only, and the guest list was suitably star-studded, including the British actor John Mills in attendance with his wife, Mary, and young daughter Hayley. Inside, Walter Mirisch, Wilder, and Lemmon watched as the film played to a packed house and was met with thunderous applause.

The next day, at a press reception held at the Savoy Hotel, Wilder was, predictably, asked about Marilyn. His reply was more measured than previously but was still biting: 'She is unique. I'm still not sure after

12. Sikov, p. 427
13. Windsors preview, *Daily Herald*, 14 May 1959, p. 2
14. Freedland, p. 774
15. Windsors preview, *Daily Herald*, 14 May 1959, p. 2
16. London Pavilion Goes Gay For Premiere of "Some Like It Hot," *Kinematograph Weekly*, 21 May 1959, p. 7

directing her whether she is a good actress or not, but she is brilliant at putting over a comedy line. She has that rare charm of being completely oblivious of her physical endowments.'[17]

With the film's popularity now seemingly established, the next logical step was a focus on awards season. In October, Leon Roth of the Mirisch Company wrote to Roger Lewis outlining plans 'to make a drive for major Academy Award nominations.'[18] This was scheduled to begin on 1 December and continue through January the following year – timed precisely to coincide with the period when ballots would be sent to Academy members.

The strategy focused on a steady stream of advertising, with plans for one or two ads per week – twelve in total. The entire campaign was to run exclusively in industry publications like *Variety* and *The Hollywood Reporter*. To support the effort, they proposed a starting budget of $12,000, which would include the hiring of a dedicated publicity officer to drive the campaign for its duration.

They also planned to bring Saul Bass on board. Widely regarded as the most influential graphic designer of his time, Bass, often working closely with Elaine, his wife and creative partner, revolutionised visual storytelling. By the late 1950s, he had begun moving seamlessly between poster design and title sequences, forging a bold, modern style that made his work instantly recognisable.

His film credits already included iconic designs for *The Man with the Golden Arm* (1955) and *Vertigo* (1958), among others. Wilder, a longtime admirer and supporter of Bass, had already collaborated with him on the title sequence for *The Seven Year Itch* and the advertising campaign for *Love in the Afternoon*.

Bass's eventual campaign for *Some Like It Hot* is widely regarded as some of his most inventive and accomplished work. Bass created a series of distinct advertisements; each built around a central visual concept that played with the film's themes in witty and unexpected ways.

---

17. Rare Charm, *Daily News (London),* 15 May 1959, p. 3
18. Box 1 Folder 5, Mirisch Corporation Records (Collection 1146). UCLA Library Special Collections, Charles E. Young Research Library, University of California, Los Angeles.

Each graphic told the story visually, without relying on stills from the film. The trade reviews and predictions of award success became part of the composition, and the words are shown being poured into alcohol bottles, inside a musical instrument case, a sailing boat bobbing inside a bathtub and making up the flattened body of a gangster. It is a striking and sophisticated campaign that certainly captures attention.

The 1960 award (honouring films released in 1959) season kicked off with one of the most prestigious honours in Hollywood – The Golden Globes. First established in 1944 by the Hollywood Foreign Press Association, the ceremony had become a major indicator of industry recognition. That year's event took place in March, at the iconic Cocoanut Grove nightclub in the basement of the Ambassador Hotel, Los Angeles.

Marilyn Monroe was in attendance and won "Best Actress – Musical or Comedy," before being photographed beaming as she clutched her award. She wasn't alone in her victory – Jack Lemmon took home "Best Actor" in the same category, and the film itself was awarded "Best Motion Picture – Musical or Comedy."

Next came the 32nd Academy Awards, held on 4 April at the magnificent RKO Pantages Theatre in Hollywood. *Some Like It Hot* was nominated for multiple Oscars, including: "Best Actor" for Lemmon, "Best Director" for Billy Wilder, "Best Adapted Screenplay" for Wilder and Diamond, "Best Art Direction (Black-and-White)" for Ted Haworth and Edward G. Boyle, "Best Cinematography (Black-and-White)" for Charles Lang, and "Best Costume Design (Black-and-White)" for Orry-Kelly.

Curtis later admitted he was deeply disappointed not to receive an Oscar nomination. While acknowledging that Lemmon's nod was 'richly deserved,' he said his 'heart ached' at being overlooked. 'Nothing. Nothing.'[19]

The anticipation surrounding the awards that year was memorably captured in a striking illustration by artist Al Hirschfeld, whose unmistakable line work and sly wit had become a beloved part of American visual culture.

Hirschfeld had begun his career in the publicity department of Goldwyn Pictures. He later worked as an art director at both Universal

19. Curtis & Golenbock, p. 216

and Selznick Pictures before going freelance, spending time in Paris in the mid-1920s and eventually returning to the U.S., where he was commissioned by the *New York Herald* and became a regular contributor to the *New York Times*. Rather than designing illustrated film posters, an art form that had waned by the late 1940s in favour of photographic marketing, Hirschfeld found his niche in newspapers and magazines, creating caricatures that became synonymous with Broadway, Hollywood, and the awards season.

A hallmark of his work was the hidden inclusion of his daughter's name, NINA, concealed at least once in nearly every drawing he made after her birth in 1945. Beginning at the suggestion of a reader, Hirschfeld also started placing a number next to his signature indicating how many "NINA's" were hidden in that particular drawing, adding an interactive challenge that readers came to love even more.

In 1956, he began producing publicity sketches in association with United Artists, often joining film crews on location. He travelled the country by train, visiting UA sets and filling a sketchbook with vivid impressions of films in production.

For the 1960 Academy Awards, Hirschfeld created a delightful composite illustration of the "Best Actor" and "Best Actress" nominees, drawn in character and in costume. Among those featured were Charlton Heston in *Ben-Hur*, Doris Day in *Pillow Talk*, Jack Lemmon as Daphne, Katharine Hepburn in *Suddenly, Last Summer*, Audrey Hepburn in *The Nun's Story*, Paul Muni in *The Last Angry Man*, and James Stewart in *Anatomy of a Murder*.

Expectations had been high, but the film was up against *Ben-Hur*, William Wyler's epic that dominated the night with a record-breaking eleven Oscar wins. Despite being nominated in so many categories, *Some Like It Hot* walked away with only one – given to Orry-Kelly.

There's a fascinating surviving recording of the costume design award presentation. Bob Hope, the evening's host, introduced the actors Arlene Dahl and her husband Fernando Lamas. Dahl began:

> "In motion pictures the classic function of the costume designer is to provide clothing that furthers the story, its theme and its mood. And to help actors better realise the characters they portray."

Lamas added:

> "This year, because of the wide variety of stories selected for the big screen, our costume designers faced an even greater challenge to authenticity than ever before."

Dahl continued:

> "This then is not a fashion show but a parade of the brilliant achievements of our industry's costume designers."

As the nominees were read – Edith Head (*Career*), Charles LeMaire and Mary Wills (*The Diary of Anne Frank*), Helen Rose (*The Gazebo*), Howard Shoup (*The Young Philadelphians*), and Orry-Kelly – actresses walked down a catwalk modelling a costume from each film. When the woman in the iconic *I'm Thru With Love* gown walked the stage, Lamas audibly said, "Wow."

When Orry-Kelly was announced the winner, he skipped onto the stage to the tune of *Runnin' Wild* and charmed the audience with his brief acceptance speech and Australian accent: 'Thank you … particularly Tony Curtis and Jack Lemmon.' Then with a mischievous grin, he added: 'As Louella would say – "They never looked lovelier."'

Despite not being nominated Tony Curtis was there and even presented one of the evening's awards, but Monroe was absent. In fact, she only ever attended the ceremony once, in 1951, when she presented the Oscar for "Best Sound Recording" to Thomas Moulton for his work on *All About Eve*, a film in which she had a small supporting role. Despite her appearances in numerous critically acclaimed films, and many co-stars' assertions of her incredible talent, she was never nominated for an Academy Award.

Though overlooked as a nominee, she was a member of the Academy. A series of letters traces her induction. In October 1958 whilst filming *Some Like It Hot* she had received an official invitation on Academy letterhead, signed by then-president George Stevens. In January the following year, Monroe finally responded, apologising for the delay, explaining she had been 'indisposed and away,' and asked for further details regarding the Academy's by-laws. A reply from executive director Margaret Herrick followed, enclosing the requested documents. Finally, as the film was premiering, Monroe received her formal welcome along with a membership card.[20]

Wilder, suspecting *Some Like It Hot* would be overwhelmed by *Ben-Hur*'s dominance, also chose not to attend the ceremony. Instead, he went to a private viewing party where, in a rare lapse of control, he drank heavily – reportedly consuming a dozen martinis – before locking himself in the bathroom. According to those present, Kirk Douglas had to break the door down, carry him to his limousine and send him home.

Wilder eventually recovered enough to praise Saul Bass's campaign illustrations for the film, telling him, 'Brilliant, brilliant. I laughed and laughed. So did everyone – but I still didn't get an Oscar.' Then, pausing for effect, he added, 'Maybe your designs made people think the movie was going to be as funny as the advertisements.'[21]

Despite Oscar disappointment the film continued to collect accolades across the international industry landscape. Jack Lemmon won the British Academy of Film and Television Arts (BAFTA) for "Best Foreign Actor." Wilder was nominated for "Best Film from Any Source" at the same ceremony. He was also recognised by his peers with a nomination for "Outstanding Directorial Achievement in Motion Pictures" from the Directors Guild of America. Meanwhile, the Writers Guild of America honoured Wilder and Iz with the award for "Best Written American Comedy" for the screenplay.

In the end, *Some Like It Hot* could be considered an absolutely resounding success, far exceeding the cautious hopes of those behind it. By 1962, in addition to all the awards, the film had grossed $14 million in the United States alone.

And it all helped solidify the Mirisch brother's reputation as the era's standout independent production house. In its first six years of operation, the Mirisch Company produced twenty three films for release through United Artists, earning an impressive thirty five Academy Award nominations and winning sixteen.

In 1972 Walter and Marvin (Harold died in 1968) reflected on some of their successes including *Some Like It Hot*. 'We look back to it with

20. Julien's Auctions, *Property From the Estate of Lee Strasberg*, Lot #313, 17 November 2016 https://bid.juliensauctions.com/lot-details/index/catalog/180/lot/83198
21. Bass, Jennifer & Pat Kirkham. *Saul Bass: A Life in Film & Design*, Laurence King Publishing, 2016, p. 156

fond memories. The potential of film in those days, though didn't compare with the potential of film today, even with the attraction of star names like Marilyn Monroe and Jack Lemmon and Tony Curtis, wasn't as great. Were we to have *Some Like It Hot* now, I think it would be a much more immense success than it was at the time it was made.'[22]

Although the company was eventually formally acquired by United Artists the brothers continued producing films for them under various corporate names, still working out of their familiar rented offices at Samuel Goldwyn Studios, just as Wilder and Diamond did too. Remarkably, that old complex is still with us although it has changed hands and names over the decades. Warner Bros. purchased the site in 1980 and renamed it Warner Hollywood Studios; it was later sold to private investors, eventually becoming The Lot at Formosa.

As it happens, I have unknowingly stood outside it myself. Back in 2023 – long before I'd begun formally researching this book – I was in Los Angeles working on a project about the nightlife of Golden Age Hollywood. I stopped at the Formosa Café, had two very good cocktails and some excellent dim sum, and found myself drawn to the building across the street. It looked intriguing, studio-like, so I took a few photos intending to look it up when I got home. I had no idea at the time that I was standing in front of somewhere that would come to mean so much to me and hold such a fascinating place in Hollywood history. What a missed opportunity!

United Artists continued its remarkable ascent through the 1960s. In stark contrast to many of the traditional Hollywood studios, which either collapsed or were absorbed into larger conglomerates during the turbulent years that followed – they not only survived but actually thrived. They built a strong television division and released a string of major hit movies, including *West Side Story* (1961) and *It's A Mad, Mad, Mad, Mad World* (1963). They also capitalised cleverly on the transatlantic appeal of "Swinging London," collaborating with director Richard Lester to bring *A Hard Day's Night* (1964) and *Help!* (1965) to the screen – effectively introducing The Beatles to American film audiences.

One of UA's most lucrative moves, however, was backing the company that had acquired the screen rights to Ian Fleming's James Bond novels. The

22. United Artists Series 99AN/MCHC 82-046, box 5 folder 14, *Wisconsin Center* for Film and Theater Research.

film franchise launched in 1962 with *Dr. No*, and by the time *Thunderball* arrived in 1965, it was popular enough to pull in nearly $26 million – making it the sixth highest-grossing film of the entire decade.

Hollywood was, again, facing mounting challenges. The movie-going habit that had once been a weekly ritual was rapidly declining, and ever escalating production costs meant that every film carried enormous financial risk. Yet, when the formula was right – when they found the perfect combination of story, star power and marketing – films could still become major events and generate massive profits.

As the 1960s progressed, UA also managed to pivot smoothly towards the increasingly influential 16-24 year-old audience – the demographic actually buying most of the movie tickets at that point. With the nostalgic *Bonnie and Clyde* (1967), *The Graduate* (1967), and *Easy Rider* (1969), the studio aligned itself with the cultural and cinematic shifts of the era.

They were then acquired by the San Francisco-based Transamerica Corporation and began operating under the formal banner United Artists – A Transamerica Company.

However, it faltered under the new management and began haemorrhaging money, prompting the return of former executives Arthur Krim and Robert Benjamin. Their response was swift and severe – they slashed overheads, including cutting one-sixth of its global workforce, and gradually began rebuilding their fortunes.

The steady income from the James Bond franchise helped keep UA afloat during these uncertain years, but the real revival came in the mid-1970s with a stunning streak of Best Picture winners: *One Flew Over the Cuckoo's Nest* (1975), *Rocky* (1976), and *Annie Hall* (1977). Bond remained a steady draw with *The Spy Who Loved Me* (1977), and the *Pink Panther* series also performed well at the box office.

But power struggles and internal discord ultimately led Krim, Benjamin, and other key executives to depart and launch a rival studio, Orion Pictures. However, despite the turbulence, 1979 turned out to be United Artists' most profitable year to date, with hit films like *Manhattan*, *Moonraker*, and *Rocky II* drawing large audiences.

Meanwhile, the original generation that had built the original company were dying. Charlie Chaplin had passed away on Christmas Day in 1977, and Mary Pickford in May 1979. It was a symbolic end of an era. By the 1980s, they was struggling to stay relevant in a new Hollywood landscape that would be dominated by big-budget blockbusters and franchises like *Star Wars* (1977), *Raiders of the Lost Ark* (1981), *E.T.* (1982), and *Back to the Future* (1985). A string of high-profile flops damaged them further. As Charles Schreger of the *Los Angeles Times* put it: 'Quite simply, UA, a company that was viewed historically as vibrant and innovative, has fallen into the hands of the money men.'[23] United Artists was eventually purchased by MGM and folded into the newly formed MGM/UA Entertainment Corporation, marking the end of that particular era.

23. Bergan, Ronald. *The United Artists Story*, Octopus Books, 1986, p. 293

Chapter Fifteen

After the Hot Air Cooled

In September 1959, Monroe and Wilder crossed paths once more – at one of the most talked-about social events of the year, hosted by Twentieth Century-Fox. The guest of honour was Nikita Khrushchev, leader of the Soviet Union and First Secretary of the Communist Party, then midway through a high-profile thirteen day tour of the United States.

The dinner took place in the studio's famed Café de Paris, a commissary where everyone on the lot ate. Built in the late 1920s, it had earned a reputation as the most glamorous of all the studio canteens. When it opened, stars like Will Rogers and Fifi D'Orsay were among its first guests, and by 1932, vibrant Art Deco murals depicting Hollywood legends and world capitals had been added to the decoration.

With only 400 seats available, the Khrushchev gathering was very exclusive. While a few major names, such as Ronald Reagan and Bing Crosby, declined the invitation for political reasons, the guest list still glittered with stars, including Frank Sinatra, Dean Martin, Judy Garland, Tony Curtis, Kirk Douglas, Zsa Zsa Gabor, and Henry Fonda.

Guests were asked to arrive by noon and Wilder showed up at 11:45. To his surprise (and amusement) he found Marilyn Monroe already there, seated with director Joshua Logan. Wilder couldn't resist getting a dig in the press, joking that someone had finally managed to get Monroe to arrive on time and suggesting that Kruschev would therefore be better suited to direct all her films.

When she spotted him, Marilyn ran over and the two embraced. A few months later, Wilder told columnist Art Buchwald that they had called a truce and were 'good pals again,' even acknowledging that he might considering working with her again if the right project came along. When reminded of his earlier vow never to direct her again, Wilder laughed, comparing it to the dislike you feel for your dentist when he is working on you but that the next day 'you're playing golf with him again.'[1]

Wilder and Diamond had thrown themselves immediately into their next project – *The Apartment* (1960), an unconventional black-and-white romantic comedy. A bittersweet story laced with infidelity, loneliness, tragedy, and unrequited love, it starred Shirley MacLaine, Fred MacMurray, and Jack Lemmon.

Over a career spanning 45 years, more than seventy films, and eight Oscar nominations, Lemmon built a reputation as one of Hollywood's finest actors. He formed a long and fruitful screen partnership with Walter Matthau, making eleven films together, and he also reunited with Tony Curtis for Blake Edwards' *The Great Race* (1965) which was co-produced by Lemmon's Jalem Productions and Curtis's Reynard Productions.

But for many, it is his decades long collaboration with Wilder and Diamond – including *The Fortune Cookie* (1966), *Avanti!* and *The Front Page* (1974) – that remains his most enduring legacy, particularly *Some Like It Hot*. Lemmon himself acknowledged the film's remarkable longevity, noting that it generated more correspondence from audiences around the world than any other project he had worked on. He also marvelled at how while some of his other films enjoyed bigger initial box-office returns, *Some Like It Hot* seemed to grow in stature with each passing year.

Wilder and Diamond were equally as impressed by Lemmon. As Iz put it, 'Before the picture was even previewed, we were already searching for another vehicle for Jack Lemmon. Our reasoning was simple – we felt that nobody in his right mind would make a picture without Jack Lemmon.'[2] Or as Wilder said: 'Happiness is working with Jack Lemmon.'[3] Lemmon hadn't hesitated either; after hearing the outline of the premise, he signed on to the role of C.C. "Bud" Baxter before a single page of the script had been written. As soon as the casting was announced there was a buzz with

1. Wood, p. 160
2. United Artists Series 99AN/MCHC 82-046, box 5 folder 14, Wisconsin Center for Film and Theater Research.
3. Rolston, p. 18

some predicting 'It could very well make Jack Lemmon the biggest star in the business.'[4]

The Apartment also reunited several key collaborators from Wilder and Diamond's earlier projects. Adolph Deutsch returned to compose the film's poignant background score. Alexander Trauner, who had worked with Wilder on *Witness for the Prosecution*, came in as art director. Hair stylist Alice Monte and makeup artist Harry Ray were also back on board and, in Ray's case, properly credited this time!

Filming took place once again at Samuel Goldwyn Studios, where Trauner was tasked with designing ten major sets, including the lobby of the insurance company, a Chinese restaurant interior, and Baxter's modest apartment. The insurance office set was a technical marvel. Covering 18,000 square feet of stage space, it was dressed with more than $4 million worth of borrowed equipment, everything from thirteen IBM calculators to punch card machines and sorters.

By any standard, the scale was enormous. As one report put it, 'collectively, these sets constituted the largest construction programme ever assembled for an independent black-and-white picture.'[5] Enough lumber to build a dozen three-bedroom homes was used, and a full-time crew of forty workers laboured for nearly four months to complete the job. The final price tag for the sets alone approached half a million dollars.

When it hit the screens, *The Apartment* caused quite a stir. Its frank look at adultery, moral compromise, and the loneliness lurking behind New York office windows shocked some critics and audiences, but that didn't stop it becoming both a commercial success and a beloved film.

It was nominated for ten Academy Awards and won five in total, including "Best Director" and "Best Motion Picture" for Wilder and "Best Art Direction (Black-and-White)" for Trauner and set decorator Edward G. Boyle. Wilder and Diamond also picked up the award for "Best Screenplay." At the 33rd Academy Awards held in April 1961, the two men walked up onto the podium together, shaking hands as

4. United Artists Series 99AN/MCHC 82-046, box 5 folder 14, Wisconsin Center for Film and Theater Research.
5. United Artists Series 99AN/MCHC 82-046, box 5 folder 14, Wisconsin Center for Film and Theater Research.

they went. Their speeches were as perfectly pitched as one of their scripts:

"Thank you, I.A.L. Diamond," said Wilder.
"Thank you, Billy Wilder," replied Diamond.

Wilder continued to make notable films mostly with Iz. There was *The Private Life of Sherlock Holmes* where he finally fell in love with filming in colour and *Fedora* (1978). Their final feature, *Buddy Buddy* (1981), brought them together with Lemmon and Walter Matthau once again.

In 1980 they were honoured with the Writers Guild of America's "Laurel Award for Screenwriting Achievement." Wilder was presented with the American Film Institute (AFI) "Life Achievement Award" in 1986, and in 1987 he received the "Irving G. Thalberg Memorial Award."

The following year came a devastating blow. Diamond called Wilder to his house and, without preamble, told him, 'Shit! I'm dying.' He had been living with advanced multiple myeloma for four years, keeping it a secret from almost everyone. Four weeks later, he was dead.[6]

That May, Wilder paid a tribute to his friend – and in doing so did his final bit of directing. At a Writers Guild memorial service, he staged a short sketch with Lemmon and Matthau in Iz's honour. He confessed how solitary life felt without his collaborator: 'Well, it's lonely now in that office of ours. I look at that empty chair and I miss him so much. On his birthdays, maybe I should put a red rose there, like DiMaggio for Marilyn.'[7]

Wilder died of pneumonia on 27 March 2002 and was buried at Pierce Brothers Westwood Village Memorial Park and Mortuary in Los Angeles. His gravestone carries a perfectly Wilder-esque epitaph,

BILLY WILDER
I'M A WRITER
BUT THEN
NOBODY'S PERFECT

6. McBride, p. 388
7. Ibid, p. 388

A short distance away lies another stone that recalls the opening credits of a film:

JACK LEMMON
in

Lemmon had died the year before Wilder of bladder cancer. At his funeral, the frail 95-year-old remembered his friend, saying simply, 'He was a wonderful guy. I loved him dearly, and he was the best actor I ever worked with.'[8]

And on the same site, though further away, lies Marilyn herself, entombed in a crypt.

She lived only four more years after completing *Some Like It Hot.*

Until the very end, she struggled against her image and pressure from the industry as well as battling significant health issues. In May 1961, she underwent surgery related to endometriosis and a couple of months later had her gallbladder removed following a diagnosis of cholangitis. That same year, she spent a number of traumatic weeks in a psychiatric hospital receiving treatment for depression.

A potential chance to work with Wilder again had been touted when he acquired the screen rights to the hit stage musical *Irma La Douce* (1963) .

By then, the frost between director and star had definitely melted. Their encounters at various Hollywood functions had become increasingly cordial and Marilyn had even been spotted at a party following a screening of *The Apartment*. She had been in the midst of separating from Arthur Miller (they divorced in 1961), a development Wilder saw as a positive sign – an indication, perhaps, that she was beginning to steer her life and career with greater independence. Encouraged, he apparently gave serious thought to casting her as Irma, but in the end, chose Shirley MacLaine for the role, continuing the partnership with Lemmon that had worked so well before.

After completing films like George Cukor's *Let's Make Love* (1960) and John Huston's adaptation of Miller's *The Misfits*. Marilyn's final, unfinished, film was *Something's Got to Give* in 1962, with co-stars Dean Martin and Cyd Charisse. Days before filming was set to begin, Monroe became ill once again and was advised by doctors to delay shooting while receiving treatment.

8. Fuller, p. 76

However, Fox began without her whilst at the same time pressurising her to come onto the set. When she did, she was repeatedly too sick to work, but the studio accused her of faking illness and reports in the press suggested she was now too old to be a star.

Fox was already struggling financially due to recent box office disappointments as well as the soaring costs of *Cleopatra* (1963) and couldn't afford further delays or rising expenses on another project. After missing around twenty days of filming and a badly timed – but iconic – visit to New York in May, where she sang *Happy Birthday, Mr. President* to John F. Kennedy the studio fired Marilyn and began planting negative publicity about her in the press.

While she was eventually rehired to complete the picture, Monroe pushed back with a publicity campaign and collaboration on photographic projects with Bert Stern and George Barris. To *LIFE* magazine editor Richard Meryman, she expressed her feelings of frustration and betrayal about the ways actors were treated when they became ill. She complained that executives could often avoid scrutiny for their absences, whereas performers were expected to work regardless of their condition. More broadly, she argued that filmmaking was 'supposed to be an art form,' and not merely a 'manufacturing establishment.'[9]

Marilyn Monroe died late at night at her much loved home on 4 August 1962 at only 36 years old. The toxicology report revealed that the cause of her death was acute barbiturate poisoning. Her sudden death caused a media frenzy, with the press swarming her home and graphic photographs appearing in the papers.

She had often joked with Whitey Snyder that if she were to die first, she wanted him to do her makeup for her funeral. As a token of that pact, she had given him a gold Tiffany money clip engraved with the words:

> "Whitey Dear:
> While I'm still warm
> Marilyn."[10]

---

9. Marilyn on Marilyn: Conversation with *LIFE* Associate Editor Richard Meryman, *LIFE*, 3 August 1962
10. Jordan, p. 101

When the time came, he kept his promise. She was buried on the 8 August, at a funeral attended by only a few of her closest friends. To steady himself for the task, Whitey reportedly turned to gin for liquid courage. It was also said that emotionally, he never fully recovered from the experience and the loss of his friend.

Marilyn's death was, of course, a tragedy. She was still so young, with much more to give – both onscreen and off. Ever since, people have speculated about the roles she might have taken on had she lived longer, and what kind of career she might have shaped for herself in a changing Hollywood and a more permissive society. While she left a truly wonderful legacy with a body of work that showcased her talents and is greatly loved I do often think what a fantastic villain she would have made if she had ever fully escaped from the bombshell roles and further channelled the energy she bought as a psychopathic babysitter in *Don't Bother To Knock* (1952) or the murderous Rose Loomis in *Niagara*.

In the years that followed, an entire industry sprang up around her life and death. Books, films, and documentaries have pored over the details, often blurring the line between history and myth. Indeed, what Sarah Churchwell insightfully describes in *The Many Lives of Marilyn Monroe* as an industry of "trashing Marilyn" appears to exist; in her survey of 300 biographies, she found that most took a notably mean-spirited tone to say the least. Marilyn the woman became Marilyn the icon – forever frozen in time, and never quite allowed to rest. This is perhaps most apparent in the controversy surrounding the crypt adjacent to Monroe's. In 1992, Hugh Hefner purchased it for $75,000.

Hefner, who had already financially exploited her during her lifetime by buying those early nude photos and publishing them as the centrefold in the first issue of *Playboy* without her permission (or financial benefit), explained that the chance to be buried beside her was an opportunity he was not going to miss out on.

The circumstances of her death – whether accident, suicide, or something darker – have also remained the subject of endless and, at times, rather farcical speculation. Her connection to the Kennedy family has only added fuel to the conspiracies.

Another part of Marilyn's legacy lies in what happened to her personal effects and how so many of them came to be preserved, catalogued, and eventually sold. When she died her instructions had been clear – she wanted her belongings distributed 'among my friends, colleagues, and to those whom I am devoted.'[11] The majority had been left in trust to Paula Strasberg but complicated legal wranglings followed, including disputes over taxes, which meant that none of the beneficiaries named in the will received anything until 1971. In the meantime, Paula herself had died, and the estate was inherited by her husband. And, in turn, as Lee had later remarried, ownership transferred to his third wife, Anna, after his death in 1982.

Anna eventually made the decision to sell off the collection through the auction house Christie's in 1999. The interest was extraordinary. Around 75,000 people attended preview exhibitions held in six cities across three countries. The sale reportedly netted over $13 million – plus additional revenue from the printed catalogue listings.

Our fascination with Monroe's possessions extends well beyond letters and personal mementos – the costumes she wore in her films have also taken on an extra significance.

Part of this change reflects a wider and growing interest in fashion history. Film costumes, once seen as mere studio inventory, are now regarded as major cultural artefacts. That shift began in earnest when actress Debbie Reynolds purchased items from MGM's costume and memorabilia collection in the 1970s "rummage sale," laying the foundation for a vast archive she continued to build for decades. The Reynolds' Collection was eventually also auctioned off between 2011 and 2014, drawing worldwide attention.

Marilyn's costumes, including those created by Orry-Kelly, are now also seen as essential pieces of Hollywood history. One of the standout examples is the black dress she wore while singing *I'm Thru With Love*, which sold at Christie's in 1992 for $38,500. In 2016, it sold again, this time for $490,000.

That 2016 sale, held by Julien's Auctions, came after a touring exhibition – "Marilyn Monroe: The Legacy of a Legend." The lots included everything from that stunning black dress to a pair of diamond pendant earrings she wore to the *Seven Year Itch* premiere, to the fish-scale bodice from *Bus Stop* to more personal items.

Ahead of the auction, the lots were displayed in cities across Europe, Asia, South America, and the U.S. In London, it was hosted at the Design

11. Churchwell, Sarah. *The Many Lives of Marilyn Monroe*, Granta Books, 2005, p. 247

Centre, Chelsea Harbour. The subsequent sale, held on 19 and 20 November 2016, was dubbed "The Marilyn Monroe Auction of the Century."

In 2023, the V&A featured the *Runnin' Wild* dress in its "Diva" exhibition. The piece came with an impeccable pedigree: sold at Christie's in 1988 with a letter of authenticity, purchased by the BFI for its costume collection, and eventually transferred to the V&A museum the mid-2010s. It's one of around 500 film costumes preserved from the former Museum of the Moving Image's holdings. Still, even with its credentials, debate has lingered about whether the dress is *the* original or not.

Our appetite for viewing (or owning) her belongings doesn't seem to be waning either. In 2024, "MARILYN – The Exhibition" opened in London, billed as "the world's largest collection" of objects associated with the actress and drawn from the private archive of collector Ted Stampfer. 2026 has also seen – as part of the global celebrations of her centenary – a plethora of books, exhibitions and events. There was the Academy Museum of Motion Pictures in Los Angeles exhibition: "Marilyn Monroe: Hollywood Icon," which featured hundreds of posters, portraits and production documents as well as two of her Orry-Kelly designed dresses from *Some Like It Hot*. The National Portrait Gallery in London held "Marilyn Monroe: A Portrait" which brought together representations of her by some of the greatest photographers and artists including Andy Warhol, Cecil Beaton, Eve Arnold, Milton Greene and Richard Avedon. And Julien's, on 4 June – a few days after what would have been her birthday– held a huge auction "100 Years of Marilyn" which included a number of lots directly from her Brentwood home as well as pelvic scans and medical records, something which sparked a strong backlash and calls to destroy these items.

Whilst many have rightfully pushed back around the ethics about someone's personal life possessions and medical history being pored over, traded and exhibited it is true that they have become a useful resource for researchers – offering tantalising glimpses into the everyday details of her life and helping to counter the myths that continue to circulate. From these we can determine the extent of her physical struggles and read her acting notes on how to portray Sugar's experience on the yacht, while the letters to her friends and family reveal more about how she felt during filming. They are crucial insights but only partway counter the glaring absence of her voice.

For instance, we know almost nothing of her feelings about the film after it was released to the general public. Beyond her distress at an early preview, there is little on record. We can only hope that, in time, she might have reassessed and seen how deeply audiences connected with it and how legendary her performance would become.

In contrast there are no shortage of interviews and recollections to draw upon from others involved. There was the 25th anniversary celebration in 1984, when the cast and crew were invited back to the Hotel del Coronado. Many of the surviving production members showed up including actors like Grace Lee Whitney (Rosella) – who had gone on to play Janice Rand on the original *Star Trek* – and Marian Collier as well as henchman Mike Mazurki. News footage from the event also captured Lemmon, Curtis, and Wilder revisiting the locations, repeating many of the stories that had by then already become part of its legend.

Dan Aulier interviewed Billy, Audrey, Walter, Jack, Barbara, and Tony between 1999 and 2000 for *Billy Wilder's Some Like It Hot* (2001), edited by Alison Castle. Wilder and Curtis are also extensively quoted in Charlotte Chandler's *Nobody's Perfect: Billy Wilder* (2002) and Cameron Crowe's book-length *Conversations with Wilder* (1999) adds yet another layer.

The 50th anniversary was marked with Laurence Maslon's 2009 book which gathered stories, interviews, and a plethora of wonderful images to celebrate the occasion.

These, as well as numerous broadcast interviews over the years, gave everyone – except Marilyn – involved in the production time to hone their stories.

As journalist Anthony Lane observed of one of Wilder's anecdotes, 'this tale has been told many times, to the point where 'being able to ascertain whether it might actually be true' becomes difficult. He added that Wilder himself was 'the worst and most enjoyable offender' when it came to embellishing his own mythology.[12]

With the benefit of hindsight, opinions also shifted. Even Wilder, who had once been so publicly frustrated with her, came to fully recognises how essential she was to the film's lasting success. He later acknowledged that *Some Like It Hot* would endure not because of his direction, but because of Monroe's presence and star power.

12. Lane, p. 711

Looking back, he admitted it felt like exhaustion at the time. A sense of 'never again.' But the distance softened that. 'Well, all I can tell you is,' he added, 'if Marilyn was around today, I would be on my knees begging – please, let's do it again.'[13]

But by far the most challenging aspect of reconstructing *Some Like It Hot's* history is the heavy reliance on Tony Curtis – and the ever-evolving accounts he gave over the years.

Curtis wrote and spoke about the film at length, across multiple decades and in various formats including interviews on television and in magazines but also in books. There's *Tony Curtis: The Biography* (1993, with Barry Paris), *The Making of Some Like It Hot: My Memories of Marilyn Monroe and the Classic American Movie* (2009, with Mark A. Vieira), and then biographies by others, including Aubrey Malone's *The Defiant One* (2013) and Michael Munn's *Tony Curtis: Nobody's Perfect* (2011) both of which involved extensive interviews with him.

What makes Munn's work particularly useful is that it draws from interviews with Curtis at different stages of his life. Munn observed that Curtis's memories often reflected the emotional state he was in at the time – nostalgic and warm in the 1970s, when his career was on the rebound; bitter and erratic in the 1980s, during a time of personal turmoil, including a collapsing marriage and heavy drug and alcohol use.

That period brought some of the most troubling claims. Curtis alleged, among other things, that Monroe had become obsessed with marrying him and tried to trap him into a relationship. That a brief fling – a re-establishment of their previous intimacy – during filming in San Diego had led to her pregnancy. That Miller had found out about their relationship and the two had a physical fight on the set. Curtis later walked back some of those claims, arguing he hadn't meant to reveal so much. There is little, if any, external evidence to support any of those stories yet they have entered into Hollywood lore and recirculate endlessly.

What does run consistently through much of his storytelling, however, is a note of resentment. Joan Collins, who had worked with him in the 1970s, told Munn: 'I find it odd that a man like Tony Curtis should find it necessary

13. 61 Years of Some Like It Hot, *Marilyn Remembered,* 29 March 2020 https://www.marilynrememberedfanclub.com/61-years-of-some-like-it-hot/ accessed 6 June 2025

to still talk with such hatred about Marilyn Monroe so many years after her death.'[14]

And yet, for all the volatility and contradiction, Curtis's attitude towards the films itself also shifted over time. Whatever his personal feelings, he eventually came to realise the significance of what they had all created. Looking back years later, he concluded, that the film's success depended on the unique combination of everyone involved and was a special alchemy that could never be recreated.

And Curtis actually returned to the world created by Wilder and Diamond several more times.[15]

Initial plans for a TV pilot had begun in the spring of 1960, in co-production with Ziv-United Artists, the television arm of United Artists. During the first decades of broadcast television, there was an insatiable demand for programming. With three (and eventually four) major networks to feed in the U.S., executives were always on the lookout for content and often turned to known film's and established stage personalities to anchor new sitcoms or variety shows. Naturally, Ziv-United Artists looked to *Some Like It Hot*, one of their parent company's biggest successes, as a viable property.

There was some debate over whether the agreement that had been made with ever-savvy Lew Wasserman's MCA over the film title also covered its use on television. It didn't. A new deal was struck – they would pay $500 per episode for the rights to use the name again.

Billy Wilder was originally supposed to act as a consultant, but his other projects pulled him away. In his place, those duties would have largely fallen onto his associate producer, William Schorr. Walter Grauman, a seasoned television director, was brought in to helm the project.

The real challenge, though, was figuring out how to extend the story of Jerry and Joe into a twenty-one episode series. The teaser for the opener offered a somewhat surreal solution: Curtis and Lemmon would reprise their roles – but only briefly. As a gesture of goodwill, they spent an afternoon filming, accepting only symbolic compensation. Curtis reportedly received

14. Munn, Michael. Tony Curtis: *Nobody's Perfect*, JR Books, 2011, p. 157
15. Jack Lemmon also revived his character making an uncredited cameo appearance as Daphne in the movie *Pepe* (1960). And they were both photographed by Annie Leibovitz in 1995. Her image of "The Girls" in their underwear was published in *Vanity Fair* that same year for their Hollywood: The Power & Glamour edition.

an oil painting he'd admired from a Beverly Hills gallery; Lemmon was given a shopping spree at a high-end haberdashery.

In the setup, Jerry and Joe undergo plastic surgery to change their identities, emerging with entirely new faces – and now played by Dick Patterson and Vic Damone.

Joan Shawlee and Sandra Warner reprised their roles as Sweet Sue and Emily respectively, Mike Mazurki is again a henchman, but Sugar was absent. In her place was a new character – Candy Collins, played by Tina Louise. Candy is the girlfriend of a gangster called Studs who is revealed to be the twin brother of the original film's Spats.

With their new appearances, Joe and Jerry believe they're finally in the clear. No more disguises, no more running. But their luck doesn't hold. Federal agents soon track them down with a request they can't refuse – help bring down Studs, who's sworn to kill the musicians he holds responsible for his brother's death. And to do this they will need to slip back into their heels again.

The pilot was filmed at NBC's studios in mid-March 1961, but it quickly vanished without a trace when neither the broadcasting company nor the sponsor, Procter & Gamble, wanted to move forward with the show. While the exact reason was not publicised, one studio memo offered a telling insight: 'As this is essentially a joke show, it would be difficult to sustain on a high level.' By August, as reported by Laurence Maslon who was lucky enough to be shown the pilot by Walter Mirisch himself, internal correspondence had declared the project officially "dead." [16]

Then, in 2002, Curtis was cast in a national touring stage production of *Some Like It Hot: The Musical*, playing none other than Osgood Fielding III.

That particular musical production had been borne out of an earlier stage adaptation, one originally spearheaded by Broadway's most flamboyant and notorious producer, David Merrick. Through the mid-1950s to the early 1970s, Merrick dominated Broadway, producing nearly seventy-five shows, including hits like *Gypsy* (1959) and *Hello, Dolly!* (1964). He was equally well-known for his backstage feuds, outrageous publicity stunts, and combative relationship with critics, which earned him the moniker "The Abominable Showman."

16. Maslon, p. 160

Merrick had first crossed paths with Wilder during the Broadway transfer of *Irma La Douce*. Soon after, he approached Wilder about acquiring the stage musical rights to both *The Apartment* and *Some Like It Hot*. Wilder, who had little interest in the Broadway stage and had already turned down several similar requests, initially resisted. But Merrick was relentless. Wilder remarked on the producer's persuasive charisma – 'I'm sure even Hitler was charming when courting Eva Braun,' he quipped.[17]

Merrick eventually succeeded in convincing Wilder. His stage adaptation of *The Apartment* became *Promises, Promises* (1968), which went on to run for over three years on Broadway and an additional year in London's West End.

When it came to *Some Like It Hot*, however, Merrick ran into a predictable legal snag over the licencing of the name. As a result, the show was retitled *Sugar* and opened on 9 April 1972 at the Majestic Theatre on Broadway.

The creative team featured some legends including Bob Merrill who was responsible for the song lyrics and Jule Styne who arranged the music. Like Matty Malneck before him, Styne came with a jazz pedigree as he had studied music in Chicago and even played in clubs owned by Al Capone, during the Beer Wars era. Adding to the real life parallels his band had also toured Miami during the late 1920s.

The original cast included Robert Morse as Jerry/Daphne, Tony Roberts as Joe/Josephine, Elaine Joyce as Sugar Kane, and Cyril Ritchard as Osgood Fielding. *Sugar* ran until 23 June 1973, clocking in at 505 performances. A west coast tour, with a new cast, followed in the autumn of 1974.

In the early 1990s the finally properly named *Some Like It Hot* made its way to the West End. The production opened at the Prince Edward Theatre on 19 March 1992.

This time Mandy Perryment played Sugar, Billy Boyle took on the role of Jerry, and the show was built around rock and roll star Tommy Steele as Joe. That decision came with challenges. The original musical *Sugar* had never been designed as a vehicle for the character of Joe, so the production had to be carefully retrofitted to give him a central focus.

The touring show had done well, thanks in large part to Steele's popularity, but in London, it failed to find its footing. Despite the title recognition and familiar story, it closed at a reported loss of nearly one million pounds.

---

17. Ibid, p. 163

But in the early 2000s Curtis was thrilled by the prospect of being involved in the revival. It was a striking piece of stunt casting, and one that brought a great deal of publicity. He threw himself into the role, spending months learning his lines and training to dance. While he had some prior experience on stage, this marked the first time he would sing and dance in a full-scale musical production.

Reflecting on the role, Curtis said:

> 'I want to make him different from Joe E. Brown's Osgood. Brown was an extraordinary comedian. But I wanted to make my Osgood frivolous, very extravagant. Billy Wilder wanted a more graphic millionaire, with a lot of old millionaires in rocking chairs, not good for anything anymore. I want my Osgood to be freer, looser, more like a kid playing.'[18]

Only one day after his 77th birthday – Curtis stepped onstage in Houston to open the run. Over the course of the next year, he performed in 237 shows across multiple cities, finishing in Portland on 6 May 2003. Not bad for someone with health problems who'd had heart bypass surgery almost a decade earlier.

The tour was long and demanding and he admitted it was gruelling. But he clearly relished the experience, especially the opportunity to deliver the famous final line. Reviews were mixed with many critics noting that while his enthusiasm was undeniable, his singing and dancing sometimes fell short.

It was to be his last big acting challenge. He did, however, get one final opportunity to reference the film in a nude photoshoot for *Vanity Fair* to mark his 80th birthday. His pet Yorkshire Terriers "Daphne" and "Josephine" held in front of him, playing a vital role in preserving his modesty. Tony Curtis died in 2010 and was buried in Palm Memorial Park Cemetery near Las Vegas.

Over time, the reputation of the film itself has also grown, along with its cultural significance. From the 1960s it became a fixture on television, and in the early 1980s it was released globally on VHS, in the United Kingdom with a "U" certificate, framing the film as no longer shocking but as family

18. Ibid, p. 173

entertainment. In 1989, the Library of Congress selected it as one of the first twenty-five films to be preserved in the U.S. National Film Registry, recognising it as "culturally, historically, or aesthetically significant."

In 2000, the AFI voted it the funniest American film of all time in its "AFI 100 Years ... 100 Laughs" poll. It also appears regularly in surveys of the greatest films ever made, including *Variety*'s 2025 list of "The 100 Best Comedy Movies of All Time" where it came second to *The Naked Gun: From the Files of Police Squad* (1988).

There have even been rumours of a (thankfully not ever realised) remake starring Scarlett Johansson, Ashton Kutcher and Shia LaBeouf. Plus, a reenvisaging of the musical when, in 2022, S*ome Like It Hot* returned to Broadway. The production was met with acclaim and earned thirteen nominations at the 76th Tony Awards, including "Best Musical." And as of 2026, the touring production is still going strong!

And as the next major milestone approaches, there will no doubt be further opportunities to revisit *Some Like It Hot* once more and to spend time considering its true legacy as well as the lives of those who helped create it.

After all, three quarters of a century "makes a girl think!"

Chapter Sixteen

Legacy – The Final Reveal

There is no question that *Some Like It Hot* continues to connect with audiences.

It's, of course, an enduring classic which incorporates many different genres including crime, comedy and romance. It's even part musical (but not enough of one to put you off if that's not your type of thing) and part buddy movie. It also has the rare distinction of having been deemed satisfactory to Wilder and Diamond. Joseph McBride relates how Barbara believed that it was 'the one picture that both of them said they wouldn't change a line if they had to do it over. And this was from two men who second-guessed themselves for years after a picture was out of their hands.'[1]

However, for many it is the ending – especially that final line – that stays in the memory and gives it such lasting appeal. But it wasn't necessarily going to be that way.

Over the years stories have circulated about the various conclusions that were contemplated for the film.

Over lunch with Charlotte Chandler while she was researching his biography, Wilder described an idea that had been considered before finishing the first draft. She noted down his summary and shared it with Diamond who added a few details of his own. In this particular version the ending was to be filmed in a bustling 1920s nightclub in Havana. Sugar Kane performs on stage 'singing in bad Spanish' while Joe and Jerry, out of drag, play in the band. While it is clear that Joe is still in love with Sugar and gazes at her adoringly Jerry seems disengaged – bored of his new life and still being on the run. His expression shifts to dismay when

1. McBride, p. 388

he recognises Osgood entering the club, with a woman on each arm, and smiles in recognition.[2]

It was apparently not the only proposal for an alternative ending. George Raft once said that Marilyn Monroe proffered it should close with Sugar and Spats dancing a tango. It makes for a good tale, but it is questionable – mainly because Spats is no longer around by that point, on account of having been rubbed out.

It has even been suggested that Wilder and Diamond were left scrabbling around for an idea either after Marilyn had left the set in anger after learning the film would not end on a close-up of her, or when she unexpectedly failed to appear for the final day of shooting. Neither of which can be true.

In truth, the ending had mostly been decided from the start. Much of the scenario and final dialogue is already there in the first draft of the script. What was not yet fixed was a killer last line.

The eventual end line itself had been in play for some time. At first, it was placed in an earlier scene set in Joe and Jerry's room at the hotel, after Curtis climbs in through the window following Junior's date with Sugar on the yacht.

Lemmon is already in the room, and it is clear that Daphne is still very much in charge. She has been out dancing with Osgood and has enjoyed herself. At one point, Jerry practically forgets he is a man, so caught up is he in Osgood's attention and the thrill of being engaged. After all, this is his chance to marry a millionaire.

Joe reacts in shock, pointing out the absurdity of the situation and reminding him that he is not actually a woman. To which Jerry would respond "Nobody's perfect."[3]

Wilder decided the line disrupted the flow and didn't suit the rapid pace of the scene, so it was dropped. Instead, he arrived on set with a pair of maracas, handed them to Lemmon, and explained that he should use them throughout the scene – speaking a line, then giving the maracas a shake, adding a little dance in between. Lemmon, who had carefully prepared the scene in his own way, was taken aback and protested that it was madness, asking Wilder to let him perform it differently. But Wilder stood firm,

2. Chandler, p. 222
3. Curtis & Vieira, p. 188

telling him he was free to try his own way, yet there was no chance he would be talked out of the idea. In the end, Lemmon followed Wilder's instruction.

Despite the director's assurances, Lemmon phoned his girlfriend Felicia and told her he believed the scene would be a disaster and that Wilder had lost his touch. However, he later came to understand where he was coming from, reflecting that while the addition of the maracas initially unsettled him it ultimately proved to be a great decision, since without the rhythmic intervention, audiences would have missed much of the dialogue as they laughed through his lines.

All this meant that the line was still available when Diamond and Wilder came to resolve the final third of the script. The story demands that Joe and Jerry return to their original identities. For Joe, this leads to his romantic ending in the back of the motorboat with Sugar.

But crucially this is not where the film's final emphasis lies. Curtis himself confirmed no one really believed in the couple's long-term future together: 'That's why the picture doesn't end on Marilyn and me. Billy knew that [Joe and Sugar would not last]. As soon as that toothpaste would have been empty, he'd be gone.'[4]

So, if the end isn't Sugar and Joe then it has to be Osgood and Jerry, where he confesses that he too hasn't been truthful to his beau.

Iz described the writing process on how to deal with this reveal: 'I mentioned a line I'd considered using at some earlier point. And Billy said, "Do you think it's strong enough for the tag of the picture?" And I said, "I don't know."'[5]

Wilder, speaking years later at Diamond's memorial, remembered it a slightly different way: 'We needed a final line, a final, final line, a spleen-shattering belly laugh. And Iz came up with "Nobody's perfect." We were not crazy about it, but it was late at night, and we were pooped. So we decided, "Let's put it on paper so they can mimeograph it," fully expecting to find something *really funny* when the time came to shoot the scene. That just goes to show you how little we know.'[6]

4. Gehring, Wes D. *Joe E. Brown: Film Comedian and Baseball Buffoon*, McFarland & Company, 2006, p. 181
5. McBride, p. 402
6. Ibid, p. 402

Wilder may have been doubtful, but Iz had been much more confident than he seemed. As he said at the time: 'We're not going to find anything better. It's much stronger than he thinks it is. And I'm going to go in there tomorrow and basically I will kill him if he doesn't put it in.'[7]

When the film was later shown in preview, the final line received a strong audience rection, confirming the view that it was no placeholder – it was a great line at the end of a clever sequence. If you haven't watched it for a while then I urge you to go now and revel in its genius. Just as the first cut to Joe and Jerry in women's clothing makes us accept the disguise without question, the understated ending feels inevitable, and therefore an acceptable outcome.

In the exchange, Daphne attempts to reveal why their marriage is impossible, listing increasingly desperate objections, while Osgood calmly dismisses each one. Even when she finally admits her true identity, Osgood responds with simple acceptance rather than shock.

The extended sequence works because it draws in the audience with rhythm and tempo before flipping their expectations. Diamond explained that viewers often think they can anticipate a punchline. However, he argued that the comedy comes from withholding that reaction and a deliberately flat response would often prove most effective.

It's a rhythm joke but the ending is also incredibly striking for its ambiguity and this, I would argue, is the reason why the film still resonates with so many people today – because we can place any interpretation we want on it.

For some, Osgood's reaction to Jerry's reveal is not meant to be read into too deeply. He simply shows an easy-going nature. He does not want to make a fuss and accepts things as they come.

Curtis offered his own, rather unconvincing, interpretation of the relationship to the *New York Times* in 2002: 'I think Osgood has had so many affairs with beautiful women, he's happy to have this spiky person who fights back and walks all over him. Maybe he's relieved to have found companionship. "Nobody's Perfect." It's a way for Osgood to say, "Just be my friend."'

7. Ibid, p. 403

For others, including one of Wilder's biographers – Ed Sikov, the conclusion is rather different: 'Brown's line is openly gay, there's no question about that. The line is meaningless otherwise.' [8]

In this scenario Wilder and Diamond created a deliberately ambiguous line that would be understood, by some viewers at least, to indicate that Osgood is clearly still anticipating a future with Jerry.

And as Steven Cohan has pointed out, some of the advance promotion in Los Angeles at least seemed to acknowledge the queer possibilities of the film. A set of adverts, that were not distributed nationally, were created to be personalised with the local cinema's name and phone number.

One showed a rather saucy photograph of Daphne with the line: "For a Good Time Call Chelsea 0-0000 [insert theatre's telephone number] … And If A Man Answers – Don't Hang Up – It's Me Jack Lemmon!" beneath the bold promise: "COMING SOON – AND SIZZLING! 'SOME LIKE IT HOT.' The Freshest, Maddest Hunk of Entertainment In The Whole Wide World!"

Another placed Josephine in a modest pose, accompanied by the text: "She's Young … She's Engaged … She Uses After-Shave Lotion."[9]

But when asked later about the final line both Wilder and Diamond denied any suggestion that their intent had been to imply any ongoing relationship between Osgood and Jerry. In fact, when answering this question, they were not ambiguous at all and instead are frequently openly homophobic and transphobic not to mention very defensive.

In one of the less offensive takes Iz upheld that the film was entirely straight, saying: 'The whole trick in the picture is that, while the two were dressed in women's clothes, their thinking process was at all times a hundred percent male. When there was a slight aberration, like Lemmon getting engaged, it became twice as funny. But they were not camping it up. They never thought of themselves as women. Just for one moment Lemmon forgot himself – that was all. The rest of the time, Curtis was out to seduce Monroe, no matter what clothes he was wearing.'[10]

Wilder echoed the same view and added his own reflection: 'But when he [Lemmon] forgot himself it was not a homosexual relationship. It was

8. Sikov, p. 424
9. Cohan, p. 83
10. Gemünden, p. 117

just the idea of being engaged to a millionaire. It's very appealing. You don't have to be homosexual. Despite these denials it's worth noting that it isn't the only Wilder film that has been argued to have queer overtones – with *Sunset Boulevard*, in particular, cited as an example. It isn't even the only one that features a wig reveal – in *Stalag 17* Shapiro whips off his wig when "Animal" finds his Betty Grable impersonation a little too convincing. Unlike in Osgood's case the action works to snap him out of the illusion.[11]

It is hardly surprising that Wilder and Diamond tended to downplay such interpretations – or at least allowed themselves the cover of plausible deniability. For all its tentative progressivity, when it comes to women's sexuality and behaviour (but let's not go as far as calling it a feminist film!), there were still some boundaries that were pretty much impossible to broach in 1950s America. Queer themes were, to put it mildly, not well received by censorship boards, the Legion, or the PCA, and beyond that, the wider context was deeply hostile. Homosexuality was a criminal offence in the United States at the time, and the social stigma was immense.

Importantly the film never mocks the protagonists even whilst using the premise to stretch conventional ideas about gender and sexuality to their limits. But it is hard to judge how much intent there actually was on the part of the writers and the subject is never tackled or addressed directly leaving us only with inference.

The actual shooting script, however, goes further than the finished film and I think gives an indication of their true intentions, despite what Wilder and Diamond later claimed. It ends with the stage direction: "Jerry looks at Osgood, who is grinning from ear to ear, claps his hand to his forehead. How is her [sic] going to get himself out of this? But that's another story – and we're not quite sure the public is ready for it."[12]

And nevertheless, in the final cut, as Osgood turns towards him with a besotted expression, Jerry is left silently quizzing himself. The spoken last line may be "Nobody's perfect," but the end is wordless.

11. Ibid, p. 117
12. Maslon, p. 181

Index